THE REIFICATION OF DESIRE

Toward a Queer Marxism

KEVIN FLOYD

UNIVERSITY OF MINNESOTA PRESS

MINNEAPOLIS • LONDON

An earlier version of chapter 3 was published as "Rethinking Reification: Marcuse, Psychoanalysis, and Gay Liberation," *Social Text* 66 (2001): 103–28; reprinted with permission of Duke University Press. An earlier version of chapter 4 was published as "Closing the (Heterosexual) Frontier: *Midnight Cowboy* as National Allegory," *Science and Society* 65, no. 1 (2001): 99–130; copyright 2001 the Guilford Press; reprinted with permission of the Guilford Press.

Published by the University of Minnesota Press
111 Third Avenue South, Suite 290
Minneapolis, MN 55401-2520
http://www.upress.umn.edu

Library of Congress Cataloging-in-Publication Data

Floyd, Kevin.
The reification of desire : toward a queer Marxism / Kevin Floyd.
p. cm.
Includes bibliographical references and index.
ISBN 978-0-8166-4395-0 (hbk. : alk. paper) — ISBN 978-0-8166-4396-7 (pb : alk. paper)
1. Socialism and homosexuality. 2. Queer theory. 3. Marxism. 4. Marxist criticism. I. Title.
HX550.H65F66 2009
335.4—dc22
2009003357

Printed in the United States of America on acid-free paper

The University of Minnesota is an equal-opportunity educator and employer.

CONTENTS

ON CAPITAL, SEXUALITY, AND THE SITUATIONS OF KNOWLEDGE

One evening in December 1996, Judith Butler delivered a plenary presentation that would appear the following year as an essay called "Merely Cultural."[1] In this essay, Butler posits a certain conservative Marxist reinforcement of schisms within the Left: a representation of "new social movements" as "merely" cultural, a reactionary dismissal of these movements as insufficiently engaged with questions of material production. The plenary itself quickly took on a certain notoriety, for understandable reasons: it was delivered at a conference in Amherst, Massachusetts, sponsored by the journal *Rethinking Marxism*—to an audience, that is, about which we can reasonably assume some significant level of interest in Marxism, and some other significant level of allegiance to it. The highly charged character of the presentation was certainly in part a product of the skeptical response of many Marxist intellectuals to efforts to "rethink" the tradition to which they are committed, a skepticism vocalized even—or especially— at the conferences *Rethinking Marxism* periodically sponsors. Although I attended the conference, I missed Butler's presentation. Others who were there are likely to remember the snowstorm that hit western Massachusetts that evening. I was not the only one who found it impossible to avoid missing the plenary, after dinner in Northampton and given the time it would take to negotiate the roads leading back to Amherst. Secondhand accounts of Butler's presentation and the audience's response did not keep me, in the following weeks and months, from wondering now and then what kind of storm I would have experienced in that room, and how it would have compared to the one outside.

Butler's critique, like her work generally, proceeds from an explicitly antiheteronormative point of view, and her controversial presentation and subsequently published essay marked a schism between Marxism and queer theory. Even her essay's unusual conditions of publication seemed to perform the assumption that these two fields of inquiry were of interest to distinct, even polarized audiences: after appearing initially in the second in a series of special issues of *Social Text* devoted to the current state of queer studies, the essay appeared the following year in *New Left Review*.[2] In the early to mid-nineties especially, a schism between Marxism and queer theory was impossible not to notice if you were reading in both at the same time. Doing this meant, for example, coming to terms with Foucault's, not Marx's, formative influence on queer theory. This was also the period in which queer theory began offering sustained and formidable interventions in social theory, a shift that could even be said to mark the emergence of queer theory proper. This shift was announced by a number of influential publications that appeared in the early nineties, notably Eve Sedgwick's *Epistemology of the Closet,* which combined literary analysis with far from exclusively literary claims, indeed with a genuinely paradigm-shifting analysis of the most basic structuring of Western knowledge itself by the hetero/homo divide; Butler's *Gender Trouble* and *Bodies That Matter,* two texts that should have made it impossible any longer to account for gender without also accounting for the normalization of heterosexuality; and a collection of essays explicitly identifying itself as a queer intervention in social theory, appearing initially as the first special issue of *Social Text* devoted to queer studies and soon thereafter as the volume *Fear of a Queer Planet.* A number of different contributors to this collection discussed the ways in which certain blindnesses to sexuality and its politics characterize Marxism in particular.[3]

It is all the more striking, then, that in the last decade or so, a trend has developed in queer thought that one wouldn't necessarily have had much reason to expect: a greater openness to the kind of direct engagement with Marxism that emphasizes its explanatory power as much as its epistemological limitations, and a distinct though by no means unrelated development, a widespread critical consideration of the dynamics of capital in its current, global, neoliberal phase.[4] A strong sense of Marxism's limits, of its tendency to elide questions of sexuality, was central to and even constitutive of what we might call queer theory's early stage. This field has since developed new ways of thinking sexuality's relation to capital, and especially heteronormativity's relation to capital, a development marked especially by a rich consideration of the ways in which this relation is mediated by a range of normalizing regimes and forms of social hierarchy, including those that operate along axes of gender, race, and nation. A great deal of recent work in queer studies that takes the contemporary United States as its focus, for example, has been either tacitly or explicitly informed by the restriction, in that same time and place, of the very horizon of mainstream lesbian and gay "political" imagination to the terrain of rights as rights have themselves been articulated within a neoliberal moment.[5] This antiheteronormative critique of capital, then, needs to be understood in relation to at least two potentially contradictory horizons: the impact on queer social life of contemporary regimes of capital accumulation, and the abiding sense of Marxism's blind spots that informed queer thought from the beginning.

With this general understanding of its context, this book revisits certain arguments that have been formative for Marxism or formative for queer theory, arguments we might even call canonical, bringing those arguments together to suggest some of the ways in which they can be read in relation to each other, simultaneously with and against each other. The chapters that follow bring both of these perspectives to bear on a series of historically and nationally specific conjunctures to theorize these conjunctures in their terms, but also, and more importantly, to think through the explanatory capacities as well as the limitations of these same terms. This book understands Marxism and queer theory as forms of critical knowledge, as critical perspectives on social relations that operate from a subordinated situation within those relations. Marxism and queer theory will refer here to ways of knowing the social which are ultimately inseparable from specific histories of collective praxis. This book is primarily concerned with these distinct forms of knowledge themselves, with epistemological categories and presuppositions. It is about what this introduction's title calls the situations of knowledge, about the determinacy of these categories and presuppositions, their historical embeddedness, as well as their situations relative to other forms of knowledge, the way in which they are defined in relation to what they exclude.

This book's basic methodological orientation is drawn from Marxism. I forthrightly frame key insights from queer thought in Marxian terms.

But far from representing just another effort, at this late date, to trump a queer form of critique with a Marxian one, the implications of bringing Marxism and queer theory together in such a fashion turn out to be rather more complicated. Centrally motivating this book's focus on the epistemological is a wish to nudge Marxism into developing a greater capacity to speak to certain dimensions of social and historical reality powerfully illuminated in queer theory's relatively brief history, dimensions that Marxism has little history of acknowledging, much less examining—or at least to suggest ways in which some of Marxism's fundamental terms have tended to keep this from happening. In explicitly approaching the insights of queer critical practice from a Marxian perspective, my central objective is to indicate some of the ways in which this very move requires a fundamental rethinking of that perspective itself. To examine queer critical practice from the vantage of Marxian critical practice will in this way also mean doing the reverse, simultaneously and inseparably. It will mean considering the way in which, when certain insights from queer thought are brought to bear, certain Marxian terms retain an explanatory power, but only with significant revision. This book critically appropriates—both employs and rethinks—two categories that have been central to a specific but influential strand of Marxist thought as it has taken shape over the last century, categories that could use, it seems to me, some queer invigoration. These categories are *totality* and *reification*. My introduction explains how this book rethinks these categories, and highlights some of the implications of this rethinking.

TOTALITY

I want to begin moving toward a more detailed elaboration of this book's objectives by revisiting some potentially familiar ground and by suggesting some of the ways in which this ground may not be so familiar after all. Perhaps the most basic way of understanding the impasse between Marxism and queer theory that persisted through the nineties, and to a lesser extent still does, is in terms of Marxism's traditional emphasis on thinking a totality of social relations. Skeptical dispositions toward Marxism, in the domain of queer thought and elsewhere, have long been articulated with reference to Marxism's totalizing theoretical practices. While reference to "totalization" sometimes seems to involve little more than the easy reiteration of a pejorative buzzword, queer skepticism about Marxian efforts to think totality has also been more than justified in the face of a persistent Marxian tendency to deprioritize questions of sexuality when those questions were acknowledged at all, to subordinate these questions to other, more "total" concerns—to represent sexuality, in other words, not only as "merely cultural" but as always already localized and particularized.[6] I don't think it is too much to say that this tendency within social theory generally, and in Marxism especially, centrally conditioned queer thought as it emerged in the early nineties.

The critique of what was eventually called heteronormativity emerged as a critique of discourses localizing and particularizing sexuality and its politics, as an insistence that the normalization of heterosexuality can be understood only in terms of its operation across a broad social field. In his introduction to *Fear of a Queer Planet*, an introduction that can now be seen to have anticipated many of the field's subsequent developments, Michael Warner pointed out not only that "materialist thinking about society" had especially been characterized by a tendency to elide questions of sexuality from its understanding of the social, but that this very elision only served to reinforce an objectively totalized heteronormativity.[7] And *Epistemology of the Closet* had famously opened with an invigorating challenge, the assertion that "an understanding of virtually any aspect of modern Western culture must be, not merely incomplete, but damaged in its central substance to the degree that it does not incorporate a critical analysis of modern homo/heterosexual definition."[8] Developing some of the implications of Sedgwick's argument, Warner's introduction announced that queer critique was "at the point of having to force a thorough revision within social-theoretical traditions." Warner insisted that the normalization of heterosexuality is "deeply embedded" not only in "an indescribably wide range of social institutions" but also in "the most standard accounts of the world."[9] These accounts included not only dominant ideologies about democracy, nationalism, and the so-called market but also a range of critical knowledges that fall under the heading of social theory, knowledges that did not simply, innocuously exclude any account of sexuality but excluded it in such a way that a widespread social tendency to universalize heterosexuality by particularizing homosexuality was reinforced.

To this representation of a totalizing Marxism's symptomatic sexual blindnesses, it is important to offer an initial response, now from a Marxian vantage, that the effort to think totality is itself a critique of ontological and epistemological particularization. Marxian practices of totality thinking critique capital's systemic, privatizing fragmentation of social production especially and of social life more generally. This privatization takes on a dizzying range of forms in the ongoing historical development of capitalist social relations. Capital's enforcement of a strong differentiation of public from private, for instance, is based on its naturalization of private property but is also ultimately inseparable from an ongoing differentiation of social labor, including a gendered division of labor, a division between manual and intellectual labor, and an atomizing, disciplinary specialization of knowledge itself. The Marxian critique of capital then endeavors to comprehend what this ontological and epistemological atomization makes it impossible to apprehend: capital as the systemic, global source of this enforced social dispersal. If Marxism has long been criticized for a tendency to emphasize sameness rather than difference, for imposing a form of epistemological "totalitarianism," it is more accurate to say that it refutes epistemological fetishizations of difference. If Marxism aspires to understand the mediations that articulate different horizons of social reality, if it tends to emphasize connection rather than differentiation, this is because a social and epistemological severing of connections is precisely one of capital's most consequential objective effects. In this respect, totality thinking is a rigorously *negative* practice, a practice opposed to the kind of positive imposition of totality of which Marxism has long been accused— an imposition referring, from a Marxian perspective, not to thinking at all but to the objective, enforced social atomization that is capital itself. Preemptive rejections of this kind of critical practice have too easily led to what Steven Best called, in a critique of poststructuralism written twenty years ago, an epistemological "dictatorship of the fragments."[10]

Qualifications of this general way of understanding Marxian efforts to think totality will soon be necessary here, but I want first to suggest that this very practice of totality thinking provides, at the same time, a way of understanding a certain *convergence* between Marxian and queer accounts of the social. As the last three paragraphs may well have already begun to imply, a critical disposition toward particularizing knowledges is one of the characteristics queer thought and Marxism most saliently share in common. I would even propose that queer thought can be understood as a distinct variation on the effort to think totality. To the extent that the boundaries of queer thought are defined in relation to its own versions of excluded, *unembraceable* forms of epistemological perversity—and in spite of queer thought's distinctive and unusual capacity for epistemological perversity—perhaps this proposal is perverse indeed. But queer studies' constitutive refusal of any facile localizing or particularizing of sexuality and its politics persistently gives the lie, I think, to any easy assumption that this form of critique consistently and rigorously sidesteps totality thinking. To the contrary, a refusal of sexual particularization, a refusal of sexuality's routine epistemological dissociation from other horizons of social reality, has given rise here again to particularization's dialectical opposite. As Warner put it in what would become one of queer theory's most widely cited assertions, "the preference for [the term] 'queer' represents, among other things, an aggressive impulse of generalization; it rejects a minoritizing logic of toleration or simple political-interest representation in favor of a more thorough resistance to regimes of the normal."[11] A constantly expanding focus on the way heteronormativity is thoroughly entangled with a host of social horizons that appear at first to have nothing to do with sexuality has been a recurring feature of some of the most trenchant work in the field. How else are we to understand Sedgwick's early, formative challenge, her insistence on the centrality of homosexual/heterosexual definition to "virtually any aspect of Western culture"? How else to understand the implications of a title like *Fear of a Queer Planet* (with its insurgent echo of Public Enemy's *Fear of a Black Planet*)? Even Lee Edelman's more recent provocation, in his reading of the psychoanalytic death drive, to the effect that *any* political emphasis on futurity already operates within a heteronormative logic, elaborates its own Lacanian logic of the social as such.[12] And one can understand in a similar fashion the recent flourishing of work on queer temporalities, work that critiques heteronormative logics that operate even in the way time itself is experienced and understood.[13] I hasten to add that this tendency is hardly exhaustive of a field in which some of the most prominent work has indeed scrupulously avoided anything that smacks of totality thinking. Important examples here include the work of Butler and Leo Bersani, for instance, work that in different ways suggests that scrutinizing the discursive complexities of the sexual body is at least as important as the sustained examination of that body's concrete social location.[14] And few specific interventions in queer studies have aspired toward an analysis

of totality as forthrightly as does Warner's introduction. But queer elaborations of heteronormativity's varied social demands have also consistently
maintained that any representation of sexuality in isolation from these
other dimensions of the social, any representation of sexuality as always
already localized, particularized, or privatized, is a misrepresentation of
the social as well as the sexual.

Any such "impulse of generalization" is likely to call forth differentiation as a critical response, and the queer form of generalization that
Warner's essay anticipated has hardly evolved smoothly. It has given rise
to important critiques of the gendered, racial, and indeed global blindnesses persistently risked by the abstraction "queer," to an increasingly rich
attention to other axes of hierarchized social differentiation that the term
has a well-established capacity to exclude. But the aspect of this ever-
growing body of work I would highlight is the way in which it has expanded and internally differentiated, rather than constricted, the domain
of queer thought. A critique of various forms of heteronormative assumption within other critical knowledges—knowledges of race, ethnicity, gender, and diaspora among them—has within the very domain of queer
studies been joined with an immanent critique of its own blindnesses, a
critique facilitated by these same knowledges. The two more recent intro-
ductions to special issues of *Social Text* devoted to the state of queer studies, in 1997 and in 2005, are revealing here. They articulate just as strongly
as Warner's earlier introduction this constitutive queer refusal of the analytic isolation of sexuality from a broad range of social and historical horizons. These texts introduce the new work their respective volumes collect,
and gloss the recent work that constitutes their ground, by emphasizing the
importance of analysis in which sexuality is understood to be, as the introduction to the 2005 issue put it, "intersectional, not extraneous to other
modes of difference." They underscore the indispensability of a dynamic
critical movement "across, between, among various social domains and
political experiences," which is simultaneously an exercise in "traversing
and creatively transforming conceptual boundaries," a movement the 1997
issue called "transexion."[15] These discussions perform a critique of ontological and epistemological dispersal and segregation, emphasizing inter-
sections between instances of social hierarchy that, while operating in qualitatively different ways, are also constitutive of each other. Queer studies
continues in this respect to be informed by a critique of epistemological

particularization, by a genuinely dialectical refusal to isolate sexuality from other horizons of knowledge. Its ongoing development appears here to operate in terms of a consistent pursuit of connections with other fields of critical knowledge and an equally consistent critique of the elisions of difference those same connections risk. These conjoined, multidirectional forms of critique create a dynamic within queer studies of simultaneous expansion and internal complexification, even as this interaction between queer studies and a range of other knowledges constantly raises the question of the extent to which they are in fact "other." These more recent developments in queer studies can to this degree be understood not in terms of a persistent rejection of generalizing impulses but in terms of a critique immanent to this generalizing impulse itself, a critical dynamic in which analytic intersection and differentiation, at the level of the field and sometimes at the level of specific interventions in the field, tend to operate in tandem.

I would propose, then, an initial reading of the relation between Marxian and queer forms of critical knowledge in terms of simultaneous divergence and convergence, convergence here taking the form of a common critique of epistemological particularization, a common "impulse of generalization," a common emphasis on totality thinking. I underscore this commonality not to understate the persistent and obvious ways in which Marxism and queer theory diverge but because this very commonality will ultimately make it possible to see this divergence in a different light. What are some of the ways in which the limitations of Marxian categories are thrown into relief by competing efforts to think totality? What might Marxian versions of totality thinking look like if they really did incorporate a rigorous account of the complex heteronormative dimensions of the social totality they aspire to map? What if they tried to account for insights produced within queer theory rather than, say, always framing sexual questions in classically Marxian terms, assuming that capital mediates sexuality in relatively consistent, predictable ways, in terms of traditional understandings of privatization and commodification, for example?

Though Marx's work explicitly critiques a totality of capitalist social relations, Georg Lukács's *History and Class Consciousness* played a key role in making the epistemological category of totality central to Marxian analysis. What Lukács pivotally introduces is a representation of totality thinking as *totalitätsintention,* a totalizing intention or *aspiration* to totality, an aspiration that for Lukács is a practical rather than a purely theoretical

matter, an aspiration that cannot be separated, finally, from a specific history of collective praxis. "The plenitude of the totality," he writes, "does
not need to be consciously integrated into the motives and objects of
action. What is crucial is that there should be an aspiration toward totality."[16] I want to propose not just that totality thinking has been central
to the development of queer forms of critique but that queer critique has
tended to take the form of this kind of aspiration, especially inasmuch as
the limitations of this aspiration have been registered, again, immanently,
as a scrutiny of the exclusions risked by the abstraction "queer," for example. Though an examination of the terms in which Lukács theorizes this
aspiration will be important in the following section, for the moment I
want to emphasize that the term *aspiration* underscores the epistemological potential as well as the social and historical embeddedness and limitations, the necessary abstraction, of any such critical effort. This implication
is highlighted in one of the most richly suggestive examples of Fredric
Jameson's ongoing (even career-defining) defense of Lukács. Jameson has
insisted on the continuing importance of the category of totality as tenaciously as any contemporary critic, and here he characterizes the aspiration
to totality elaborated by *History and Class Consciousness* as an "unfinished
project." Defending this text from the persistent charge that it elides difference, that it operates according to a naive logic of identity and posits a
simple teleology of alienation and reconciliation, Jameson contends that
its emphasis on totality is the most crucial component of its analysis. Here,
he argues, is where the text opens up a way of accounting for difference
rather than identity. Jameson's essay represents an effort to account for
competing critical perspectives, to think these perspectives in terms that
exceed the "merely cultural"; he highlights the importance of the "new
social movements," but the way in which he understands Marxism in
relation to these movements is radically different from the way in which
Butler's essay understands it. Jameson emphasizes especially the capacity
of *History and Class Consciousness* to facilitate a certain dialectical understanding of the distinct forms of critical knowledge immanent to each of
these movements. Lukács opens a way of thinking about "the epistemological priority of the experience of various groups or collectivities," as Jameson puts it.[17] Jameson stresses the social and historical conditions under
which new forms of critical knowledge develop from within a socially
subordinated position, taking his cue from what was, when the essay was

published, the relatively recent theoretical elaboration of a feminist critical standpoint (which itself drew explicitly on what Lukács called a proletarian standpoint).[18] He raises the question of the specific epistemological
capacities of these various knowledges "from below," critical capacities
that both emerge from and inform a determinate, socially situated history
of praxis, which result from what Jameson calls a specific "social phenom-
enology," a distinctive "group experience":

> Owing to its structural situation in the social order and to the specific forms
> of oppression and exploitation unique to that situation, each group lives the
> world in a phenomenologically specific way that allows it to see, or better
> still, that makes it unavoidable for that group to see and to know, features
> of the world that remain obscure, invisible, or merely occasional and sec-
> ondary for other groups.[19]

Jameson underscores the qualitative, irreducible differences between "various negative experiences of constraint," between, for instance, "the *exploitation* suffered by workers and the *oppression* suffered by women and
continuing on through the distinct structural forms of exclusion and alienation characteristic of other kinds of group experience." This way of thinking totality, he adds, can account for socially and historically differentiated
"epistemological potentialities" as well as "blocks and limits to knowledge."[20] This reading of Lukács frames differences internal to a social
totality in terms of the divergent social situations from which the critical
practice of totality thinking itself emerges. In the face of a Marxian tendency to localize sexuality, this reading begins to suggest ways of understanding Marxian and queer aspirations to totality as both analogous and
irreducibly distinct. Indeed, this reading implicitly extrapolates from *History and Class Consciousness* an understanding of totality one would hardly
have expected this text to provide, a positioning of divergent social movements not as subordinate to Lukács's proletarian subject but as operating
on the same level as that subject, with the same degree of social and political consequence. Highlighting the need to account for the objective situation that distinguishes specific movements, as well as the potential and
the limitations of the specific critical aspirations to totality they develop,
Jameson proposes that Lukács's text "has yet to be written," that it "lies
ahead of us in historical time."[21]

Central to this reading of *History and Class Consciousness* is an insistence that no critical effort in totality thinking can ever be innocent, can ever proceed from a position outside the totality that effort aspires to know. The implications of this proposition, which I now want to emphasize, are both structural and historical. In structural terms, first of all, all such efforts are limited simply by virtue of being socially situated and determinate. With reference to Sartre, Jameson has elsewhere distinguished between two different versions of the effort to think totality, one that "sometimes seems to suggest that some privileged bird's-eye view of the whole is available, which is also the Truth," while the other "implies exactly the opposite and takes as its premise the impossibility for individual and biological human subjects to conceive of such a position, let alone to adopt or achieve it"—an experiential, cognitive impossibility that is itself the product of capital's fragmentation of social relations.[22] Aspirations to totality approach the universal, rather, from the vantage of a specific location within that web of relations, a vantage that necessarily abstracts that totality in coloring everything it sees, but also makes possible broad understandings of social reality unavailable to other perspectives. This is the undeniable difficulty of which the various forms of skepticism about totality thinking are a necessary symptom: any given instance of this properly critical, negative practice will necessarily also omit an infinite range of other mediations, other forms of social differentiation. Efforts to think totality will necessarily posit an internally as well as externally bounded totality, a totality operating at some inevitable level of analytic abstraction, a level evident in the very exclusions that mark from the beginning the limits of that effort. This book's own version of this aspiration will hardly be an exception, for example, prioritizing as it does an analysis of the capacities and limits of two specific forms of critical knowledge.

A useful illustration of this defining characteristic of totality thinking, of the way in which such efforts are necessarily immanent rather than transcendent, is the logic by which Marx leads the reader through the first volume of *Capital*. The text moves through a range of specific vantages on the totality of capitalist social relations, a movement underscoring the way in which each of these limited perspectives conditions everything that can be comprehended from within it. The text gradually moves, for example, from the sphere of commodity exchange, where capital appears one way, to that of production, where it appears another way. But even within exchange, the text moves through the different vantages of buyers and sellers of commodities, for instance. The opposing vantages of capital and labor, meanwhile—opposing vantages on the set of social relations that contains both of them—are introduced in Marx's discussion of the sphere of exchange, even as the very distinction between these perspectives ultimately leads that discussion from the sphere of exchange into that of production. Even the crucial contradiction between value and use value introduced in the first chapter implies the opposing perspectives on capital represented, respectively, by capitalists on the one hand and laborers on the other.[23] The totality of capital, Marx suggests, can be accounted for only through this movement through a range of particular, immanent points of view. *Capital* in this respect avoids the "bird's-eye view" moment, the moment of direct, transcendent omniscience. If it unambiguously prioritizes certain perspectives over others—its "critique of political economy" takes the form of a clear prioritizing of the perspective of production over that of exchange, for example—it just as rigorously underscores the immanence of the vantages it prioritizes. What we might call *Capital*'s narrative temporality consists of this recurring articulation and subsequent displacement of what Marx repeatedly calls "our present standpoint." Any pretension to a bird's-eye view is revealed here to be the effect of a failure to account, within the very effort to think totality, for the specific social location of that same effort.

But Marx's rigorous emphasis on capital's internal differentiation brings us also to the historical implications of Jameson's rereading of Lukács. If capital's internal differentiation only becomes more complex as it develops, this implies that new forms of social differentiation—and new perspectives immanent to that set of relations—emerge in the course of that development. While the early and to some extent persistent polarization of Marxian and queer forms of critical knowledge is certainly indicative of competing intellectual lineages, undeniable methodological divergences between Marxian and Foucauldian modes of analysis, for example (however much some of us want to insist, as this book will insist, that Marx's and Foucault's respective bodies of work are hardly as incommensurate as is sometimes suggested), these intellectual divergences cannot alone explain this polarization, which needs instead to be understood in terms of broader historical developments.

Marxism emerges, for example, from within capital's ongoing imposition of new forms of social differentiation, specifically from within the broad

social consolidation of an opposition between two distinct classes—in contrast with earlier stages in capitalism's development, when the production
and exchange of commodities overlapped with unevenly persistent aspects
of feudal social relations, when the class opposition between capital and
labor was not yet broadly dominant. A distinctly queer critical vantage
on social relations also emerges from within capital's ongoing internal differentiation. In a North American context, for example, John D'Emilio
pointed out long ago that a homosexual form of subjectivity emerges in
relation to developments in the division of labor, especially in relation to
a growing system of wage labor.[24] Familiar aspects of this trend include industrialization's displacement of ever larger numbers of people from rural
areas into urban ones, a displacement that opens up the relatively new
possibility that a large portion of the nation's population can survive economically outside the family unit, a unit gradually becoming much more
central to consumption than to production.

The increasingly varied forms of social differentiation that capital imposes in its development in the United States open up, in other words, a
broad social distinction between heterosexual and homosexual forms of
subjectivity. And the implications of this pivotal instance of social differentiation are, within the confines of the United States, both as total and
as uneven as the differentiation of capital from labor. Heterosexual identification begins, however gradually and unevenly, to turn into a social norm
from the early twentieth century. The ongoing requirements of sexual normativity compel this new form of identification as a means of minoritizing
homosexuality. From the late nineteenth century, as historians have long
argued, sexual subcultures in the United States articulated a hugely varied
range of new forms of minority sexual identity.[25] But this range of identities is also conditioned by broader social forms of minoritization, by this
more abstract, more broadly social differentiation between two opposing
forms of sexual subjectivity. The meaning of subjectivity I would emphasize here is not personal or collective identification but an immanent perspective on social relations, a way of seeing and knowing those relations.
Heterosexual and homosexual subjectivities refer in the present context to
binarized, oppositional social locations, to social—not individual—subject positions, perspectives from which potentially divergent and indeed
opposed forms of knowledge emerge. Homosexual subjectivity here signifies a socially and historically subordinated location within this specific

horizon of social differentiation. This is a location that some unpredictable set of specific persons will wholly or partially, permanently or temporarily or intermittently inhabit, or through which they will pass, a location mediated by "entrances" and "exits," as Lauren Berlant and Michael Warner have put it.[26] If to speak of a queer vantage or aspiration is once again to risk the abstractions imposed by the term "queer," to risk eliding the ways in which sexuality is constitutively interfered with by other axes of social difference and hierarchy, that is because "queer" is not merely a terminological abstraction; it also refers to a form of social abstraction. If the term emerges as a slur, from within a history of heterosexist hatred and violence, and then begins gradually to be redirected in the service of a critique of the sexual normativity that legitimates such hatred and violence, it to this extent presupposes the earlier social differentiation of heterosexual from homosexual subjectivity. This is the case even, or especially, given the way in which the term has been brought to bear in critiques of this very distinction. A new form by which capitalist social relations are categorically differentiated, a form of differentiation compounding and complexly interacting with a host of other forms, is in this respect a condition of possibility for a queer form of critical knowledge.

In the next section, I specify further capital's differentiation of the social into heterosexual and homosexual forms of subjectivity, the socially abstract character of this differentiation, and the epistemological capacities this form of differentiation facilitates. But first it is worth pointing out that Jameson's term "group experience" is an imprecise way to refer to the kind of critical knowledge I am trying to suggest here, insofar as the term "group" implies some relatively stable set of identitarian or communitarian boundaries. "Group experience" might instead be taken to refer to a specific kind of collective, practical experience that develops from within increasingly complex forms of social differentiation. The queer vantage to which I am referring should indeed be understood as irreducibly collective. Mediating the relation between this subordinated social position within capitalist social relations, on the one hand, and the forms of critical knowledge that emerge from within this position, on the other, is the complex history of social and political practice, the panoply of specific articulations of lesbian, gay, antihomophobic and queer struggle, which emerge from within certain "experiences of constraint." This is a history of struggles that take a range of relatively radical or liberal forms, from early lesbian and gay activism's communist roots, to the more conservative homophile movements of the fifties, to gay liberation and ACT UP, among a host of other organized efforts. The generation of what I am calling queer critical knowledge has as its ground this history, which presupposes and is conditioned by a distinction between heterosexual and homosexual subjectivity, however justifiably critical queer practice has been of much of this history. Queer thought in this way operates in the context of a history of competing forms of critical knowledge production, competing critiques of compulsory heterosexuality, which cannot be separated from practice, which both emerge from and feed back into practice. And the queer critique of sexuality's epistemological particularization is again itself as dynamic as it is limited; these limitations are elastic rather than given. This form of critique carries a capacity to open out into broader epistemological horizons, to account for unpredictably variable dimensions of social reality. This queer vantage on a social totality is in these ways a highly mediated product of social differentiation.

For all of Marxism's self-representation as a critique that speaks for the human race as such, its particularity is disclosed precisely in its inability to grasp horizons of social reality that forms of critical practice like queer practice endeavor to grasp, endeavors that are conditioned, facilitated, even provoked by this same inability. The claim I have made, that an aspiration to totality is shared in common by Marxian and queer forms of critical practice, will in this way lead necessarily—according to the very logic by which totality thinking has been practiced in a prominent version of Marxist theory—to the blind spots imposed by that same logic. How, then, might we characterize, from a queer point of view, the epistemological "blocks and limits," as Jameson puts it, that mark the boundaries of this influential form of Marxist thought?

REIFICATION

In the version of totality thinking closely identified with the work not only of Lukács and Jameson but also of prominent members of the Frankfurt school, including Adorno and Marcuse, totality's dialectical other is reification. Lukács's introduction of totality's centrality is ultimately inseparable from his introduction of reification's centrality; what he introduces is in fact a dialectic in which reification and totality are methodologically

bound together. In its effort to mediate these competing critical aspirations to totality, this book insists on the importance of a critical movement
through the concept of reification, a concept that, as we shall see, has a
distinct relevance to the queer form of critical knowledge under consideration here. Reification refers to a certain misapprehension of capitalist
social relations; it identifies the very process of social differentiation within
capital as fundamentally and objectively mystifying, as preempting any
critical comprehension of the social. No mere subjective illusion, this misapprehension is as socially and historically determinate as capital itself.
History and Class Consciousness extrapolates this concept from the opening
chapter of *Capital,* where we find the famous theory of commodity fetishism: the way in which capital, even as the social division of labor grows in
complexity, represents varied, qualitatively different use values as quantitatively commensurate exchange values. Dynamic, productive social relations between people take the form of (exchange value) relations between
static, autonomous things, things that appear to be independent of people.
In this way, social differentiation is the contradictory other side of formal
equivalence. Reification compels an experience of privatization and isolation, an experience of exchange relations as impermeable to human intervention. The aspiration to totality then refers to historically determinate
knowledge that is also praxis capable of negating reification, a critical stance
vis-à-vis this dispersal and compartmentalization of social life. This dialectic binding together the categories of reification and totality, I will argue,
in providing the tools for a critical account of mediation, of capital's simultaneous unity and internal differentiation, also provides the tools for situating sexual normalization, as well as queer critique and the history of praxis
it presupposes, within the broader social processes of capital.

A queer reading of this dialectic will require a critique of the concept
of reification. The capacity of this term, which has been so central to so
much of Marxist thought, to lend itself nonetheless to highly abstract
employments, to conflict with some of Marxism's key methodological priorities—social and historical specificity, for example—is relatively familiar.
If Marxist intellectuals have repeatedly examined the category of totality,
even if only in the effort to defend it in the face of broad skepticism—
Jameson's work is again perhaps the most prominent example here—Marxism has more consistently presupposed than scrutinized the meanings of
reification. Edward Said warned of the ease with which the concept can

become a "reductionist implement," emphasizing especially that any representation of reification as "total" has a tendency to lead to the category's greater and greater abstraction, so that reification is said to be so pervasive that it determines everything. The category can encourage, as Said puts it, a kind of bad infinity whereby it becomes a way to explain ever broader horizons of human experience, turning into "too inclusive, too ceaselessly active and expanding a habit of mind," the result being an inevitable attenuation of whatever explanatory power it might have had. Said adds, rightly, I think, that this ceaseless expansion was finally the direction intended by Lukács himself with his emphasis on the total character of the process to which this term refers.[27]

Reification's capacity for metaphysical explanation especially is inseparable from its radically dehistoricizing capacity. This concept has been used to explain all kinds of imaginable human experience, up to and including religious experience. It has lent itself to epistemological encroachments that exceed not merely the boundaries of the capitalist mode of production but also the boundaries of the social and historical as such. The concept of reification typically grasps capitalist development as a narrative of decline, for example. Lukács's formative use of it has appropriately been accused of presuming some prior, harmonious integration of subject with object, some earlier moment of unproblematic, organic social unification. Capital's subsequent differentiation of the social thereby becomes a kind of brutally dehumanizing interregnum between the idealized periods of organic social wholeness and harmony that presumably both precede and follow it. Here *History and Class Consciousness* is read not as an unfinished project but as a conservative project, having fundamentally failed to disentangle itself from the metaphysical reading of history characterizing Lukács's pre-Marxist work. *The Theory of the Novel,* with its explicit longing for what it retrospectively posits as an earlier historical period marked, as the title of its opening chapter puts it, by "integrated civilizations," is often exhibit A in such accounts.[28] Does the concept of reification then *necessarily* presuppose this kind of fall from organic unity, a Fall less historical than romantic and ultimately religious, less socially specific than lapsarian? Is this category as inherently metaphysical as the narrative of social decline that so frequently frames its uses might suggest?

Timothy Bewes's book-length reconsideration of reification thoroughly rehearses the well-established contemporary intellectual skepticism about it, a skepticism fueled precisely by this capacity for seemingly endless abstraction, by the way in which the concept, according to some accounts, "approximates everything to a single narrative," as Bewes puts it. Bewes underscores the concept's capacity especially for metaphysical and religious explanation, rightly emphasizing that reification is among the most easily reified concepts, that the term is "all too susceptible to the process it denotes." His study begins with a discussion of reification's potential "obsolescence" in light of its abstraction in general and its metaphysical generalization in particular, remarking, for instance, that the concept could be used, given the narrative of decline it so often presupposes, to refer to the fall from grace, from organic wholeness, elaborated in the Eden myth. Then, within a page, Bewes also suggests that reification's reference to the objective, material isolation of broad processes—the "thingification" of those processes, as he puts it—could just as easily explain Christ's incarnation of the divine.[29] If these examples seem extreme, they are extreme examples only of a metaphysicalizing tendency that has haunted this ostensibly Marxian category ever since Lukács established its importance.

How could such a term contribute to analysis that calls itself historical and materialist if its capacity for metaphysical analysis is so elastic that it can accommodate a dialectic of sin and redemption? Bewes's thorough consideration of the way in which the term has lent itself to religious forms of explanation unfolds, as it turns out, in a volume that forthrightly endorses this tendency. In the face of the term's potential obsolescence, as he sees it, for precisely this reason, Bewes's response is to advocate the term's religious expansion. Contending that the relation between Lukács's Marxist work and his earlier, explicitly metaphysical work is best understood in terms of continuity rather than discontinuity, and contending that this is a strength, not a weakness, he develops a sustained consideration of reification as a form of religious anxiety, finding the concept at work in the writings of religious thinkers from Søren Kierkegaard to Flannery O'Connor. "Rather than discard the concept of reification on the grounds of its covert religiosity," Bewes endorses a religious transcendence of mere historical periodization, seeking to "discard the prohibition on 'religiosity' within critical thinking—or rather, to *mediate* the opposition between secularism and religion," and in this way "to rehabilitate the concept of reification." It is not simply, for Bewes, that the concept is implicitly religious or idealistic;

the concept itself, he contends, ultimately attests to "the *innate religiosity* of mankind and the world."[30]

My rethinking of reification moves in precisely the opposite direction. I argue that it remains an indispensable concept despite its traditional limitations, that those limitations are indeed traditional, not definitive. Though theorizing sexuality in terms of reification may at first seem like yet another expansion of the concept beyond useful limitations, this effort in fact emphasizes reification's historically and socially specific operation. A critical vantage on the social we can call queer emerges, as I have suggested, from within a century-long history of struggle against compulsory heterosexuality, a history that itself is conditioned by capital's internal differentiation of social relations. We could put this another way by saying that a queer aspiration to totality emerges from within the process of reification. But to the extent that this is the case, an understanding of reification in terms of ever greater social mystification itself mystifies the determinate relation between capitalist development and this history of struggle. In this context, one rises from the abstract to the concrete, as Marx puts it, by accounting for capital's complex dispersal of social life as an aspect of a reifying dynamic with potentially surprising consequences. To think sexuality in reification's terms is to begin to see the way in which reification refers to a social dynamic that opens up critical vantages on the totality of capital as much as it closes them down.

I want to begin to flesh out this critique in the same way I began to flesh out what I meant by totality thinking, by referring again to the work of the most prominent contemporary critic whose work is organized centrally around a dialectic of reification and totality. In *The Political Unconscious,* Jameson employs this dialectic, while also drawing on a Freudian hermeneutic, to elaborate what he calls the "ideological limits" of certain discourses that operate within the horizon of capitalist development, the fundamental repression by these discourses, he claims, of "History" as such. At one of its more startlingly dialectical moments, his analysis makes reference in turn to the ideological limits of Freudianism itself, positing reification as a condition of possibility for a certain abstraction of sexuality characteristic of psychoanalytic discourse:

> The psychoanalytic demonstration of the sexual dimensions of overtly non-sexual conscious experience is possible only when the sexual "dispositif" or

apparatus has by a process of isolation, autonomization, specialization, developed into an independent sign system or symbolic dimension in its own right; as long as sexuality remains as integrated into social life in general as, say, eating, its possibilities of symbolic extension are to that degree limited, and the sexual retains its status as a banal inner-worldly event and bodily function.

Recall the familiar opening words of this text's preface: "Always historicize!"[31] What kind of historicizing practice does the concept of reification enable Jameson to perform here? What kind of future and what kind of past does this way of historicizing sexuality presuppose? We could find ourselves asking, for example: What historically precedes this reification of sexuality? What kind of prior social integration does this formulation posit? When, for example, was sexuality ever as integrated into social life as eating (leaving aside the question of the social and historical integration of the practice of eating itself)? Jameson appears to recapitulate the Lukácsian narrative of reification as a movement away from some prior, retrospectively posited moment of organic social unity, though here that movement does not necessarily imply decline. We could also ask questions about the objective social and historical effects of reification this passage presupposes, about what some of the historical consequences of this reification of sexuality might be. In at least one important sense, *The Political Unconscious* employs the concept of reification in a way that is more historical than metaphysical; Jameson's critique insists on the explanatory power of the Freudian hermeneutic even while positing reification as one of Freudianism's conditions of possibility. But his study also explicitly separates that hermeneutic from its basis in sexuality, from what Jameson calls its historically specific content, and in this way suspends the question of the broader historical repercussions of this specific instance of reification.[32] How, for example, might we think about this reification of sexuality in relation to the critique of Freud that was foundational for queer studies—Foucault's—a critique that makes Freudianism's normalizing historical impact *inseparable* from its content? One of the lessons of Foucault and queer studies generally is that sexual knowledges like psychoanalysis have their own social effectivity. A Foucauldian perspective would, for example, insist on the way in which the clinical institutionalization of psychoanalysis produces qualitatively new ways in which sexuality is disciplinarily normalized, including the production of new forms of sexual subjectivity. What historically subsequent chains of determination can result from the dynamic of reification, and can these be adequately understood in terms of the possible outcomes the concept of reification typically presupposes, total mystification or total negation?

One of the crucial innovations of *History and Class Consciousness* was its reestablishment of the importance of subjectivity in the face of a deterministic, mechanistic fetishizing of the objective within the contemporaneous official Marxism of the Second International.[33] Lukács cogently locates a dialectical alternative both to objective determinism and to subjective voluntarism by emphasizing how subjectivity is everywhere conditioned by—though by no means a simple function of—objective historical developments. Reification here unfolds objectively and as part of this unfolding also compels a passive, "contemplative" subjectivity even as it provides at the same time for the objective potential for class consciousness, for a collective proletarian subject's active, practical breaking of reification's spell. But it is not enough to say that Lukács reestablishes the importance of subjectivity: for entirely understandable reasons, perhaps, given the fetishizing of the objective to which *History and Class Consciousness* responds, Lukács methodologically *prioritizes* reification's subjective over its objective moment, ultimately and radically abstracting the objective. Lukács on the one hand proposes that Marxism is, first and foremost, a critical method. *History and Class Consciousness* is one of the twentieth century's most influential defenses of dialectical method, a text that famously opens with the claim that Marxian "orthodoxy" refers "exclusively" to method. Lukács insists on the historical specificity of concepts and the constant correction of concepts by history, arguing that historical change compels conceptual change. He refers to the "delusion of confusing the intellectual reproduction of reality with the actual structure of reality itself."[34]

But simultaneously and inconsistently, Lukács takes issue with the separation of method from reality, thought from being, and in this respect insinuates their ultimate coincidence and identity: the privileged moment of this identity is his insistence on the proletariat's distinct capacity for a knowledge of society adequate to its object. This identity results from the contention that for the proletariat, self-knowledge coincides with knowledge of the social totality. Lukács specifies reification's objective moment in terms of the proletariat's capacity to understand itself as both subject *and object* of the process that is capital: as soon as the proletarian subject knows itself, it also knows the truth of this process. The method he employs in this respect recapitulates Hegel's prioritizing of subject over object, as opposed to the prioritizing of objective reality over subjective negotiations of it on which Marx's foundational critique of Hegel insists—and as Lukács ultimately admits in his 1967 preface.[35] If the subject is the more crucial moment for Lukács precisely because he wants to underscore the importance of class consciousness, his analysis of the reified object is by contrast highly elliptical. He argues, for example, that reification's objective result is to "freeze" the social appearance of what he calls false immediacy. The reified object is to this extent delineated entirely in terms of the subject's experience of that object as radically ahistorical and beyond that subject's control. The dynamic of reification can in these terms only become quantitatively more intense or be negated absolutely by proletarian praxis. Here the object is ultimately folded back into the subject— we might even say folded back prematurely—before objective mediations of that subject are adequately registered. And in this respect, Jameson's defense of *History and Class Consciousness* as an unfinished project, his contention that it provides a way to account for the internal differentiation of capitalist social relations into a range of irreducibly distinct ways of encountering and understanding those relations, is a reading that is as generous as it is suggestive and would ultimately require a more thorough critique of the text than he provides. Reification itself needs to be rethought if this aspiration to totality is to be rethought; the discourse of reification introduced by Lukács is, again, a discourse in which each of these categories implies the other.

How, then, might we further specify reification's objective moment? This moment, first of all, has two contradictory aspects, as Lukács insists: social labor is atomized into the competitive, individuated labor of private persons, obscuring its fundamentally social character, even as the products of these dispersed labors are placed in a relation of formal equivalence. Social differentiation, again, has equivalence, sameness, as its constitutive other side. Second, however, reification is a more general concept than commodification, a concept referring to a broader, more complexly mediated social dynamic: no longer confined to the abstraction of social labor and commodity exchange per se, reification refers to an objective normalizing of formal abstraction throughout the totality of social life. Lukács's

argument that reification is objectively total unfolds in largely epistemological terms; it is based primarily in his discussion of the reification of
knowledge. He elaborates reification's objectivity almost exclusively in terms
of an increasing pervasiveness of epistemological formalisms that dominate
the subject, knowledges that are themselves abstract, equivalent products
of a deepening division of labor. We can then begin to specify reification's
objective moment by underscoring the way in which, for Lukács, ever
greater degrees of reification mean ever greater degrees of epistemological
differentiation. These formal knowledges eliminate any larger sense of what
Lukács calls the "ontological totality," any sense of knowledge's material
and historical substratum, and give themselves over instead to their own
isolated, internal protocols. His primary concerns are the deactivating
impact that these knowledges have on the subject, and the proletarian
potential for a critical, practical knowledge of totality that can negate this
negation. These knowledges do not then merely "reflect" the formal abstraction of commodity; they actively mediate capital and have their own
objective social effects. But Lukács elides whatever effects these knowledges
may have beyond this induction of a passive, "contemplative" subjectivity.

To more thoroughly specify this concept would thus entail a more thorough historicizing of the objective determinations and repercussions of
these formal knowledges that emerge in relation to new forms of social
differentiation. And if a generation's worth, now, of queer critical practice
has highlighted any single social phenomenon, it is the normalizing effectivity of sexual knowledge. As I argue in detail in chapter 1, what Foucault
identifies as the twentieth-century sexual knowledge regime exemplified
by the psychoanalytic culmination, around the beginning of the twentieth
century, of a longer-term historical "deployment of sexuality" should be
understood as a product of reification. Lukács emphasizes, for example, the
way in which specialized knowledges reify bodily attributes: the scientifically managed factory, in his analysis, reifies not only the body's capacity
for labor but skill itself. The factory expropriates, disembodies, and reifies
the very technical knowledge of the production process. With the emergence of this regime of sexual knowledge, sexual desire is also reified: a
bodily capacity is epistemologically abstracted in the form, for example, of
qualitatively new heterosexual and homosexual subjectivities. This is an instance of objective social abstraction with historical repercussions far beyond
the specific history of Freudianism. The following chapters propose that

this reification of sexual desire is a condition of possibility for the development of queer forms of critical knowledge.

The term "queer," I have suggested, refers to an abstract form of subjectivity, a vantage on social relations opened up by capital's ongoing differentiation of those relations. It is now necessary to be more precise: this is a *reified* form of subjectivity, a subjectivity that begins to disclose the limitations of the standard Marxian account of reification. Where Lukács's method prioritizes subjectivity, Foucault's method famously prioritizes objectivity. This, of course, means not that he neglects subjectivity but that he underscores the capacity of these knowledges to discipline not consciousness but bodies themselves and to produce new forms of subjectivity in the process. What this book identifies as a reifying abstraction of sexual desire then regulates bodies in turn, in a normalizing attribution of sexual subjectivity; I will in this way take issue with Lukács's contention that reification produces only two different kinds of subjectivity, passive contemplation and the potentially critical, negative standpoint of the proletariat. While Foucault represents history in terms that posit a narrative of decline even more unwaveringly, perhaps, than the narrative of reification we encounter in Lukács, his work also facilitates an understanding of the way in which regimes of sexual knowledge have complex social effects. Reification in this respect seems to have a radically unfreezing social impact: far beyond the two different kinds of subjectivity Lukács allows, reification is a condition of possibility for a new form of critical, antiheteronormative knowledge, which may not make Lukács's "ontological totality" less legible so much as provide a new critical perspective on it. To begin to move away from this concept's capacity for theoretical bad infinity, we might begin to examine the divergent significations of reification rather than taking its meaning as established. We might begin to understand the social differentiation this concept seeks to grasp in terms of an opening as well as a closing of horizons of critical and, yes, political possibility.

Subsequent Marxian employments of the concept—by no means only Lukács's—tend to recapitulate this prioritizing of subject over object, representing reification's objective moment more or less exclusively in terms of increasingly damaging degrees of social abstraction. The very aspiration to totality that underpins the Marxian discourse of reification is thereby compromised by its own fundamental terms. This tendency is perhaps nowhere more in evidence than in precisely those revisions of the concept that represent critical subjectivity as all but liquidated, as in the narrative of reification one encounters in the work of the Frankfurt school, where reification morphs into an instrumental reason that has saturated and neutralized the very psyche of Lukács's proletarian protagonist. In certain respects, the Frankfurt school's divergence from the account of reification in Lukács could hardly be more apparent. Whereas Lukács elaborates the dynamic of reification in terms of the loss of an organic social wholeness, a less and less accessible "ontological totality," Adorno, for example, revises this concept by emphasizing, to the contrary, reification as a pervasive and all but inscrutable social logic not of difference but of sameness, a logic not of differentiation but of commodity equivalence. Adorno's elaboration of nonidentity thinking emerges from an understanding of reification as operating according to a social logic of identity.[36] But these accounts of reification, which emphasize opposing sides of the dynamic of differentiation and sameness to which I have referred, also share in common the narrative of decline they articulate—or presuppose. Whether a social identification of subject and object is (for Lukács) lost or (for Adorno) violently enforced, what reification can hardly be seen to do is open up potential new horizons of critical leverage. While the discourse of reification tends in some respects to recognize both sides of a dialectic of quality and quantity, it also typically posits a largely quantitative narrative whereby critical capacities suffer greater and greater degrees of paralysis, a narrative that closes down opportunities for any account of reification's more complex social and historical results.[37] This prioritizing of reification's subjective moment becomes extreme in Bewes's study, where the emphasis is far less on reification's objective, historically specific social impact—the division of social labor receives scant attention in this account, for example—and critical possibilities are displaced by a kind of Kierkegaardian anxiety toward reification that Bewes reads as somehow constitutive of the process of reification itself. My study recasts the concept of reification in such a way that the dynamic to which it refers is revealed to do much more than, as *The Political Unconscious* suggests, ideologically repress history.

FROM THE ABSTRACT TO THE CONCRETE

I began this discussion by highlighting a certain convergence between Marxian and queer forms of critical knowledge, a convergence that itself led inevitably, as I suggested, toward an examination of reification, an examination that underscored instead the way in which these respective forms of critique diverge. I want now to suggest the way in which this emphasis on divergence itself begins to lead us back in the other direction, the way it can bring us to a different understanding of how these forms of critical knowledge can operate together. This book will maintain that to specify reification's objective moment in this queer fashion is also to concretize this concept in Marx's sense of the term, and to discern a certain inconsistency between the typical practice of the dialectic of reification and totality and the methodological priorities evident in Marx's work. I argue, in fact, that this queer reading of reification and totality exemplifies, simultaneously, Marxian as well as queer forms of critical practice.

Marx's method of theorizing a totality of social relations turns fundamentally on the practice of concretizing the very abstractions that theory requires. His work performs this method, but he rarely steps back to offer sustained elaborations of it, more often articulating it in relatively brief comments scattered throughout his corpus. One of these rare exceptions, a notoriously elliptical one, is found in the section of his introduction to the *Grundrisse* called "The Method of Political Economy." Here he frames his method in terms of an ongoing movement between the concrete (objective, determinate social totalities) and the abstract (categories the thinking subject must necessarily employ to grasp the concrete). The concrete is not, he makes clear, the empirically given; to comprehend the concrete in its complexity, the thinking subject has to engage in a certain practice of abstraction. This subject has to distill in thought, in conceptual form, the concrete's constitutive determinations, and only through this process can the concrete be theoretically reconstructed with anything resembling validity.

This reconstruction does, however, necessarily *begin* with the empirically given, with what Marx calls the "imagined concrete." In a key passage, Marx considers the extent to which the category "population," for example, can account for the totality to which it refers. This concept, he argues, leads necessarily to a series of "more simple concepts," "thinner abstractions" that internally differentiate this totality by identifying its multiple determinations:

> The population is an abstraction if I leave out, for example, the classes of which it is composed. These classes in turn are an empty phrase if I am not

familiar with the elements on which they rest. E.g. wage labor, capital, etc. These latter in turn presuppose exchange, division of labor, prices, etc. For example, capital is nothing without wage labor, without value, money, price, etc. Thus, if I were to begin with the population, this would be a chaotic conception of the whole, and I would then, by means of further determination, move analytically towards ever more simple concepts, from the imagined concrete towards ever thinner abstractions until I had arrived at the simplest determinations. From there the journey would have to be retraced until I had finally arrived at the population again, but this time not as a chaotic conception of the whole, but as a rich totality of many determinations and relations.[38]

In this conceptual movement from an abstract unity to an internally differentiated one, the "imagined concrete" itself, first of all, turns out to be an abstraction: a chaotic abstraction, one that requires specification. Marx delineates a double movement: first, a movement through a series of these increasingly simpler abstractions, concepts that identify various determinations within a social totality, which internally differentiate what began as a chaotic conception of totality. In a second movement, unity is reestablished, but here an internally differentiated unity replaces a chaotic one. These simple abstractions are themselves concretized by establishing the simultaneous differentiation and connection between the various determinations to which they refer—by establishing, for example, the social process of capital of which social class, wage labor, and value are all defining moments. "Along the first path the full conception was evaporated to yield an abstract determination; along the second, the abstract determinations lead towards a reproduction of the concrete by way of thought."[39]

Theoretical abstractions, in this account, can be more or less chaotic, more or less concrete. In the two movements Marx describes here, movements leading to the establishment in thought of an internally differentiated whole, theoretical abstractions are concretized: a chaotic conception of totality is concretized by way of ever simpler abstractions, and then these simple abstractions are themselves concretized in turn through an establishment of their determinate interconnections, through a more complex reconstruction of the totality with which the process began, now understood "as a rich totality of many determinations and relations." The specification of concepts and the specification of totality are here inseparable.

Even concepts that are not chaotic, as Marx emphasizes, vary in their level of complexity; they operate at different levels of abstraction. Capital is a more complex, abstract concept than price, for instance. Reification is a highly complex abstraction referring to a broad set of social phenomena—even in Lukács's account, before one approaches subsequent elaborations and expansions of the term. Reification is also a chaotic abstraction to the extent that it fails to account for key aspects of this complexity—to the extent, for example, that it excludes any rigorous understanding of the objective moment of the social dynamic it seeks to grasp. It is chaotic to the extent that it accounts for social differentiation in the abstract terms of a quantitatively deepening mystification of social relations, for example. And as soon as Eden and Christ's resurrection begin to appear within reification's purview, we have arrived at a vertiginously chaotic conception of the whole.

In a crucial turn, Marx then underscores the ways in which the thinking subject who aspires to move beyond a chaotic conception of the whole is already embedded within the very totality for which thought would account. He emphasizes that the concrete "appears in the process of thinking . . . as a process of concentration, as a result, not as a point of departure, even though it is the point of departure in reality and hence also the point of departure for observation and conception." Social reality remains ontologically prior to its conceptual reconstruction. One of the implications here is that this reconstruction operates at *some* level of analytic abstraction, if only because the thinking subject is already socially conditioned, limited, situated within a determinate position within the social totality, a position that defines, as I suggested earlier, both the extent and the limitations of what it can know. I have emphasized the way in which the social situatedness and determinacy of the subject who aspires to grasp totality are underscored in *Capital* by the text's avoidance of direct omniscience, its restriction of its own perspective on capital to a movement through a series of specific, limited vantages internal to capital. In the *Grundrisse,* Marx similarly underscores this situatedness and determinacy by identifying this thinking subject in explicitly social rather than individual terms, by insisting on the knowing subject's determinate situation. "The subject, society, must always be kept in mind as the presupposition."[40] On the one hand, then, the concrete is the object that thought seeks to grasp; on the other hand, thought also "plays" object, as it were, to the concrete's subject: the concrete for which thought seeks to account is also thought's material situation, what Stuart Hall calls in his reading of this passage "a privileged and undissolved 'moment' within a theoretical analysis."[41]

This objective, determinate social situation of thought is further complicated by the fact that social reality is also historically dynamic. The determinate situation of the thinking subject is conditioned both socially and historically; this subject is itself a product of a specific historical juncture within capital's ongoing internal differentiation. Marx articulates a dynamic method that is determinate in relation to the dynamism of history itself: just as concrete social totalities change qualitatively in their historical development—capital is expansive, dynamic, it has opened conditions of possibility for a history of queer critical practice, for example—that totality's reconstruction in thought is itself always historically conditioned. If thought by definition proceeds at some level of abstraction, necessarily requiring exclusions, all thought is also historically determinate, and the limitations of any specific critical effort will be dictated not only by the abstract character of thinking as such but also by the historically conditioned character of the effort itself. If concepts produced within a specific, historically determinate situation remain open to historically subsequent deployment, they also require examination of the extent to which this historical relocation itself affects their meaning. Concepts as they are deployed within subsequent situations require critical, historically situated scrutiny. To evade this scrutiny is to fail to account for the concept's historical determinacy, and the result is likely to be a more chaotic, less concrete concept. The aspiration to totality elaborated within the dialectic of reification and totality that I consider in the subsequent chapters falls short of its objectives to the extent that the theoretical abstractions it brings to bear are insufficiently concretized—to the extent, for example, that the complex historical repercussions of reification's objective moment are erased.

Marx's method insists in this way on a movement in two opposing but equally important directions, a development of categories adequate to the complexity of historically determinate social relations, and an ongoing examination, as those relations continue to develop, of the explanatory capacity and limitations of those same categories. Just as historical development is conceptualized, so concepts are themselves historicized; conceptual abstraction and an insistent emphasis on social and historical specificity here operate in tandem, each accounted for from the vantage of the other. "Viewed apart from real history," Marx writes in *The German Ideology*, "these abstractions have in themselves no value whatsoever."[42] The divorcing of concepts from their historical determinations, a habit Derek Sayer has called the "violence of abstraction," is by no means limited to nondialectical forms of analysis.[43] This dehistoricization of concepts is sometimes referred to as a reification of concepts, but, as Bewes points out—and as his study, in my view, ultimately demonstrates—there is perhaps no Marxian concept as vulnerable to reification as the concept of reification itself.

This book takes the position that the interpretive horizon of Marxism is open rather than closed. But this will not mean that Marxism represents some ultimate interpretive horizon, as, for example, *The Political Unconscious* maintains (famously or infamously, depending on your point of view). It will mean, more modestly, that Marxism is open to the extent that it recognizes the historical specificity of even its most basic categories and the way in which those categories are subject to forms of scrutiny every bit as specific. Marxism is open to the extent that it retains a capacity for immanent critique of its own determinate limitations and demands that such a critique be ongoing—just as queer critique, as I indicated earlier, has been characterized centrally by an immanent critique of the blindnesses imposed by its own operative categories. An effort from within Marxism's terms to account for the horizons of social reality that Marxism has tended to erase needs to be joined with an immanent scrutiny of those same terms. When these two imperatives fail to operate together, what can result, for example, is the endlessly expansive use of a category like reification, reification as bad infinity, shorn of any attention to the way in which its meaning will have to change if it is to retain its ability to account for constantly changing social relations. Marxism itself is in this respect an always unfinished project, constitutively open to rereadings of its terms. Even Foucault, that supposed theoretical opponent of Marx, took the position that this openness was not only characteristic of Marxism but one of its strengths.[44] Marxism's epistemological limits, its finitude, are not static and never given in advance. These limits should be understood instead in terms of the way Marxism is practiced within specific social and historical situations.

As I indicated earlier, for example, Lukács's privileging of reification's subjective moment is in part a response to the privileging, in the official

Marxism of his time, of capital's objective development over the forms of subjectivity it produces. That same methodological privileging can now be viewed, from a queer perspective, in a substantially different light. Reification, to the extent that it defines capital's ever greater internal differentiation in terms of mystification, will hardly be able to account for new perspectives on the social that this internal differentiation makes possible. One way to account more concretely for reification's inherent logic of differentiation, then, is to critique the concept from a perspective that itself emerges from within this ongoing differentiation. To scrutinize this Marxian category from a queer vantage is to scrutinize it from a historically situated vantage and to discern the way in which the social dynamic of reification, far from only preempting critical understandings of capitalist social relations, has also opened up new critical understandings of those relations.

In the indispensable discussion of reification to which I referred earlier, Said emphasizes that "theory is a response to a specific social and historical situation of which an intellectual occasion is a part," and that concepts are transformed whenever they are employed within a different situation. Concepts are transformed to the extent that they travel, as he puts it.[45] In suggesting the ways in which reification is a condition of possibility for the queer aspiration to totality to which I referred at the beginning of this introduction, this book sketches what we might call a queer variation on the dialectic of reification and totality. Theoretically framing queer critical practice and some of its conditions of possibility in terms of this dialectic, this study also accounts for ways in which this practice and these conditions diverge from some of this dialectic's traditional assumptions. This book contends that this queer aspiration to totality now makes it possible to see the ways in which reification was a condition of possibility for a new form of social differentiation that emerged at the beginning of the twentieth century, an opposition between heterosexual and homosexual forms of subjectivity, and thus also for this same queer aspiration itself. Marxian aspirations to totality need to be understood in relation to what they tend to elide, elisions that include heteronormativity's multiform and invisible horizons, horizons it has taken this same queer vantage on totality to elucidate. What the vantage of queer critical practice can propose is a critique of fundamental Marxian categories that is also entirely consistent with Marx's method. Indeed, a queer critique of the reification/totality dialectic that is also a Marxian concretizing of this dialectic is my most basic objective, an objective that insists throughout on the simultaneous convergence and divergence of these open, unfinished forms of critical knowledge.

REGULATION

This book emphasizes the way in which this queer variation on reification and totality is mediated by stages in the relatively specific history of capital accumulation in the twentieth-century United States. The discourse of reification, moving as it does from the specifics of commodification and the division of labor out toward the kind of epistemological forms and capacities these dynamics tend to produce, hardly in itself provides an adequate basis for understanding capital's operation at this historically and nationally specific horizon. Such a basis is, however, provided by the discourse of regulation theory, a discourse that has also focused much of its attention on the twentieth-century United States.[46] Regulation theory emphasizes that the accumulation of capital, if it is to be sustained over long periods, must always be institutionally secured at a range of different levels, from corporate and governmental forms of regulation to a normalization of everyday social practices. Perhaps the only characteristic that regulation theory and the discourse of reification share is their common effort to grasp capital's historical development in conceptual terms. While both discourses are simultaneously theoretical and historical in emphasis, while both endeavor to conceptualize capital's historical logic, regulation theory operates at a different level of abstraction. It represents an effort to establish a set of historically grounded concepts that can negotiate the distance, as it were, between highly theoretical accounts of capital, on the one hand, and historically detailed elaborations of socioeconomic development, on the other.[47] Regulation theory focuses not on capital's general laws of motion but on the historical and institutional specifics of accumulation in a relatively well-defined period and location. It emphasizes that the history of capitalism cannot be understood without accounting for broad and recurrent corporate and governmental efforts to forestall accumulation crisis, strategies that have punctuated capital's history, which indeed have had to be as persistent as the threat of crisis itself. Though the character of specific efforts to mitigate crisis can never be predicted in advance, these efforts typically implicate, in one way or another, capital and labor as well as government. Though they operate at the level of class struggle and are in this way relevant to questions of class consciousness, the respective emphases of regulation theory and the discourse of reification are in the main quite divergent. In highlighting capital's constant tendency to undermine the very institutional preconditions that ensure the prospects for additional accumulation, regulation theory emphasizes not what the discourse of reification emphasizes—capital's potent capacity to misrepresent its constitutive relations and processes—but the fundamental social volatility that capital's objective contradictions consistently produce, and the socially broad, historically conditioned strategies necessary to keep crisis at bay.

Central to this discourse is the relation between two key concepts. The first is the *regime of accumulation,* which refers to a macro-level, relatively cohesive coordination of production, distribution, and consumption sustained over an extended period. Fordism, regulation theory's primary example of such a regime, identifies an unusually (even anomalously) coherent consolidation of the production-distribution-consumption circuit that resulted in strong levels of accumulation in the United States from, very roughly, the early fifties to the late sixties. The second concept identifies the institutional and practical foundation that secures any functional regime of accumulation: the *mode of regulation.* A mode of regulation is a complex ensemble combining official political structures, practices, and policies with a network of broadly defined social norms and habits, an ensemble that ensures consent, at the level of everyday practical life, to the reproduction of the conditions of accumulation. Relationships between a regime of accumulation and a mode of regulation are never entirely stable; these relationships are "temporary institutional 'fixes.'"[48] The development of Fordism, for instance, as David Harvey puts it, "depended on myriad individual, corporate, institutional, and state decisions, many of them unwitting political choices or knee-jerk responses to the crisis tendencies of capitalism, particularly as manifest in the great depression of the 1930s."[49] Regulation theory emphasizes in this respect that any successful harmonizing of a regime of accumulation and a mode of regulation is only ever a hegemonic process, which is to say a potentially unstable one, and in this respect the work of Gramsci is one of regulation theory's more obvious touchstones.[50] But my study will place special emphasis on the ways in which macrosocial forms of regulation have to be supplemented with microsocial forms of normativity and discipline not unlike those highlighted by Foucault especially, and by queer critical practice generally. Regulation theory is anything but an explicitly Foucauldian means of theorizing the ways in which accumulation is normalized at the level of everyday social practices.[51] But I argue that it is precisely the more micro-level components of the mode of regulation, especially as this mode operates at the level of the body, which provide a way of understanding the relation between the dynamics of capital accumulation as they develop in the United States and the way in which a reification of sexual desire attributes to bodies certain new, normalized forms of sexual, and potentially critical, subjectivity. Social norms and practices that from a certain perspective appear cultural or "superstructural" are instead treated from this point of view as "potentially *infrastructural*," as Leerom Medovoi has put it, "as genuine conditions of possibility for the reproduction of any particular historical form of capitalism."[52] The queer variation on reification and totality that I argue unfolds in the United States during the past century is mediated by these efforts to forestall accumulation crisis. In this way, the following chapters contend that reification's objective effects must be understood not only in terms of the tenacious resilience of capital typically emphasized by the discourse of reification. They also need to be understood in terms of capital's persistent instability, in terms of its fundamental opposition to itself, and the way in which this instability is negotiated historically through a range of forms of social regulation, forms that in this respect are misrecognized insofar as they are identified as "merely" cultural or superstructural.

In addition to this emphasis on capital's persistent instability, my analysis highlights one other, major theme from regulation theory: the way in which unprecedented corporate and governmental efforts to manage social demand—to socialize a national population into a consumption norm—have been one of the defining characteristics of capitalism as it has developed in the United States since the early twentieth century. What I identify as a disciplinary social consumption has been constitutive of the reification of heterosexual and homosexual forms of subjectivity and of the gradual emergence of a queer critical knowledge of the social. Beginning in the early twentieth century, I argue, bodies are increasingly, if quite unevenly, normalized not only as heterosexual and homosexual subjects but also, and inseparably, as consuming subjects. The following chapters highlight the way in which sexually disciplined, regulated bodies, simultaneously deployed as strategies of capital accumulation, are defining aspects of the mode of regulation that begins to emerge in the United States in the early twentieth century.

While at the level of individual chapters the book develops specific Marxian critiques of certain influential arguments closely identified with queer studies, its overarching concern is to bring a queer vantage to bear on the dialectic of reification and totality, a dialectic exemplified in these pages by the work of three figures: Lukács, who made this dialectic central to an entire Marxist tradition, and Herbert Marcuse and Fredric Jameson, both of whom give sexuality a central place in their respective reformulations of this dialectic. Though the categories of reification and totality are ultimately inseparable, this book's sequence of chapters, emphasizing reification as a condition of possibility for a queer, critical vantage on the social, gradually shifts emphasis from discussions that emphasize reification to discussions that emphasize totality. The first two chapters approach the same, early-twentieth-century conjuncture from distinct vantages. In chapter 1, I develop in greater detail the claim made earlier that both Lukács and Foucault elaborate a turn-of-the-century epistemological shift defined by a reification of bodily qualities and capacities. Rejecting any assumption that *History and Class Consciousness* and the first volume of *The History of Sexuality* are simply incommensurate texts, I suggest ways in which each enables a productive rereading of the other. Chapter 2 then further considers the way in which sexual knowledges discipline bodies, and the mediation of this corporeal discipline by capital, by reconsidering one of queer theory's formative early interventions, Judith Butler's notion of gender performativity. Here I try to concretize the performative normalization of masculinity, elaborating that norm not in Butler's relatively abstract, formal register but as a socially and historically specific phenomenon mediated by capital. This discussion will require some consideration of the historical limits of Butler's terms, limits that are anything but explicit in her work. But this chapter also responds to a persistent Marxian complaint about Butler's erasure of the horizon of capital from her analysis by proposing ways in which her theory of gender in fact presupposes that horizon and is ultimately well suited to the task of thinking gender, sexuality, and reification together.

Chapters 3 and 4 also approach a specific historical period from different perspectives. Marcuse's *Eros and Civilization,* which was a major influence on the gay liberation movement, is my central concern in chapter 3. Marcuse's influence on gay liberation, I argue, should be understood in terms of a relation between the objective and the subjective—in terms of a collective political subject's negotiation of his influence, especially his conceptualization of the objectified, revolutionarily sexual body, which was inseparable from his profound pessimism, during the period of *Eros and Civilization*'s production, about revolutionary subjectivity as such. *Eros and Civilization,* that is, leaves the struggle to articulate sexual subjectivity with revolutionary subjectivity—programmatically to bridge the gap between abstract Freudian speculation and historically conditioned practice—to this pivotal political movement. Chapter 3 begins to sketch the way in which reification's objective moment opens opportunities for the formation of new forms of critical, antiheteronormative subjectivity, beginning the book's shift from an emphasis on reification to an emphasis on totality. Chapter 4 then moves to a more direct consideration of Fordism's characteristic mode of regulation by resuming the historical analysis, begun in chapter 2, of the performative normalization of masculinity. Here I frame the relation between two developments of the sixties— a national gay male formation's increasingly visible, collective working of what Butler would call the homosexual weakness in a heteronormalizing masculinity, and the development and crisis of a Fordist regime of accumulation—in terms of the way a specific narrative, the film *Midnight Cowboy* (1969), allegorizes both of them. This allegorical reading sets the stage for the chapter's final objective, a critical engagement with the work of Jameson. Here I ask how one might account for the unpredictable, objective historical repercussions of the reification of sexual desire within the terms of Jameson's rethinking of allegory. The book's final chapter returns to the topic with which this introduction began, a queer form of critical practice that has taken shape, I argue, as an aspiration to totality. Chapter 5 delineates a distinctly queer vantage on totality from within the determinate social and historical conditions that obtain in the United States after Fordism, a regulatory conjuncture most precisely characterized, I argue, as neoliberal. I conclude by considering the aspiration to totality performed by that indispensable memoir of the eighties—the opening stage of neoliberalism in the United States, and the opening stage in the AIDS epidemic in the United States—David Wojnarowicz's *Close to the Knives.*

The sequence of chapters moves through reification's objective moment to a potentially surprising, queer, subjective moment. This sequence echoes Lukács's movement, in "Reification and the Consciousness of the Proletariat," from "the phenomenon of reification" to "the standpoint of the proletariat"—an echo intended simultaneously to converge with and diverge from the reification/totality dialectic Lukács introduced into twentieth-century Marxism. Though some of my chapters develop arguments introduced in previous ones, the book offers not a continuous historical narrative but a reading of this dialectic from a queer vantage, and in relation to a series of conjunctures understood in terms of ongoing corporate and state efforts to avoid accumulation crisis. What links the chapters is finally a method, a triangulation of Marxian and queer perspectives on totality with historically specific analysis. To subject the dialectic of reification and totality to the kind of historical scrutiny Marx delineates in the *Grundrisse* is also, in the present case, to subject it to a queer kind of scrutiny. Only in relation to such a critique is it possible to understand a certain situation of Marxism, the way in which its limitations are indicative of queer horizons it routinely fails to register.

chapter 1

DISCIPLINED BODIES:
LUKÁCS, FOUCAULT, AND THE
REIFICATION OF DESIRE

The respective historical narratives unfolded by *History and Class Consciousness* and the first volume of *The History of Sexuality* could hardly diverge more radically.[1] This divergence should be understood not merely in terms of the concrete, irreducible differences between "class consciousness" and "sexuality" but also—and more consequentially—in terms of method. Foucault's narrative is presented by way of a methodological rejection of the dialectical humanism of Hegel, a rejection made more explicit elsewhere in Foucault's work but informing all of it.[2] This methodological rejection is easily as fundamental as the allegiance to Hegel that everywhere informs *History and Class Consciousness*. In this chapter, I set out to defamiliarize each narrative by way of the other, initially by homing in on a commonality: both represent as historically pivotal a period of a few decades around the beginning of the twentieth century. Lukács identifies this moment in the history of capitalism in terms of an unprecedented rationalization of production (Taylorism is his key example) and its fallout: a broad, indeed "total," reification of society. Foucault identifies a contemporaneous, similarly significant moment in the history of sexuality in terms of the psychoanalytic culmination of a more long-term epistemological "deployment" of sexuality, the psychoanalytic location of sexual pathology within the "family cell."

Bringing Foucault's anti-Hegelian analysis of sexuality to bear on Lukács's arguments is useful in highlighting both the value of the concept of reification in historicizing sexuality's relation to capitalist development and the analytic limitations that Lukács's Hegelianism enforces. What Foucault characterizes as an emerging discursive regime representing sexuality in terms of subjectivities rather than actions—for example, in terms of homosexual "species" instead of sodomitical practices—I argue can be understood as mediated by capital in terms of a growing epistemological dissociation of sexual desire from the gendered body, a reification of sexual desire as such. On the one hand, I argue that the concept of reification can enable a Marxian historicization of Foucault's terms that emphasizes the shift from a physiological to a psychoanalytic model in which sexual desire becomes a discursively independent phenomenon, an object of study in its own right and epistemologically distinct from dichotomized gender definition. On the other hand, this chapter draws on Foucault to show not only that the psychoanalytic stage in the deployment of sexuality exemplifies reification but that this insight suggests a need to rethink this concept itself, to displace it from some of Lukács's structuring assumptions.

Lukács extends Marx's arguments about the fetishism of the commodity to argue that scientifically managed capitalism reifies, in an unprecedented and indeed total fashion, properties and relations that are always ultimately social, historical, and human. Objectively, the work process in particular and social knowledge in general are increasingly fragmented, organized around specialized, predictable operations and the "principle" of "what is and can be calculated."[3] Under the influence of an increasingly complex division of labor, including an intensified division between intellectual and manual labor, social knowledge itself assumes what we might call, in a more Foucauldian parlance, the disciplinary, normalizing character of the capitalist labor process itself. The totality of the modern capitalist social formation has its structural basis, for Lukács, in factory organization. In this he is famously under the influence of Weber's argument that capitalism cannot be maintained without the rationalization of politics and law and, ultimately, of daily life itself. For Lukács and Weber alike, all aspects of social life are abstracted and standardized, reduced to formal, partial systems. Subjectively, the worker in particular and human beings in general are profoundly fragmented, reduced to so many fully predictable, calculable operations, inducing a "contemplative" relation to this objective historical development: "The contemplative stance adopted towards a process mechanically conforming to fixed laws and enacted independently of man's consciousness and impervious to human intervention, i.e., a perfectly closed system, must likewise transform the basic categories of man's immediate attitude toward the world."[4] Lukács elaborates here the formation of a distinctly modern and distinctly passive form of subjectivity. Reification enforces an objective but false, "frozen" immediacy that causes human beings to experience historical processes as natural laws that govern human life and elude human control. This frozen state of affairs can only be negated, he insists, by the collective proletarian subject that—as both subject and (exploited) object of this reifying process—is the only subject capable of becoming an agent of dialectical reunification.

In this chapter I begin my critique of this concept by emphasizing the broad, disciplinary character of the reified knowledges to which Lukács refers. I read reification not in the Lukácsian terms of a relation between knowledge and consciousness but in the Foucauldian terms of a relation between knowledge and bodies. Both Lukács and Foucault elaborate a turn-of-the-century shift from knowledges that classify bodies to knowledges that partition bodies, a shift in which bodily capacities are epistemologically disembodied, reified. The critique of Foucault I develop here is that he mystifies the very character of the regime of sexual knowledge he elaborates—specifically, its status as a product of this increasingly complex social division of labor. But my primary objective in this chapter is a critique of Lukács: I displace the concept of reification both from suppositions on Lukács's part that I identify as heteronormative and the Hegelian frame—especially the methodological privileging of subject over object—within which that elaboration proceeds.

This chapter also lays out in some detail the reification of sexual desire I contend emerges in the United States in the early twentieth century. After establishing key points of similarity between the respective turn-of-the-century histories presented by Lukács and Foucault, I read both against two developments that, I argue, mediate and concretize this reification of desire as it emerges in this specific national context: Taylorism's repercussions throughout the division of labor, and an emergent set of corporate strategies for managing social consumption—what regulation theory identifies as an emergent mode of regulation. I then examine a nineteenth-century epistemology of gender difference that was increasingly displaced during this period by an epistemology disembodying and reifying not only sexual desire but gender difference itself. The chapter concludes with an effort to specify the kind of critical appropriation of the concept of reification this juxtaposition of Lukács and Foucault necessarily performs.

CLASSIFYING BODIES, PARTITIONING BODIES

The scientifically managed shop floor of Taylorism manifests the dynamic of reification in "concentrated form" for Lukács; he insists that the deskilling of the factory would never succeed "were it not for the fact that it contained in concentrated form the whole structure of capitalist society."[5] While his central concern is consciousness, he underscores the extent to which, inside and outside the factory, knowledges emerge that reify *bodily* attributes: laborers are pervasively deskilled as a technical-managerial class emerges to enforce a systemic expropriation of the technical capacity—the knowledge—that was once indissociable from the embodied, skilled practice of labor itself. This emerging class now possesses this knowledge in the form of "science," disembodying that knowledge, expropriating it from the laborer and objectifying it within managerial discourse. As Harry Braverman puts it in his landmark study of labor deskilling, "the unity of thought and action, conception and execution, hand and mind, which capitalism threatened from its beginnings, is now attacked by a systematic dissolution employing all the resources of science and the various engineering disciplines based upon it."[6] In Foucauldian terms, a normalizing knowledge regime emerges that disciplines individual laboring bodies. But for Lukács this emergence operates dialectically: the bodies that had previously been the exclusive location of that knowledge are now disciplined by the very thing they had previously embodied, a technical knowledge now expropriated, managerial, "scientific."

Reification's objective moment refers, then, to a subjection of the worker to an expropriation of something in addition to, and qualitatively different from, the value that labor produces, an expropriation of technical knowledge and indeed a wide array of human attributes and capacities. As reification becomes "total," an abstract, formal, instrumental logic, a logic of what Lukács calls "pure calculation," becomes widespread within knowledge production in general. "With the modern 'psychological' analysis of the work-process (in Taylorism)," for example, "rational mechanisation extends right into the worker's 'soul': even his psychological attributes are separated from his total personality and placed in opposition to it so as

to facilitate their integration into specialised rational systems and their reduction to statistically viable concepts."[7] Referring also to the "specialized
'virtuoso'" of what would eventually be called the professional-managerial
class, "the vendor of his objectified and reified faculties"—his examples
from outside the factory per se include the hyperspecializations of journal-
ists and bureaucrats—Lukács insists that reification represents a moment
in which the individual's "qualities and abilities are no longer an organic
part of his personality, they are things which he can 'own' or 'dispose of'
like the various objects of the external world."[8] Subjectively, relations
between people are represented here again as relations between things,
things that in turn govern the lives of those people. But Lukács is at pains
to emphasize that, objectively, the things in question now include epistemologically abstracted and objectified bodily properties and capacities.

Historicizing knowledge in such a way as to demystify its objectifying and disciplinary character is a fundamental objective that Lukács and
Foucault share. Foucault's narrative of the formation of a psychoanalytically defined sexual subjectivity as the nineteenth century gave way to the
twentieth not only corroborates this dynamic of social reification, as I will
demonstrate, but also begins to suggest the critical value, vis-à-vis Lukács,
of his radically anti-Hegelian, antisubjectivist framing of history in terms
of its impact on bodies rather than on consciousness. Both Lukács and
Foucault elaborate the formation of historically specific forms of subjectivity in terms of the conditioning of that subjectivity by certain institutionalized forms of knowledge. For Lukács and Foucault alike, subjectivity is
embedded in a history of the way particular knowledges shape, constrain,
instrumentalize, attach meaning to, and otherwise manipulate concrete
bodily practices. For Lukács, a reified social formation induces subjective
passivity and "contemplation," while for Foucault the so-called human sciences are simultaneously constraining and productive discursive attempts
to subject human beings to epistemology, to produce the human subject
of knowledge by treating human beings the way the natural or physical
sciences typically treat the objects of the natural world.[9] In both Lukács
and Foucault, we encounter an insistence that modern subjectivity develops in relation to an epistemological regime that gives the "human" scientific, instrumental form.

In Foucault's account of sexuality's historical deployment, the decades
surrounding the beginning of the twentieth century mark a qualitative

shift that is strikingly similar to that shift elaborated by Lukács—in this case a shift from a physiologically oriented sexual science that *classifies* bodies to a psychoanalytically oriented sexual science that *partitions* bodies in its emphasis on an internally contradictory bodily psyche. Nineteenth-century sexual science is, for Foucault, epistemologically inseparable from the classification of bodies according to race within the discourse of eugenics. Sexual science classified bodies according to certain sexual characteristics, distinguishing, for instance, between "normal" sexual bodies and sexual "inverts." Inverts were routinely associated with racial degeneration; they were, after all, infuriatingly unhelpful in reproducing the vulnerable white race that eugenics discourse implicitly or explicitly posited.[10] During this period, as Foucault puts it, "the analysis of heredity was placing sex . . . in a position of 'biological responsibility' with regard to the species." This discourse of sexuality was organized around concerns about "the body, vigor, longevity, progeniture, and descent of the classes that 'ruled.'"[11] By way of the discourse of sexology, according to Foucault, the nineteenth-century bourgeoisie attempted scientifically and defensively to isolate itself from the immediately felt threat of a working class stigmatized as sexually unclean, degenerate, and dangerous.

The break with this dynamic of epistemological classification is, for Foucault, largely a credit to Freud. While Freudian psychoanalysis "resumed the project of medical technology appropriate for dealing with the sexual instinct," it also "sought to free it from its ties with heredity, and hence from eugenics and the various racisms."[12] Freudianism broke with sexology in refusing to base itself on physiology, and figures like Sander Gilman have suggested that this break was itself by no means racially neutral: "As virtually all of Freud's early disciples were Jews, the lure of psychoanalysis for them may well have been its claims for a universalization of human experience and an active exclusion of the importance of race from its theoretical framework."[13] In what Lukács would term the formalized "partial" science of Freudian psychoanalysis—especially in its insistence on an irreducible, complexly signifying "polymorphous" sexuality—desire is isolated from other bodily properties, reified into scientific discourse, developed into a means of revealing the truth, the essence of an individual subject. A bodily capacity assumes the epistemological form of a complexly, scientifically signifying system.

Foucault famously situates psychoanalysis in relation to a larger history of "confessional technologies," technologies that expose sexual information to figures of authority—religious "experts" at first (the priest in the confessional), scientific experts later (the analyst in the clinic)—who were entrusted with the exclusive ability to discern the truth of, and to make meaning of, that information. Only through such a confession—only through the mediation of expertise—could a subject understand itself. I want to stress the striking similarity between the clinic's gradual supersession of the religious confessional and the contemporaneous emergence of Taylorism: both the shop floor and the clinic—the modern, scientifically managed confessional, as opposed to the earlier, theologically managed confessional—become sites of scientific *deskilling*, sites at which knowledge is expropriated from bodies, sites at which those bodies are made into particular kinds of subjects precisely in becoming subject to scientific expertise. The epistemological objectification of the worker's technical skill and the epistemological objectification of sexual desire are both, in this sense, aspects of a more general, ongoing, reifying capitalist dynamic that Lukács elaborates.

If psychoanalysis has its prehistory in nineteenth-century sexual science, moreover, Taylorism has its prehistory in nineteenth-century forms of industrial deskilling, and indeed both of these prehistories are characterized by a dynamic of body classification. Marx's analysis in the first volume of *Capital* of the worker's gradual reduction to a mere appendage of industrial machinery runs through three major stages: simple cooperation, manufacture, and large-scale industry. Each of these stages supersedes the previous one through an ongoing dynamic of deskilling on the one hand, and the technological "subsumption" of previous forms of labor on the other.[14] This process was historically uneven and took widely different forms in different contexts, especially if one compares its unfolding within different countries. In the United States, for example, Taylorism culminated a process of industrial deskilling that had itself been under way for most, but not all, of the nineteenth century, and in highly uneven fashion given the different paces of industrialization and urbanization in different regions.[15] But across cases this history entailed the reduction of labor to isolated specialized functions and the classification of laboring bodies according to specialized tasks. Such classification typically took a spatial form, the division of the factory into different work areas. The U.S. labor historian David Montgomery mentions some of the specific workshops in a 1902 farm equipment factory, for example: machine shop, polishing department, fitting department, blacksmith shop.[16]

Given his emphasis on the impact of knowledge on bodies, Foucault's discussion of a nineteenth-century factory in *Discipline and Punish* is especially relevant here. The several shop floors of this factory were divided into sets of specialized work areas—tables arranged in rows, each inhabited by a craftsman and in some cases an assistant, including engravers, printers, dyers, and colorists. Foucault stresses that "production was divided up and the labour process was articulated, on the one hand, according to its stages or elementary operations, and, on the other hand, according to the individuals, the particular bodies, that carried it out: each variable of this force—strength, promptness, skill, constancy—would be observed, and therefore characterized, assessed, computed and related to the individual who was its particular agent. Thus, spread out in a perfectly legible way over the whole series of individual bodies, the work force may be analyzed in individual units." The labor discipline of the factory during the period between the earliest stages in the deskilling of the independent artisan and full-fledged Taylorism subdivides a certain spatial concentration of laboring bodies into distinct kinds of laboring bodies, "the disciplinary space" being "always, basically, cellular."[17]

But the shift within sexual science from a logic of body classification to a logic of body partitioning ultimately has its basis in specific mediations that intervene between and connect these two histories of deskilling, mediations that are historically much more complex than Lukács's analysis itself equips us to discern.

TEMPORALITIES OF LABOR AND DESIRE

Harry Braverman's classic account of labor deskilling in the United States frames dramatic shifts in the national division of labor as a product of Taylorism, while Michel Aglietta emphasizes in the foundational text of regulation theory that the unprecedented corporate effort during this period to manage the rate of capital accumulation was centrally an effort to manage social consumption.[18] Braverman's and Aglietta's respective analyses approach the period from divergent perspectives, Braverman defining it in terms of the emergence of monopoly capitalism, Aglietta in terms of a theory of regimes of accumulation. I bring these perspectives together here to emphasize the structural and historical connections between changes in the division of labor and this increasing effort to manage social consumption, and the mediation of the reification of sexual desire by both.

Lukács explicitly connects intensifying reification with an increasingly more complex division of labor—the increasing specializations of laborers and bureaucrats alike, for instance—but Braverman makes possible a more detailed account of this relation. He stresses that, like all innovations in productive technology, scientific management had as its aim an increase in labor productivity, which entailed a simultaneous decrease in the demand for labor power. Fundamental to Marx's analysis of the movement from simple cooperation to manufacture to large-scale industry is the insight that these technological innovations facilitate a more rapid accumulation of capital by increasing labor's productivity, which also tends to decrease the portion of new value extracted from labor power. In Braverman's succinct formulation, "the purpose of machinery is not to increase but to decrease the number of workers attached to it."[19] But because of pressures of competition, capital must be expanded if only to be preserved; the need to maintain the rate of profit makes this a situation of potential accumulation crisis—overaccumulation, that is, of idle, uninvested capital on the one hand and idle, uninvested labor on the other—a situation in which ways of reinvesting this newly "freed" capital and labor must be located if crisis is to be avoided. The ongoing imperative to locate new sites at which to bring capital and labor back together is in this respect basic to the ongoing expansion and complexification of the division of labor.[20]

One form such sites took in the wake of Taylorism was a range of new service industries created with the increasingly urban U.S. population in mind. As industrialization pulled the population out of rural, agrarian areas and into urban centers, new branches of production came into being to fulfill new needs, to compensate, in particular, for the corrosion of older, smaller-scale forms of cooperative social and family production and self-sufficiency. These earlier forms of social organization tended to be locally organized (maintaining close connections between agrarian regions and small towns, for example) and were distinguished by a significant overlap between familial and productive practices; these were social relations not yet dominated, that is, by a logic of exchange value. The rise of a broad service industry in the United States is in part a story about how this logic came to dominate U.S. social relations, beginning with capital's gradual, extensive conquest of goods production over the course of the nineteenth century. As capital is accumulated in more and more technologically efficient, productive industries, labor is also displaced from them, and these accumulations of capital and labor are subsequently reinvested in the production of new goods as well as services. Increasingly, the population relies more and more heavily on what Braverman simply calls "the market": a market "not only for food, clothing, and shelter, but also for recreation, amusement, security, for the care of the young, the old, the sick, the handicapped. In time not only the material and service needs but even the emotional patterns of life are channeled through the market."[21] Goods production is gradually assimilated to the commodity form, followed by the commodification of preexisting services, followed by a cycle of production including new services, many of which replace older alternatives, assimilating social life more generally to the commodity form. As Marx puts it in the *Grundrisse,* the ongoing production of surplus value reaches a stage at which it "requires the production of new consumption; requires that the consuming circle within circulation expands as did the productive circle previously. Firstly quantitative expansion of existing consumption; secondly: creation of new needs by propagating existing ones in a wide circle; *thirdly:* production of *new* needs and discovery and creation of new use-values."[22] And crucially, Braverman emphasizes that the new forms of labor ultimately produced by this dramatic restructuring of social production embrace "the engineering, technical, and scientific cadre, the lower ranks of supervision and management, the considerable numbers of specialized and 'professional' employees occupied in marketing, financial and organizational administration, and the like, as well as, outside of capitalist industry proper, in hospitals, schools, government administration, and so forth."[23]

This last point especially begins to suggest the way in which the pivotal Freudian stage in the deployment of sexuality was mediated in the United States by a specific moment in the ongoing history of social efforts to manage accumulation. The disciplinary and commodifying institutionalization of psychoanalysis is deeply implicated in the structural and historical repercussions of Taylorism: as part of an emerging differentiation of service industries, it is one site at which capital and labor were reinvested in the early twentieth century, an example of the highly specified, reifying knowledges that Lukács represents as products of an increasingly complex division of labor, especially a broadening division between mental and manual labor.[24] The widespread social deskilling of the subject, which I framed in the previous section as a key aspect of reification, is another way of articulating what Braverman calls "the atrophy of competence." As he puts it, "the population finds itself willy-nilly in the position of being able to do little or nothing itself as easily as it can be . . . done in the marketplace by one of the multifarious new branches of social labor."[25] And this perhaps especially applies to things it had never occurred to the population to do for itself before. One effect of Freud's famous 1909 lectures at Clark University was to accelerate significantly the spread of his ideas within the scientific and medical professions in the United States. Within a decade, psychoanalysis virtually dominated American psychiatry, which by that point could already claim the largest number of analysts in the world. For younger analysts especially, Freudianism represented a dramatic improvement over an earlier, physiologically oriented psychiatry.[26] And between the wars, this emergent field began to have a substantial impact on other fields as well, including criminology, education, and social work.[27]

If there is a distinction to be maintained between "consumer" or "mass" culture as discourses like cultural history tend to define these terms, on the one hand, and the new forms of knowledge that developed in the United States along with it, on the other, consumption in this more narrow, "cultural" rather than "social" sense is nonetheless entangled with these knowledges in complex ways, playing an important role in disseminating and popularizing them, for example. Richard Ohmann makes this point when he argues that the magazines he takes to exemplify an emergent early-twentieth-century form of "mass" culture—publications marketed to a developing professional-managerial class—played a significant role in this kind of dissemination.[28] The promulgation of Freudian ideas within a broadening and deepening normalization of consumption in the United States occurred rapidly, as Eli Zaretsky points out. The mass coverage of psychoanalysis quickly surpassed the coverage of other kinds of therapy; the Hearst newspapers reported on the analysis of Mabel Dodge Luhan; Hearst himself later tried to persuade Freud to come to Chicago to study Leopold and Loeb; and Freud's nephew, Edward Bernays, the "Father of Public Relations," began to disseminate his uncle's ideas within his own emerging profession.[29] This scientific, clinical component of a more internally differentiated social production here also becomes, in Foucauldian terms, a component of a larger discursive formation, a larger *episteme* that includes, for example, popular and legal discourses, a discursive horizon that expands far beyond the specific domains in which the labor of psychoanalysis takes place.[30]

Indeed, the crucial point that Braverman at best leaves implicit is that consumption, bound together as it was in these ways with new epistemological disciplines, itself begins to assume during this period an increasingly normalized, regulatory character. Abstractions like the "universal market" are symptomatic of the extent to which, as a function of the productivist lens through which Braverman examines the changing division of labor, consumption remains undertheorized in his account, assumed even to take care of itself (even as the term "monopoly capital" implies corporate control over distribution as well as production). Even before scientific management began to revolutionize production, corporations recognized the maintaining of sufficient demand to avoid a crisis of overproduction as a persistent problem. U.S. manufacturers, economists, and merchants were by the late nineteenth century acknowledging that the inducement of demand was a serious dilemma facing an era of increasing productivity, a problem that a less haphazard, more engineered approach to marketing could potentially solve.[31]

Aglietta characterizes what he calls the "transformation of the conditions of existence of the wage earning class" during this period, by which the commodity relation "penetrates into their whole mode of life," in terms of the uneven but unmistakable displacement of a primarily "extensive" regime of accumulation by a primarily "intensive" one.[32] These terms identify two historically specific, broadly defined modalities by which capital accumulation is managed. During the primarily extensive, nineteenth-century stage in industrial development in the United States, the crises that plagued capitalism were mollified to some extent through a geographic expansion of production, a complexification of the division of labor, and the "safety valve" of the "open frontier." In the second, primarily intensive stage, capitalism's inherent crisis tendencies are held at bay for extended periods through a coordination of consumption with production. Both the implementation of Taylorism and this broad effort to coordinate production with consumption were highly uneven between the wars, indeed so uneven and haphazard that regulation theory typically explains the depression that followed a decade of dramatically intensified mass marketing in terms of a temporary if striking failure of this coordination.[33] Only with the Fordist regime of accumulation did the coordination of production with consumption reach its apex; Fordism secured the longest sustained boom in the history of U.S. capitalism, from roughly the early fifties to the late sixties, and its success was largely the result of a range of forms of governmental, Keynesian intervention in the managing of accumulation.

Earlier efforts to coordinate production with consumption were largely restricted to the private sector. But even here the acceleration of demand inducement was as unmistakable as it was uneven. Elements of increased demand inducement that began during this period included dramatic increases in capital concentration and in the pervasiveness of finance capital and trusts, which in turn facilitated greater intercorporate control not only of investment and competition but also of marketing. But these developments unfolded alongside a still strong tendency to keep labor costs to a minimum, resulting in a series of labor disputes in the twenties and thirties, especially over the implementation of Taylorist production norms. So resocializing laborers into a consumption norm also had to be an effort to neutralize their potential for radical action, as well as to commodify and incorporate social norms characteristic of traditional, agrarian ways of life, including the importance of self-sufficiency and thrift, localized culture, extended family networks, and communitarian and familial values; the persistence of such norms tended, moreover, to be reinforced by the constant arrival of immigrants into the labor force. The struggle during this period to implement a national consumption norm, in all its unevenness and contradiction, is perhaps best exemplified by the man for whom regulation theory named the Fordist regime of accumulation. Few people during the interwar period took the lead from Henry Ford's attempt to induce what we might call a local consumption norm by paying his workers higher wages and by micromanaging the personal lives that were to benefit from those wages. They were more likely to mimic Ford's readiness to employ hired guns to intimidate strikers. The point I would emphasize is that a normalization of social life operating increasingly at the moment of consumption rather than production was as definitively under way as it was riddled with contradictions during this period.[34] Underscoring both an increasingly deskilled factory experience and early-twentieth-century commercial compensations for it, the Lynds, for example, discover that the residents of "Middletown" attach value to work only in terms of the money they earn doing it, the money they can then spend on the increasingly wide array of commodified leisure activities available. It is this aspect of labor, "rather than the intrinsic satisfactions involved, that keeps Middletown working so hard as more and more of the activities of living are coming to be strained through the bars of the dollar sign," and as the city's residents witness the waning of "a system in which length of service, craftsmanship, and authority in the shop and social prestige among one's peers tended to go together."[35]

The uneven imposition of an intensive regime of accumulation begins to produce during this period a broad reification of social life, including a reification of sexual desire that operates centrally in the dimension of time. Capitalist production tends to quantify labor time into interchangeable, measurable units, and Taylorism intensifies the systematic abstraction and quantification of labor time already under way in the nineteenth-century history of industrial deskilling I glossed earlier. Abstraction and quantification are already under way, specifically, in the displacement, by a system of wage labor measured by the hour, of preindustrial forms of artisanship measured by the quality as well as the quantity of use values produced. Within preindustrial, largely agrarian processes of production—processes characterizing many regions of the United States well into the nineteenth century—labor is as inseparable from personal life, from the life of the family as a simultaneously producing and reproducing unit, for instance, as it is from lunar and seasonal cycles. Within these processes, time is apprehended as something dependent on, a pure function and product of, specific social practices. Moishe Postone, in his extended consideration of capital's abstraction of time, distinguishes between what he calls "concrete time" and "abstract time." Concrete time depends on events, is a function of those events. Abstract time is uniform, homogeneous, independent of events and indeed determining of those events. Concrete time is a result of, and is measured *by*, activity; abstract time itself conditions and is a measure *for* activity.[36]

In the gradual institutionalization of wage labor, one historically specific spatiotemporal environment is gradually destroyed, and a new one, increasingly dominated by the commodity's abstraction of time, begins to supersede it. Time changes from a dependent to an independent variable vis-à-vis labor; it becomes labor's normative measure. Taylorism culminates this process of transformation by making time into something independent and determining of the practice of labor, by reducing the entire working day to quantifiable labor time. It represents a major defeat of workers' individual and collective efforts to maintain some control over the pace at which surplus value is extracted (resistances that were a key source of the labor disputes of the twenties and thirties). This reduction of the laborer to an abstract quantity of labor power measured by the hour produces, as Lukács notes, an experiential disconnect between the practice of labor and the products of labor. And this disconnect can only intensify as productivity increases. To the extent that the quantity of abstract labor time necessary for a given output can be decreased—and labor time is abstracted at the moment of production precisely so that it may be decreased—capitalist production increases the temporal rate at which value is extracted from labor, and atrophies the laborer's cognitive, experiential capacity to connect the activity of labor with what it produces.

But Lukács, in generalizing the proletarian experience of scientifically managed labor far beyond the boundaries of the factory, also conflates the practice of labor with the life of the laborer, obscuring the way in which this loss of control over the rhythm of work intensifies another, closely related disconnect already developing in the United States by the mid-nineteenth century and accelerating after the Civil War: the experiential disconnect between the time spent working and the time spent not working.[37] Lukács's analysis in this way also obscures central aspects of the way in which reification unfolds in the specific time and place under consideration here. The abstract, estranged products of labor are increasingly consumed within an equally abstract time. The managing of consumption within an emerging intensive regime of accumulation, the attempt to ensure that effective demand keeps pace with increases in productivity, is (as the Lynds suggest) a compensatory intervention mediating—normalizing, regulating, commodifying—personal life. This intensive corroboration of production with consumption, in other words, entails a simultaneous disarticulation of the two at a cognitive, experiential level. This intervention of consumption reinforces the experiential disarticulation of labor from labor's products, especially a stark division between labor and personal life as the time of each becomes increasingly abstract, personal life increasingly as deskilled as labor, as I have suggested, and commodified by an emerging complex of compensatory service industries. Labor and leisure become more starkly differentiated precisely as they are coordinated within a larger unity, the quantified temporal measurement of both.

And as the Lynds also suggest, subjectivity itself is increasingly inter-pellated, we might say, within the space-time of leisure, at the moment of consumption rather than production, as consumption intervenes to com-pensate for ever more routinized, tedious, deskilled work environments. And crucially, this quantified mediation of the personal imputes to sub-jectivity distinct temporal rhythms of its own. In this sense subjectivity, while no less reified than Lukács would maintain, nonetheless becomes something other than purely passive, contemplative. I argued earlier that abstracted, reified objects include not only the products of abstracted labor power but also epistemologically objectified bodily properties. The division of labor, as Lukács points out, produces increasingly independent spheres that have a life of their own; new forms of industry are given over to their own internal logic. Psychoanalysis in this respect represents the epistemological abstraction of a "partial function" now made "autono-mous," as Lukács puts it, a function that "develop[s] through [its] own momentum and in accordance with [its] own special laws independently of the other partial functions of society."[38] What Lukács, who frames this pervasive epistemological partiality in terms of an increasing inability to see the "ontological totality," also fails to recognize is the way in which these epistemological "partial functions" open up new horizons of knowledge.[39]

With the buying and selling of psychoanalytic knowledge of the self, for example, sexual knowledge becomes knowledge of a reified, abstract tem-porality, a temporality specific to sexual desire. Far from being integrated into other temporalities, the psychoanalytic narrative of sexual develop-ment, a narrative in which fundamental, polymorphous sexual impulses are repressed and then repetitively, symptomatically manifested, attributes to sexuality a temporality that sets it apart from social life, that represents it as independent of other social temporalities; indeed, psychoanalysis takes an additional step and contends that the temporality of desire is centrally determining of social life. Sexual desire assumes the form of a temporality of symptomatic repetition. Rather than being a dependent function of spe-cific bodily capacities and practices (understood in terms of a reproductive cycle, for instance), this temporality becomes, in Postone's formulation, a "normative measure" for desire itself. Psychoanalysis represents sexual desire entirely in terms of this new temporality, makes it a function of this tem-porality, which thereby becomes the fundamental means by which sexual-ity is articulated, comprehended, known. The reifying disembodiment of sexual desire, its epistemological independence from and determination of the body, takes the form of the attribution to sexuality of this abstract temporality and is evident in the extent to which this temporality defines desire itself.

Capital had already reduced the laboring body to an exploited strategy of accumulation at the moment of production; now the sexual body is transformed, as this intensive regime emerges, into a supplementary strategy of accumulation at the moment of consumption.[40] Access to this sexual, temporal knowledge of self is to be had only through commodity exchange, the increasingly normalized consumption of psychoanalysis, which in its role in this emerging, intensive effort to manage the rate of accumulation deskills the sexual body so that that body can serve as a means to this end. Psychoanalysis deploys that body as a strategy that supplements and sustains, as Aglietta insists, the analogous strategizing of the laboring body. The reification of sexual desire, then, emerges from within capital's structural volatility, an aspect of capital that regulation theory has been much better equipped than the discourse of reification to recognize. It was this historically specific effort to stave off a crisis of accumulation that opened a national horizon in which personal life is epistemologically disciplined by exchange value, in which the sexual body is increasingly known in terms of an abstract, reified temporality. But this sexual body was mediated and disciplined not only by changes in the division of labor and the modalities by which accumulation was managed, but also by epistemologies of gender. The mediation of Freudianism itself by preexisting, normalized gender knowledges begins to indicate the much broader social implications of these specific aspects of reification.

REIFICATION AND THE GENDERED BODY

Gender differentiation is fundamental to the pivotal Freudian moment in the deployment of sexuality that Foucault traces. As the family gradually became a consuming rather than a producing unit, one of the things for sale to this family was psychoanalytic knowledge of itself, a knowledge of the sexual body as partitioned within and by the family. The gradual shift from a physiological to a psychoanalytic regime of sexual knowledge, from an epistemology of body classification to one of body partitioning, entailed an unprecedented sexual charging or "affective intensification," as

Foucault puts it, of the family space. Foucault defines the "deployment of alliance" that preceded the deployment of sexuality as "a system of marriage, of fixation and development of kinship ties, of transmission of names and possessions." Alliance, however, begins to lose its significance in the course of economic and political developments to which it is increasingly less central, developments that can "no longer rely on it as an adequate instrument or sufficient support." This emerging regime of sexual knowledge is then gradually "deployed" from "the fringes of familial institutions," he emphasizes, from outside the "family cell," and proceeds to saturate that cell with highly coded sexual meaning that seems at first to threaten but ultimately reinforces familial relations of alliance by radically changing the nature of those relations.[41] This sexual saturation culminates in a psychoanalytic universalization of desire that at the same time reinforces the family structure, framed as this universalized desire is, for example, by a differential, Oedipal positioning of parents in relation to children, fathers in relation to mothers.

The Freudian stage in this deployment, in other words, entailed a certain kind of disembodiment. As part of a range of institutional discourses and practices designed to manage the procreation of couples, the nineteenth-century stage in the deployment of sexuality articulated a scientific classification of sexually pathologized bodies situated at the margins of "normal," "healthy" (i.e., familial) affective life: the hysterical woman, the perverse adult, and the masturbating child. But psychoanalysis is the outcome of a transformation of this epistemological constellation of marginalized bodies into an epistemology by means of which a simultaneously disembodied and abnormal desire is located within the family cell itself. The pathologized, intrafamilial figures that both extend and supersede earlier, pathologized extrafamilial figures include "the nervous woman, the frigid wife, the indifferent mother—or worse, the mother beset by murderous obsessions—the impotent, sadistic, perverse husband, the hysterical or neurasthenic girl, the precocious and already exhausted child, and the young homosexual who rejects marriage or neglects his wife." Increasingly subject to the emergent form of sexual knowledge that would ultimately result in Freudianism, "the family was the crystal in the deployment of sexuality: it seemed to be the source of a sexuality that it actually only reflected and diffracted. By virtue of its permeability, and through that process of reflections to the outside, it became one of the most valuable tactical

components of the deployment."[42] A typology of extrafamilial pathologized sexual bodies is, according to this narrative, transformed in the late
nineteenth century and the early twentieth into a pathologized, disembodied familial dynamic that normalizes pathology as such, placing its origin within the family. This stage in the development of sexual knowledge
dissociates pathology from particular bodies; a universally pathological
sexual desire, a desire organized around the incest taboo, is universalized,
reified.

One of my objectives throughout the book is to read theoretical claims
both with and against specific historical conjunctures, especially theoretical claims that endeavor to account for historical developments. Here I
want to examine Foucault's suggestion that the pathological desire that
psychoanalytically saturates the family cell is ultimately dissociated from
bodies located outside that cell. The distinction he maintains between a
normality located within the early-nineteenth-century family, for example, and a pathology located outside it begins to reveal the limitations of
his narrative's ability to explain how sexuality was deployed in a U.S. context. Reading this narrative against some of the most basic claims made by
normalized knowledges of gender in the nineteenth-century United States,
certain pervasive anxieties about *normal* male sexuality become notable
in their very absence. Foucault associates the nineteenth-century phase of
the deployment of sexuality with "the need to form a 'labor force' (hence
to avoid any useless 'expenditure,' any wasted energy, so that all forces
were reduced to labor capacity alone) and to ensure its reproduction (conjugality, the regulated fabrication of children)."[43] And few forms of energy
caused the nineteenth-century middle class more concern about its potential for "waste" than the peculiar form of sexual energy that this normalized knowledge regime attributed to the male body, energy that was the
apparent motor force of both labor and "conjugality." This regime maintained—frequently in the face of, and indeed in reaction against, evidence
to the contrary—that men are biologically suited to active, public forms
of social activity (in government, in business), while women are biologically suited to a private, domestic existence. Representing gendered physiology in such a way that it was possible to derive and legitimate a gendered
social hierarchy, this discourse represented the male body as sexually autonomous and sexually active, as housing a potentially explosive sexual desire,
and the female body as sexually dependent and *reproductively* active, as

dominated by a maternal cycle. While this regime of sexual knowledge represented both male and female physiologies as housing limited amounts of bodily energy, properly harnessed for procreative and productive activity in the case of one and for procreative and nurturing activity in the case of the other, it also attributed to men an ability to control their energies that women were believed to lack. The nineteenth-century middle-class ideal of manhood was the "self-made" man, the man of "character," the man who succeeded in mastering and disciplining the chaotic, disruptive sexual urges attributed to his always potentially plagued body. Male desire was in these terms properly harnessed for production and reproduction, and any squandering of that energy would by definition take place frighteningly beyond the reach of the family cell's domesticating power—in morally degraded quasi-public spaces like the brothel, for instance.[44]

This discourse of the body, as numerous scholars have pointed out, bore broad anxieties about the social chaos produced by the boom-and-bust industrialization of capital. This knowledge regime manifested an effort on the part of the white men who produced it to sustain forms of social differentiation that capital seemed everywhere to be threatening, to rigorously binarize a host of axes of social hierarchy: between men and women, between whites and a panoply of racialized, infantilized others, between an emerging middle class and laborers increasingly deskilled, robbed of economic autonomy, and stigmatized as a result. We might think of this knowledge regime as an effort to compel, as it were through the prism of ostensibly stabilized corporeal difference, a misrecognition of capital's systemic chaos. In Foucault's terms, sexuality is here a tactic, an instrumentality, a "point of support, . . . a linchpin, for the most varied social strategies."[45] But this tactic was itself riddled with contradictions. Dana Nelson, for instance, has suggested its contradictory dynamic of interiorization and exteriorization. This discourse in one respect represented the chaos of industrial capital as explosive desires internal to the white male body. National anxieties about social disorder, and about the developing capitalist economy, were here "reroute[d] . . . into the psychological interior of the American boy/man."[46] But those bodies external to the family cell can also be understood in terms of a stigmatizing epistemological projection of this male capacity for pathology, a writing of abnormality onto that range of other bodies consigned to the absolute outside of idealized domestic space. This outside extends, of course, far beyond those bodies

Foucault lists, to include bodies located in a range of stigmatized classed, racialized, and gendered locations: prostitutes and other "fallen women," slaves, Native Americans, immigrants, even working-class white men, who were pathologized insofar as they were viewed as constitutionally less able than their middle-class betters to contain their sexual urges.

The normalized figure of husband and father is in this sense irreducible to the distinction between the family cell's inside and outside on which Foucault insists, the spatialized distinction ultimately compromised by that cell's psychoanalytic saturation with pathological desire. This particular body is every bit as much a repository of potentially disruptive sexual energy as those extrafamilial bodies in which Foucault locates sexual pathology, a body situated both inside and outside the family cell, straddling its membrane, constantly struggling against the many temptations to waste that energy, temptations encountered everywhere in domesticity's sexually volatile outside. If sexual volatility seemed to be projected everywhere, if white manhood defined itself in opposition to this horizon of pathologized others, the white male body was also defined fundamentally in terms of a corporeal combination of pathology and normality, a combination manifested in tests of "character," in his distinctive ability to master his own sexual energies. In the revered, anxiety-producing white male body, the opposition between normality and pathology was itself corporealized.

This contradictory combination was often framed in generational terms, in the terms of a narrative of maturity. If the male body was by definition a closed energy system, a hydraulic, "spermatic economy,"[47] health required the conservation of that energy. Male adults took the initiative in educating male adolescents about the dangers of depleting their limited reserves. Masturbation was a particular concern, represented as a practice that would sap those reserves, ushering in any number of devitalizing maladies. Advice manuals for young men that urged them to restrict sexual activity to procreative activity, and to preserve the rest of their energy for productive work, became pervasive as early as the 1830s.[48] Male sexual self-control as a form of discipline is represented here as fundamental to upward mobility in the age of socially chaotic industrialization. Foucault maintains that as sexuality is psychoanalytically deployed within the family, saturating it, sexual pathology is itself normalized; psychoanalysis represents a pivotal moment in the deployment of sexuality, for Foucault, precisely in its normalization and universalization of pathology. But that pathology was already normalized in the male body, a body scientifically understood in terms of a temporality of immature, destructive sexual instincts with the capacity to enervate that body, and the mature containing of those instincts necessary to its health and productivity. In this respect, we might understand the gradual institutionalization of psychoanalysis in the United States, its saturation of the family cell with pathology, less in terms of a pathology previously located in bodies outside the family cell than in terms of a pathology dissociated from the body distinctively located both inside and outside the cell. If the psychoanalytic reification of desire took the form of a distinct temporal rhythm attributed to desire, this temporal articulation of mature repression with the immature lack of it was in this respect less the invention of psychoanalysis than its disembodying universalization of a temporality previously and exclusively imputed not to the encounter between the psychic and the social but to the white male body itself, a corporeally contained encounter, we might say, between maturity and immaturity. This disembodiment of desire, this universalizing location of desire within the family, allows the saturation of the family space with the internal sexual conflict and struggle that only Father had previously had to face. Desire is here scientifically abstracted, dissociated, stripped from the male body as a condition of possibility for the saturation of all bodies.

The turn-of-the-century reification of sexual desire I have been considering is in this way mediated not only by changes in the division of labor and the managing of social consumption but also by contemporaneous gender epistemologies: sexual desire is in this sense dissociated not from "the body" but from a particular kind of body, a body known in historically specific and gender-specific ways. This attribution of a disruptive sexual economy to the male body represents an epistemological and historical precursor to the moment of reification I am situating around the beginning of the twentieth century; it represents a prehistory of that moment. This sexualized instance of reification, together with emerging attempts to manage social consumption, begins to suggest the value of a Marxian reframing of Foucault's methodological distinction between the family's inside and outside in terms of capital's increasing regulation of that border. A reification of desire unfolds as the family is increasingly saturated not only with pathology but also with commodities, amid the normalized consumption characteristic of an emergent, intensive regime of accumulation, from within capital's emergent distribution of a new sexual knowledge of self. As this cell ceases to be a significant unit of production and gradually becomes instead a significant unit of consumption, this specific example of reification develops within a broader horizon of reification, within what I have characterized as the increasingly consolidated differentiation of the equally abstract, quantified space-times of labor and leisure. Foucault certainly insists that sexuality arose as a tactic by which an emergent bourgeoisie differentiated itself both from the proletariat that emerged along with it and from the ancien régime. But in his elaboration of the Freudian moment in sexuality's deployment, he also concentrates on the family cell itself, effectively abstracting its outside (beyond the handful of pathologized somatic types he notes as inhabiting that outside), focusing on sexuality's intrusion into it and obscuring the role of this intrusion in a larger strategy by which the family's very conditions of existence were increasingly managed as part of an effort to maintain a vigorous rate of accumulation. Foucault's unrelenting focus on microsocial levels of cause and effect, on microsocial relations of force, produces a representation of sexuality as an autonomous tactic, an instrumentality that transgresses a spatial barrier, compromises the membrane separating inside and outside, as if of its own accord. But it is not instrumentalized sexuality per se but this much larger-scale effort to manage accumulation, to forestall crisis, that begins to compromise this particular membrane, that provides access to this new sexual knowledge of self. "Sexuality," to the extent that Foucault's narrative represents it as "deployed" by no agent other than itself, is a phenomenon he thereby fetishizes in the classically Marxian sense of the term. Here Foucault mystifies what Lukács demystifies, the status of epistemological abstractions—the abstract temporality that psychoanalysis imputes to sexual desire, for instance—as products of an ever more complex division of social labor.

The very temporal articulation of mature repression and immature, polymorphous impulses meanwhile begins to suggest the way in which this radically new, reified form of sexual desire is itself persistently mediated by gender distinction. Incest, again, lies "at the heart of" this new form of desire "as the principle of its formation and the key to its intelligibility": with psychoanalysis, "the main elements of the deployment of sexuality" are developed along the family's "two primary dimensions: the husband-wife axis and the parents-children axis."[49] Desire is now scientifically organized around gender difference on the one hand and generational difference on the other (it is no longer only the father who is sexualized but the mother as well; it is no longer only the parents but the children as well)—organized, that is, into a narrative of sexual development. This scientific model partitions bodies, universalizes a distinction between immature and mature sexuality, and organizes sexuality temporally, reifying it into a coded set of pathological behaviors and a hermeneutic of repression and symptomatic repetition.

The schema of twentieth-century sexual definition that Eve Kosofsky Sedgwick proposes in that formative text of queer theory, *Epistemology of the Closet,* begins to elucidate the complex mediation by gender difference of this reification of desire, as desire was articulated within a regime of sexual knowledge exemplified, but not exhausted, by psychoanalytic discourse. Sedgwick influentially elaborates an irresolvable epistemological contradiction, operative in the last hundred-odd years, between a universalized sexual desire, on the one hand, and an assimilation of desire to majority and minority sexual subjectivities, on the other. While the latter schema delimits the capacity for same-sex desire to a minority population identified as homosexual, and cross-sex desire to a majority population identified as heterosexual, the former presupposes a sexual desire irreducible to and disruptive of subjectivity as such.[50]

One implication of Lukács's analysis of reification is not only that reification cognitively dissociates subjectivity from objectivity but that subjectivity is itself ultimately objectified. On the one hand, an ongoing dynamic of reification outside the factory—in the discourses of science, for instance—is based on the disconnect I characterized earlier between subjective cognition and experience and the objectively existing world, so that the world of objects is understood in terms of "calculation" and sundered from any acknowledgment of the subject's participation in the production of those objects. Sexual desire, for example, becomes an isolated, autonomous, epistemological object; it is dissociated from, made independent of and irreducible to, any particular subject. But ultimately, on the other hand, the human sciences objectify the subject in the very act of comprehending it. Subjectivity is reified, in other words, not only in the form of passive, contemplative consciousness; subjectivity itself becomes an epistemological object. New forms of subjectivity articulated, for example, in terms of the gender of the body they sexually objectify—heterosexual and homosexual subjectivity—are themselves epistemological products of reification's objective moment. These binarized, indissociable subjectivities reassimilate sexual desire to gender distinction in a qualitatively new form, making subjectivity itself a function of the gender of the body that desire objectifies.[51] Lukács, in other words, provides a way of situating within the ongoing differentiation of capitalist social relations what Sedgwick calls "radical and irreducible incoherence,"[52] a way of distinguishing between two mutually constitutive and similarly self-deconstructing articulations of reified desire: desire as an epistemologically autonomous, universal object, and majority and minority sexual subjectivities defined in terms of the gendered, bodily object orienting them. Within a psychoanalytic temporality of desire, this distinction becomes one between an immature sexuality irreducible to and subversive of gender difference, and a mature sexuality mediated by gender difference (though that same psychoanalytic narrative has certainly also played a part wherever homosexual subjectivity is itself understood in terms of psychic regression). The "definitional incoherence" with which Sedgwick deconstructively binds universalization to minoritization, in other words, instantiates the partial, always troubled mediation of the reification of desire by gender difference.

Sedgwick's schema suggests, moreover, that wherever this newly autonomous desire is mediated by an epistemology of gender difference, it is assimilated to a gendered distinction between sexual subject and sexual object in which either gender can inhabit either side of the relation. This desire is mediated in terms both of the gender of the body that desire objectifies and of the gender of the body that does the desiring, and is mediated in such a way that the character or direction(s) of desire at any given moment have no necessary relation to the particular gendered bodies inhabiting the positions of sexual subject or sexual object. Desire, in other words, no longer names a relation between the embodied male subject of desire and any number of potential objects—a female body, another male body, even the male subject's own body, the out of control, immature, masturbating youthful one—but a relation between desiring and desired positions that are bound together and irreducible to the particular genders involved. The dissociation of sexual desire from male physiology then implicates male as well as female bodies in both sexual objectification and sexual subjectification. This regime of sexual knowledge represents female bodies as sexual subjects in a way they were not before—attributing capacities for either heterosexual or homosexual desire to female bodies (attributions that were initially relatively indistinct in that the very notion of an independently desiring female subject was radically new, inconsistent with nineteenth-century gender epistemology)—and represents male bodies as sexual objects in a way they were not before, attributing capacities for heterosexual desire to female bodies and for homosexual desire to male bodies.

And this reification of desire compels a reconstitution of the very gender epistemology that mediates it. Closely related to Sedgwick's universalizing/minoritizing distinction, for example, are the equally contradictory "tropes of gender" through which, she maintains, sexual desire has been understood. On the one hand, a trope of "inversion" differentiates between desiring subject and desired object in terms of gender difference, orienting the subject of desire to an object of the opposite gender: "desire, in this view, by definition subsists in the current that runs between one male self and one female self, in whatever sex of bodies these selves may be manifested." Inversion is manifest, for instance, in a late-nineteenth- and early twentieth-century physiological conception of same-sex desire as embodied by sexual "inverts," as well as in the ongoing gendering of gay men as "sissy" or "femme" and lesbians as "mannish" or "butch." The opposing but equally persistent trope is that of gender "separatism," which identifies desiring subject with desired object in terms of gender sameness. According to this trope, it is "the most natural thing in the world that people of the same gender . . . should bond together also on the axis of sexual desire."[53] This trope is operative wherever lesbians are understood to be fundamentally more feminine than straight women—in notions of the woman-identified woman and the lesbian continuum, for example[54]—and wherever gay men are seen as fundamentally more masculine than straight men, as in gay male culture's persistent idealization of masculinity.

The simultaneous indissociability of and contradiction between the tropes of inversion and separatism—which would help explain, for example, an ongoing, radical uncertainty about whether gay male sexual practice necessarily feminizes any of the men involved—suggest an epistemological dissociation not only of sexual desire but of gender itself from physiology. The abstract, universalized psyche, the reified temporality of desire that defines this psyche, intervenes here between physiology and gender difference, between a physiological knowledge on the one hand and a gender

knowledge on the other, insinuating between them a kind of epistemological gap. The partitioning dissociation of sexuality from the male body
erodes the physiological terms in which nineteenth-century bodies are
gendered, remaking the gendered body in different terms, reconstituting
it according to a new episteme that drives a wedge, as it were, between
male biology and desiring subjectivity, objectifying and degendering that
active sexual energy of which the male body had, according to an increasingly displaced, superseded regime of sexual knowledge, been the only
legitimate somatic repository. As Michael Kimmel points out, *masculinity*
and *femininity*, categories that came into existence in the United States
in the early twentieth century, refer to states of being in which gender is
embodied in other than physiological terms—their nineteenth-century
physiological equivalents being *manhood* and *womanhood*.[55]

Physiological conceptions of the trope of inversion, for instance, began
to hold increasingly less explanatory power over the course of the twentieth century's first few decades. The uneven character of their displacement
by what, in Judith Butler's terms, we can call a *performative* conception of
inversion is one way, for example, to understand the distinction between
two similarly "boyish" emergent female subjects of desire: the female invert
of medical discourse, who somehow inhabited a partially male physiology
and was frequently identified in terms of anatomical characteristics identified as anomalies, and the flapper, the sexualized young single woman of
the jazz age, who "flirted with being 'cheap' and 'fast,'" as Esther Newton
has put it, "words that had clear sexual reference," a body understood to
be biologically female who nonetheless wore short hair and dresses that
hung straight down.[56] Or consider George Chauncey's suggestions about
the way in which a knowledge of sexual desire increasingly dissociated
from gender after the turn of the century seems to compel a radical re-
definition of "normal" manhood. Chauncey suggests that what we might
call the social performance of heterosexual masculinity emerged only after
a performance of male sexual inversion, a performance manifested in a
host of specific sexual identities, had become relatively visible in urban
areas like New York. An aspect of what Chauncey calls "the growing
differentiation and isolation of sexuality from gender in middle-class
American culture" was that men who understood themselves in terms of
residual nineteenth-century definitions of what constituted normal male-
ness began experiencing pressure to define their "normal" selves in terms

of heterosexual subjectivity: to define themselves sexually "on the basis of their renunciation of any sentiments or behavior that might be marked as homosexual" and in terms of "their exclusive sexual interest in women."[57] Heterosexual masculinity is here increasingly constituted by a performance of renunciation and exclusion, defined in opposition to a performance of male inversion that seemed also to perform homosexual desire—a negative definition implicated in, indeed constituted by, its opposite.

Heterosexual masculinity here begins to assume what Butler calls a melancholic form, a form conditioned by renunciation, exclusion, loss: an identification articulated in the service of a normalizing heterosexual desire, operating within the terms of a "heterosexual matrix," terms that constitute heterosexual identification precisely through the disavowal of homosexual desire. My focus in chapter 2 is indeed on the performance of masculinity in particular because, as I argue there, the loss constitutive of the heterosexual matrix presupposes a reified sexual desire, a prior moment of epistemological loss. I argue in chapter 2 that the melancholic loss constitutive of heterosexual identification has among its conditions of possibility what I have contended here is the epistemological loss to the male body of the exclusive capacity for desire, the exclusive capacity for a normalized, interiorized sexual energy, a loss that developed as the nineteenth-century regime of sexual knowledge was increasingly displaced.

Sedgwick identifies a persistent incoherence at the level of almost the last century of sexual discourse and practice as such, a history of discourse and practice that is also a plurality of histories, of multiple, uneven, interconnecting histories. Given the complex nature of this new regime of sexual and gender knowledge, the subsequent historical repercussions of the reification of desire I have tried to theorize and historicize could be pursued in any number of a potentially dizzying array of directions. Subsequent chapters will consider some of the ways in which this aspect of an ongoing social reification has opened conditions of possibility for a regulation of bodies by forms of sexual knowledge, as well as for the consolidation of certain forms of queer social formation, and indeed of what I am calling a queer aspiration to totality. Before I can say anything further about this arena of discourse and practice, it is necessary to say more, by way of a more exclusive critical engagement with Lukács, about what reification has to do with sexual objectification especially.

APPROPRIATING LUKÁCS

I have proposed that reification's objective moment, with which Lukács is concerned only insofar as it compels a form of passive, contemplative consciousness and creates conditions for the negation of that consciousness, is also a condition of possibility for heterosexual and homosexual subjectivity as such. Some critical, antiheteronormative light then needs to be shed on the specificity and limitations of the definition of consciousness underpinning Lukács's analysis. The consciousness reified in his elaboration of "the dehumanised and dehumanising function of the commodity relation" presupposes a specific humanist discourse that, as I will presently argue, implicitly but constitutively excludes nonnormative sexual practices.[58] Reification's objective moment can, again, be understood in terms of a relation between knowledges and bodies; here I consider the sexual implications of Lukács's forthright exclusion of the body from the terms of his analysis and the way in which the body returns, in spite of this exclusion, to make itself legible in that analysis.

History and Class Consciousness is both a founding document of a century-old discourse of Marxist humanism and a critical development of Kant's, Hegel's, and Marx's respective engagements with the relation between subject and object; it influentially articulates a dialectical, Marxian notion of the human in terms of this relation. Kant is both the exemplar of what Lukács calls the "antinomies of bourgeois thought"[59] and a key participant in what Eric Clarke has characterized as a discourse of "sexual humanism," a discourse with heteronormative as well as bourgeois presuppositions, a discourse in which Lukács implicates himself.[60] According to Kantian morality, as Clarke points out, any form of sexual practice in which sexual pleasure is an end in itself is immoral, because this particular end turns people into mere means to that end. Sexual pleasure as an end in itself reduces the persons involved into objects and thereby dehumanizes them. Kant's reasoning is characteristically rigorous: humans are not supposed to *be* objects because humans are supposed to *own* objects. As Kant puts it, insofar as a human being "is a person he is a Subject who can own property and other things. . . . But a person cannot be a property and so cannot be [a] thing which can be owned, for it is impossible to be a person and a thing, the proprietor and the property."[61] According to this logic, Clarke adds, "to become (sexual) property would be to become less than human."[62]

Queer studies meanwhile has developed compelling arguments about the political importance of sustaining public, queer practices that legitimate the use of the body as a pleasurable means, practices located in spaces like bathhouses and sex clubs, for instance. In particular, these practices constitute a site of resistance to contemporary enforcements of heteronormativity—resistance, for example, to neoliberal efforts to limit the horizon of struggles against "homophobia" to the right to get married and own property, a limitation that serves to assimilate homosexual practices not only to a heteronormative model of monogamy and "commitment" but to a related, uncritical identification of privacy with property.

Chapter 5 will consider these arguments at length. Here I want to emphasize that a queer interrogation of Marxist humanism can and arguably should begin with *History and Class Consciousness:* the book's importance has largely to do with its innovative emphasis on subjectivity, its success in launching the humanist discourse of Western Marxism and critiquing the scientism and economism of the contemporaneous, official Marxism of the Second International. The discourse surrounding the book also represents it as anticipating, in a Hegelian register, the arguments made in Marx's *Economic and Philosophical Manuscripts of 1844,* which were published in Germany in 1932, nine years after the publication of Lukács's text, but which Lukács himself read in 1930, in Marx's own handwritten manuscript.[63] The famous self-critique of his own text offered by Lukács in the 1967 preface was a direct product of his encounter with the *Manuscripts:* Lukács writes that "in the process of reading the Marx manuscript all the idealist prejudices of *History and Class Consciousness* were swept to one side." He acknowledges in particular that reading Marx's text made him understand that he had conflated alienation with objectification: "Objectification is a natural means by which man masters the world and as such it can be either a positive or negative fact. By contrast, alienation is a special variant of that activity that becomes operative in definite social conditions."[64] The *1844 Manuscripts* argue that, through collective social and historical labor, human beings objectify themselves in the world, re-creating the world and, in a subsequent, inevitable dialectical turn, redefining themselves. Alienation, by contrast, characterizes situations in which humans fail to apprehend these objectifications of the human *as* objectifications of the human, in failing, for example, to apprehend commodities as the products of their own collective labor, or in failing to apprehend congealed social labor (i.e., capital) *as* congealed social labor. In contrast with the *1844 Manuscripts, History and Class Consciousness* consistently takes the position that objectification—not certain specific forms of objectification but objectification as such—has its social basis in, and is indissociable from, the commodification of labor power. Lukács conflates the productive capacity of collective labor to objectify itself with the exploitation and commodification of that capacity within capitalist social relations.

One of Hegel's claims with which the *1844 Manuscripts* most emphatically take issue is that objectification is always a condition to be overcome, superseded; for Hegel, the human being is, as Marx puts it, "a *non-objective, spiritual* being."[65] The same critique can be made of Lukács. The proletarian object of knowledge—knowledge, that is, of its own objective existence (the proletariat in itself)—becomes the basis for subjective, revolutionary praxis (the proletariat for itself). The objectification of the proletariat becomes, in Hegelian fashion, the provocation for the overcoming of this moment of objectification: "Since consciousness here is not the knowledge of an opposed object but is the self-consciousness of the object *the act of consciousness overthrows the objective form of its object*."[66] This is an overcoming of the proletariat's *objective* character, an objectivity that Lukács identifies with alienation. And it is not only proletarian objectification at the hands of capital that is overthrown but social objectification in general: Lukács extrapolates from the objectification of the worker specific to capitalist social relations an insistence that the objectification of persons is by definition dehumanizing—an extrapolation with dramatic implications.

In an effort to avoid implicating himself in Engels's dialectics of nature, Lukács makes an absolute, decidedly undialectical distinction between the social world of human beings and the world of nature, insisting that the human world operates dialectically while nature does not, and forthrightly excluding the world of nature from his analysis. But not only does the natural world not operate, for Lukács, according to a subject/object dialectic; *History and Class Consciousness* excludes, fairly consistently, any acknowledgment even that the natural world is *impacted* by that dialectic, by collective human activity as such. The dialectic of subject/object is here a dialectic of consciousness to the exclusion of that other crucial version of this dialectic, the version foreground by the *1844 Manuscripts,* between the laboring subject and the material and social world of natural and artificial objects on which that subject labors, the practical interaction between the one and the other. And here Lukács distances himself not only from Engels but also from Hegel, and ultimately (if apparently unintentionally) from Marx as well. This absolute distinction between the history of human consciousness (or, perhaps more accurately, the history of *humanizing* consciousness, that is, proletarian consciousness) and the natural world implicitly but unmistakably situates the materially existing human body within the natural world. Among the results, as Lukács puts it in the 1967 preface, are "an overriding subjectivism" that entails the "disappearance" from his analysis "of the ontological objectivity of nature upon which [the] process of [social] change is based."[67]

This elision of the body figures most strikingly in his extended critique of Kant's epistemology. For Kant, the world of things-in-themselves, the world of objects, is by definition the world external to consciousness. But in critiquing the epistemological and unbridgeable dualism that Kant posits between the cognitive, rational subject and the external world, Lukács represents the Kantian thing-in-itself as the misrecognized product of human labor. Here again—and this is the crux of his critique of Kant—Lukács makes no meaningful distinction between objects and commodities. In categorically identifying all Kantian things-in-themselves with alienated products of the subject's activity, Lukács represents the world as if it were created out of nothing. He offers no acknowledgment—which you get unmistakably and every step of the way even in Hegel—that the subject works on some kind of objective, material substance that preexists it and serves as the necessary obstacle to the subject's self-realization. The irony of this exclusion becomes yet more striking when Lukács contends that Kant implicates himself in the reification of social life by draining all things-in-themselves of any particular content, by abstracting the thing-in-itself, by reducing it to a mere form. In failing to recognize the multiplicity of specific ways in which the human body is objectified, Lukács himself produces a similar analytic reduction.[68]

Here is where the results of the "idealist prejudices" of *History and Class Consciousness* most starkly reveal themselves. Lukács's delineation of objectivity is limited to objectivity's inducement of a passive subjectivity and of a potential for active subjectivity: he represents this inducement and this potential as compelled by objectivity as such. Proletarian subjectivity is dynamic and historical, characterized in terms of a capacity to break a static, "frozen" objectivity. The proletariat, as he puts it, is "that 'we' whose action is in fact history": to this extent, history's objective dimension is attenuated; it becomes instead a pure subjective capacity.[69] Lukács's privileging of subjectivity ultimately produces a mystification of objectivity's social and historical specificity, including the specificity of objective persons and the social and historical objectification of human capacities in the world, and including the specificity of reification's objective moment. As Andrew Arato has put it, "if one disregards the problems of concrete synthesis, if one presupposes that the identical subject-object already exists (at least *in itself*), and that it can be sociologically described, then history no longer can have secrets for us. Indeed, as Lukács charged against Hegel's absolute subject, history no longer exists at the moment its agent is completely known."[70]

For Lukács, "consciousness" is not only an epistemological but a moral category, and while his text explicitly makes an epistemological argument, an argument about knowledge, it also makes, more implicitly, a moral argument with sexual implications. The book has little to say, at least explicitly, about sexual objectification per se, or even about the sensory capabilities of persons as materially existing bodies, as objective biological beings—an issue the *1844 Manuscripts,* by contrast, emphasize at length. Human bodies do, however, appear through the cracks, as it were, of this insistent methodological exclusion, rarely but tellingly. This realm of material, biological beings can be understood, in deconstructive fashion, as a constitutive outside of Lukács's argument that inevitably makes itself legible in the very course of that argument. Lukács uses marriage, for instance, as Kant characterizes it, as an example of reification. He quotes Kant: "'Sexual community' [Kant] says, 'is the reciprocal use made by one person of the sexual organs and faculties of another . . . [and] marriage . . . is the union of two people of different sexes with a view to the mutual possession of each other's sexual attributes for the duration of their lives.'"[71] Kant argues that only within the marriage contract is this kind of sexual objectification acceptable—and in this sense Kantian morality is, as Clarke argues, unmistakably heteronormative—whereas for Lukács even this form of sexual objectification is immoral and dehumanizing. This distinction is significant: to the extent that one wants to develop an antiheteronormative critique of Lukács's analysis, it is important to point out that his analysis is not so much heteronormative on its own terms—this would presumably require a more sustained consideration of sexuality, or at least of the body as a sensuous entity, than Lukács offers—as hetero-normative from the vantage of a contemporary queer politics that insists on the legitimacy, within antiheteronormative spaces, of the sexual objec-tification of bodies.

More strikingly, Lukács also contrasts proletarian objectification with narcissism, which he uses as an example of the sexual objectification of the body as articulated by what he identifies as the reifying science of psy-chology. He then goes on to compare this objectification of the body with the objectification of the slave's body, the body of what he calls "an *instru-mentum vocale*"—without troubling to make any moral distinction at all between narcissism and enslavement.[72] For Lukács all three forms of ob-jectification—the objectification of the proletarian's, narcissist's, and slave's respective bodies—are equivalently *immoral;* the distinction on which he insists is *epistemological:* knowledge of the social totality is, again, only possible from the standpoint of the proletariat. Only the proletariat's real-ization of its own objectification is simultaneously a realization of the character of capitalist social relations. In the examples of narcissism and marriage, then, Lukács associates sexual objectification with an immoral-ity and inhumanity that has its basis in commodification and its superses-sion in revolutionary proletarian praxis.

By contrast, the first volume of *Capital* insists that the human being "sets in motion the natural forces which belong to his own body, his arms, legs, head and hands, in order to appropriate the materials of nature in a form adapted to his own needs. Through this movement he acts upon external nature and changes it, and in this way he simultaneously changes his own nature."[73] And to the extent that *History and Class Consciousness* and the *1844 Manuscripts* both represent key moments in the develop-ment of a Marxist humanism, it is then worthwhile to underscore briefly the ways in which these texts diverge. Marx's central concept of "species being," for example, implies not only that biological existence is in no way subordinate or secondary to consciousness but also that biological existence is in no way excluded, as in Lukács, from history as such. "A non-objective being," says Marx, "is a *non-being.*"[74] For Marx bodies are sensory objects impacted, developed, and remade within the ongoing social and historical production of humans by humans. The insistence of the *1844 Manuscripts* on the ongoing objectification, through collective labor, of human desires and capacities in the world, and the resulting historical dynamism of this world, together necessarily imply (as this text's historicization of the senses, for example, indicates) the manipulation, the re-creation of bodies themselves, the dialectical objectification of bodies *by* the collective social body, whether or not that objectification operates within exploited social relations. Within this historical movement, one would have to include that ongoing epistemological reproduction of sexual desire that Foucault elaborates. The collective development of human faculties, capacities, needs, and desires, the realization of human powers that Marx emphasizes, would include an expansion of sexual practice, including the development of discourses (and Foucauldian "reverse-discourses") organized around the legitimacy of sexual pleasure as an end in itself—rather than, say, a procreative means—and therefore around the sexual objectification of human bodies as means to that end.[75]

Lukács would appear to be making an argument more consistent with the *1844 Manuscripts* when, near the end of "Reification and the Consciousness of the Proletariat," he unambiguously rejects ahistorical definitions of the human.[76] But the explicit epistemological and implicit moral components of his analysis fail to align, and the misalignment attenuates the force of his rejection. In his tenacious critique of Kantian epistemology, Lukács simultaneously fails to extricate himself from Kantian morality. But I want to push the implications of this claim further. Lukács's explicit argument that Kant misrecognizes mediated products of collective human labor as natural, immediate things-in-themselves at least implicitly constitutes a critique of Kant's *epistemological* naturalization of private property. But Lukács's uncritical inheritance of Kantian morality allows Kant's *moral* naturalization of private property to stand. It is precisely the inconsistency of his epistemological analysis and his moral presuppositions that allow Lukács to reproduce, in spite of himself, this moral naturalization. Lukács does nothing to denaturalize, and indeed participates, in a moral discourse of the human, a participation that cannot only be seen, from a distance of more than eighty years, as heteronormative but also, and inseparably, posits property ownership as fundamental to the very definition of the human—and this in one of the most influential texts in the history of Marxist humanism. I would underscore that it is precisely a queer critical perspective, facilitated by work like Clarke's, that throws this misalignment into relief. *History and Class Consciousness* is significantly less able than the *1844 Manuscripts* to apprehend, much less comprehend, the material, objectively existing body. So to the extent that a Marxist humanism is reestablished with the publication, within a decade of each other, of these two texts, this reestablishing is not only historically pivotal but also, from a contemporary queer perspective, more than a little ambiguous.

Legitimating homosexual instrumentalizations of the body, which has been, and I think would be by definition, a goal of any genuinely anti-heteronormative praxis, entails thinking about that form of objectification in terms that refuse a definition of the human presupposing property ownership and certainly refuse any identification of the objectification of persons as such with capital's abstraction of labor power. Reframed in terms of a relation between knowledges and bodies, reification refers to a subject-object dynamic specific to capitalist social relations by which social labor epistemologically objectifies bodily properties and capacities, and by which those objectifications in turn discipline, regulate, instrumentalize those bodies themselves, normalizing them as deskilled laborers or as sexual subjects, for example. Historically specific mediations intervene within this dynamic, including residual and emergent gender epistemologies as well as ongoing strategies for managing accumulation.

For Lukács, the subjective and objective aspects of reification are entirely commensurate, mirror images of each other, pure expressions of a single social logic. Redefined not only in terms of a relation between knowledges and bodies but also in terms of these historically specific mediations of the process by which bodily properties are objectified and by which those objectifications in turn impact those bodies themselves, reification can no longer be understood as an exclusively mystifying phenomenon, and still less in terms of a fall from a retrospectively imputed, organic social wholeness. What I have argued is a reification of sexual desire within the regime of sexual knowledge that came into existence in the late nineteenth century and the early twentieth has had radically divergent social and historical repercussions. As Foucault insists, this disciplinary subjection of bodies is both constraining and productive, productive, for instance, of "nothing more, but nothing less—and its importance is undeniable—than a tactical shift and reversal in the great deployment of sexuality."[77]

Like processes of industrialization, urbanization, and social migration, the reifying of sexual desire needs to be understood as a condition of possibility for a complex, variable history of sexually nonnormative discourses,

practices, sites, subjectivities, imaginaries, collective formations, and collective aspirations. Lukács's attribution of a fundamentally dialectical character to history—not to the history of capital but to history as such—is
an abstraction of history. While Foucault also abstracts history in occlud-
ing the status of regimes of sexual knowledge as products of social labor,
one clear strength of Foucault's method in this context is his refusal of
teleologies of reconciliation, especially his refusal to attribute a dialectical character to history as it objectively unfolds. For Foucault, relations
of power operate in a wide range of directions and are unpredictable.
Power facilitates historical dynamics that always remain open. Judith Butler characterizes Foucault's relation with Hegel in a fashion as suggestive
as it is debatable: "Foucault's analysis of modernity attempts to show how
the terms of dialectical opposition do not resolve into more synthetic
and inclusive terms but tend instead to splinter off into a multiplicity of
terms which expose the dialectic itself as a limited methodological tool for
historians."[78]

Before addressing the qualifications such a claim requires, I would emphasize that, in the case under consideration here, the terms of dialectical opposition do indeed multiply rather than resolve. Far from inducing
an exclusively passive form of subjectivity to be dialectically superseded
by the revolutionary praxis of the proletarian subject-object of history,
reification makes possible a multiplicity of new forms of subjectivity and
social practice. Qualitatively different, unpredictable, hetero- and homosexual subjects already from the beginning "splinter" off, in Butler's terms,
from the unifying dialectic of reconciliation that frames Lukács's analysis.
This new domain of sexual discourse and practice remains both structurally irreducible to capital and unpredictably determinate vis-à-vis capital—
from the emerging normalization of consumption that compromised what
I earlier called the membrane of the family cell, to the various mediations
by capital of the gradual consolidation of forms of queer sociality (a few
of which subsequent chapters will consider), even to recent interest in how
it might be possible to organize workers in more queer-friendly ways, and
queers in more labor-friendly ways.[79]

I have conceptualized reification not in terms of some quasi-Hegelian
expression of the logic of the commodity but in terms of a quantitative
and qualitative deepening of that logic through the objective, volatile expansion and retrenchment of capitalist social relations. I am proposing a

reading of the Marxian concept of reification that refuses to situate that concept within a teleology of class consciousness, or indeed any unitary phenomenon beyond the simultaneously unitary and divergent, objectively contradictory structure of capital itself, and capital's tendency to expand—to reinvest capital and labor "elsewhere"—as a result of the potential crises toward which these contradictions tend. The ongoing location of "elsewheres" on behalf of capital and the ongoing reification of social life that results always unfold unevenly, and the ways this reinvestment and reification will impact other levels of the social formation, their conjunctural repercussions, are precisely what can never be predicted. The version of the Marxian dialectic with which I have framed the category of reification is in this sense socially and historically open as well as limited, finite. Yet another benefit of regulation theory in this respect is its insistence that capital's defining tendency toward accumulation crisis is always negotiated in historically specific, unpredictable ways; regimes of accumulation and modes of regulation are by definition, as Alain Lipietz puts it, "chance discoveries."[80]

The reification of sexual desire resulted from a corrosive confrontation between historically specific knowledges of gender and historically specific efforts to ward off a potential crisis of accumulation. The mediation of each by the other at this moment gives rise, on the one hand, to a qualitatively different domain of sexual discourse and practice. But reification in this sense refers, on the other hand, to a shift from one regime of sexual and gender knowledge to another. Lukács both insists that the total character of reification is a qualitative rather than quantitative phenomenon and unfolds his theory of reification in the exclusively quantitative terms of an accumulation of increasingly pervasive layers of commodity logic, a nightmarish history to be either negated or endured. The reification of sexual desire would in these terms have its absolute negation only in some imputed, hardly imaginable future (which looks a lot like some imputed, hardly imaginable past) in which desire is integrated wholly, "organically" into concrete material life. If the dialectic is then indeed, as Butler insists, a "limited methodological tool," this claim is best understood as a critique not of Marx but of Hegel. If history does not itself operate according to a dialectical logic, this does mean that history—or the reciprocal mediation and determination of specific, objectively and subjectively abstracted histories—cannot be theorized productively in terms of the critical articulation of the abstract and the concrete that Marx's work exemplifies.

The discourse of reification as it runs from Lukács through the Frankfurt school to the work of Jameson has for so long tended to represent reification as an infinitely mystifying social dynamic that skepticism about using the category in any other way is in certain respects understandable. Subsequent chapters will nonetheless build on my suggestion here that this concept has an untapped explanatory capacity. What can be discerned as the implicit heteronormativity of Lukács's analysis, on the one hand, and his abstraction of reification's objective moment, on the other, are inseparable theoretical problems. I make similar though not identical claims, later in this book, about the work of Marcuse and Jameson.

In Lukács's insistence that reification produces an oppressive political stasis to be wholly negated, that it freezes the social as such, we reach a key moment of analytic abstraction. While this formation supposedly freezes, sexual discourse and practice somehow become yet another social horizon at which, to use the *Manifesto*'s most familiar trope, all that is solid melts—if not into air, then at least into fluid, into a Freudian confrontation, for example, between hydraulic, polymorphous force and its necessary but always inadequate repression. The discourse of reification has, as others have pointed out, failed even to do justice to Marx's own sense of capital's historical unfolding.[81] A text as basic as the *Manifesto* employs a metaphorics not of freezing but of melting to elaborate capital's social and historical fallout, insisting on its production of opportunities for liberation from certain historically entrenched kinds of taboo and prejudice, a production simultaneous with and inseparable from its atomizing violence. It is hard to find such opportunities within that total, airtight flattening of social life that—according to *Dialectic of Enlightenment,* or *One-Dimensional Man,* or *Postmodernism, or The Cultural Logic of Late Capitalism*—is reification's ultimate social logic.[82] In the most recent of these influential studies, where any "cognitive mapping" of late capitalism has become so difficult that aesthetic practices appear to offer the only possible means by which to orient oneself to the global space one inhabits, where the spatial has trumped any possible comprehension of the historical, it is for that reason all the more striking to run across remarks about the *Manifesto* as provocative and disarming as the following. Marx and Engels challenge us, as Jameson puts it, to imagine the development of capitalism positively *and* negatively all at once; to achieve, in other words, a type of thinking that would be capable of grasping the demonstrably baleful features of capitalism along with its extraordinary and liberating dynamism simultaneously within a single thought, and without attenuating any of the force of either judgment. We are somehow to lift our minds to a point at which it is possible to understand that capitalism is at one and the same time the best thing that has ever happened to the human race, and the worst.[83]

Lifting our minds to this point has not, however, been made any easier by the discourse of reification, and this is at least in part because "capitalism" turns out to be a limited way of characterizing the agent of liberation referred to here. Around a century ago, capitalist development did not itself produce, but certainly participated in the production of, a space of opportunity for a certain kind of liberatory sexual and political practice. The dangerous, collective struggle to take advantage of that opportunity would be left to a subsequent history of formations articulating a nonnormative politics of sexuality. Later in the book, I will read the dialectic of reification and totality through the lens of certain specific moments in this history. My next chapter, however, approaches from a different angle the same historical period this chapter has considered, and proposes ways in which the concept of reification, and Butler's influential theory of performative gender, can illuminate each other.

chapter 2

PERFORMATIVE MASCULINITY:
JUDITH BUTLER AND HEMINGWAY'S
LABOR WITHOUT CAPITAL

In the nearly twenty years since the publication of Judith Butler's *Gender Trouble,* critical Marxian engagements with Butler's rethinking of gender and indeed with her work more generally, while divergently focused, have tended to converge on a central point: that capital represents an interpretive horizon consistently elided from her analysis.[1] In one of the more provocative variations on this critique, Slavoj Žižek takes Butler to task for limiting her analysis to practices of signification while eliding the Lacanian Real, which is for Žižek precisely what sets limits to these practices— a Real he ultimately identifies with capital itself. Žižek levels this critique in his exchange with Butler and Ernesto Laclau; as Butler puts it in this exchange, Žižek's contention seems to be that capital "has become unspeakable" within the terms of her analysis.[2] In this chapter, I do what Butler, in her response to Žižek, chooses not to do: I question this purported unspeakability. I try to think dialectically about Butler's contention that gender is a citational practice that governs bodies, a performative norm immanent to those bodies. Even in her work on gender that followed the early interventions in *Gender Trouble* and *Bodies That Matter* (work that has been more likely to register the ways in which gender regulation operates in complex relation with specific aspects of the social, from kinship systems to reproductive technologies),[3] Butler has continued to focus almost exclusively on the traversal of bodies by disciplinary norms. My return to Butler's early work on gender suggests how the dissociation of this body from the dynamics of capital in Butler's innovative rethinking of gender

79

can be understood as symptomatic of certain forms of objective social abstraction constitutive of capital. But I will also contend that the most productive response to this dissociation is not to jump automatically from symptom to diagnosis—which has been the tendency of Marxian responses to Butler—but instead to tarry with the symptom itself, to consider the ways in which Butler's theory of gender might be read within rather than against Marxian terms. Sustained efforts to read Butler in this way have been rare. Like Miranda Joseph's reading of Marx and Butler together—an indispensable exception to the general trend—I insist here on the important contribution that Butler's notion of performative gender can in fact make to a rigorously Marxian understanding of the intermediations of gender and capital.[4]

Here I extend the central claims of chapter 1 by considering ways in which the reification of sexual desire compels a qualitatively new epistemology of gender itself. I build on the previous analysis of Lukács and Foucault by reading Butler's theory of gender together with the concept of reification. And here again my reading is triangulated, reconsidering the explanatory capacities of these ideas not only in relation to each other but within the same relatively specific, delimited national and historical period. I contend both that Butler's notion of gender performativity has certain historical limitations that the notion itself fails or refuses to register, and that the same notion opens up the possibility of a Marxian account of the way in which gender has to be understood in relation to a broader, reified social and historical horizon.

What is ostensibly made "unspeakable" within Butler's terms is in crucial ways also made unspeakable by the very terms in which Žižek's critique purports to speak it. In identifying capital with the Lacanian Real, Žižek dehistoricizes capital. Incoherently, he argues both that this way of defining the Real emphasizes "the ultimate contingency, fragility (and thus changeability) of every symbolic constellation that pretends to serve as the a priori horizon of the process of symbolization," and that this same Real represents not history but the internal "ahistorical" limit of the historical as such (that this last set of quotation marks is in fact not mine but Žižek's only compounds the incoherence of his claim). Žižek would somehow have us understand that Butler "is not historicist enough," even as capital instantiates the Lacanian Real and is to that extent "ahistorical."[5]

If performative signification is to be understood as mediated by capital, any of an incomprehensibly wide array of possible forms of mediation could be accounted for; here again the form of mediation I will emphasize is the broad social effort to manage capital's structural contradictions represented by an intensive regime of accumulation unevenly emerging in the United States during the early twentieth century. This form of mediation has the advantage of providing a more productive way of understanding the determinacy of performative norms within the mode of production that Žižek abstracts as the Real.

Performative gender norms are "corporeally enacted," Butler maintains; performativity is "a reiterated acting."[6] How, then, to concretize in Marxian terms, to think in relation to capital, this reiterated acting? Butler defines gender fundamentally in terms of its materiality. But in at least one respect, this materiality is also highly formal, in the following sense: masculinity and femininity here share in common a performative, citational form. Indeed, one of the key strengths of Butler's rethinking of gender has been that it foregrounds the way in which masculinity and femininity are bound together in a relation of interdependency, a relation that normalizes heterosexual desire, a relation Butler calls the heterosexual matrix. But one would also expect there to be a host of qualitative distinctions to be made between masculinity and femininity, to say nothing of the fact that social gender norms are only ever hegemonic, which is to say everywhere complicated by racial, class, and other social divisions. Butler certainly emphasizes the historical openness of gender norms, their capacity for subversion as well as sedimentation. But she also points out near the end of *Bodies That Matter* that "the inquiry into both homosexuality and gender will need to cede the priority of *both* terms in the service of a more complex mapping of power that interrogates the formation of each in specified racial regimes and geopolitical spatializations."[7] Concretizing a hegemonic norm of gender also means situating it socially and historically, considering the socially and historically specific *content* of that norm, a consideration that the relatively formal, philosophical register of Butler's analysis tends to preempt.

Not that this register has kept Butler's work from influencing historians of gender and sexuality. Citing *Gender Trouble* a few years after its publication, George Chauncey suggested the way in which certain early-twentieth-century normalizations of male sexuality took the form of "a

kind of ongoing performance."[8] As I proposed briefly in the previous chapter and will elaborate here, Chauncey's work on the social articulations
of male sexuality during this period strongly indicates the way in which a
policing of sexual desire routinely compelled men to gender-identify, and
to heterosexually or homosexually identify, in a fashion that should be
understood as performative in Butler's sense of the term. But certain fundamental methodological questions are then raised here, questions this
chapter will address: when one employs Butler's theory of performative
gender while also underscoring the historical specificity of one's own analysis, what happens to that theory itself? Do historically specific questions
leave the theory itself unaffected? In what ways does the historical moment
under scrutiny also "read" the theory in turn? How are we to understand
the ways in which a dialectic of concrete history and conceptual abstraction operates, or should operate, within such a scenario? In Edward Said's
formulation, to what extent can Butler's theory of gender "travel" between
different historical contexts?[9]

As soon as we begin to consider the concrete content of gender as
Butler theorizes it, for example, qualitative differentiations between masculinity and femininity immediately begin to assert themselves. Within the
specific historical period this chapter considers, divergences in the ways
masculinity and femininity are performatively articulated are themselves
a product of the reification of sexual desire elaborated in the previous
chapter. There I argued that this reification of desire dissociates from the
white male body what a hegemonic regime of sexual knowledge had in the
nineteenth century attributed to it exclusively: a simultaneously normalized and pathologized capacity for autonomous, vital sexual "energy." This
dissociation is a condition of possibility, I will argue, for the heterosexual
matrix itself. This matrix presupposes and is conditioned by what chapter 1
identified as the displacement of a regime of sexual knowledge in which
the white male body is understood to be the proper somatic repository of
the very capacity for sexual desire, by one in which this capacity is gradually and unevenly universalized—as in what Foucault calls the saturation
of the family cell with sexual pathology.

In the early-twentieth-century United States, a normative performance
of gender is still substantially complicated by the residual persistence of a
regime of sexual knowledge in which male and female bodies are defined
as irreducibly different rather than interdependent. An analysis of gender

that could focus on this period and consistently emphasize the common form shared by masculinity and femininity could only unfold at the relatively high level of analytic abstraction that Butler maintains. This chapter proceeds from a vantage that is historically specific, a vantage from which irreducible differences can be seen to complicate from the beginning what we might call the relation of equivalence within which Butler situates masculinity and femininity. This is one way in which the present effort to concretize an abstract understanding of gender by situating it historically will also necessarily disclose some of its own analytic limits: even as I try to underscore the ways in which a heterosexual matrix does indeed bind masculinity and femininity together, I also foreground what a consideration of the norm of masculinity especially can contribute to the rethinking of reification this chapter undertakes. As I will show, this norm instantiates in its own distinct fashion the pivotal displacement of one historically specific complex of sex/gender knowledge by another.

This chapter's consideration, then, of reification's mediation of—and by—a performative, citational norm called masculinity proceeds as it were outward: from the most immediate horizon of gender as Butler theorizes it, the heterosexual matrix within which gender operates, toward the dynamics of capital accumulation in a specific time and place, and ultimately toward a horizon of social reification. In these later sections, I maintain that Butler's notion of performative gender, critically and dialectically appropriated, can contribute substantially to an understanding of gender as it operates within what Lukács calls the spatialization of time that reification enforces; but here again, as in chapter 1, the concept of reification itself will not remain unchanged. Butler's work on the gendered subject does not by definition work against efforts to think gender's determinacy vis-à-vis capital. It can also contribute to more concrete understandings of that determinacy.

PHYSIOLOGY, PERFORMATIVITY, AND LOSS

Butler consistently suggests that the performance of gender is also a performance of desire, a performance intelligible only in the normalized terms of a heterosexual matrix. To perform masculinity or femininity is to perform a desire for an object of a particular gender and therefore to perform from the beginning and every step of the way a distancing, a disavowal of any desire for a prohibited object: "To the extent that homosexual attachments remain unacknowledged within normative heterosexuality, they are not merely constituted as desires that emerge and subsequently become prohibited. Rather, these are desires that are proscribed from the start."[10] Gender is here defined in terms of accepted and prohibited desires, accepted and prohibited objects.

In *Bodies That Matter* and again in *The Psychic Life of Power,* Butler characterizes this performance of disavowed desire that is also a performance of gender in terms of melancholia, an "unfinished process of grieving,"[11] terms that underscore a certain anxiety entailed by and finally identical with this performance, as well as its repetitive, always "unfinished" character—unfinished precisely because exclusion and disavowal are in this case identical with loss. What is lost is what is "proscribed from the start," the constitutive homosexual outside of what is retained, hence the always incomplete, inconclusive character of this disavowal and its necessary reiteration. What is lost as sexual object is retained, more specifically, as identification, loss being in this case a condition of possibility for identification. "Heterosexual melancholy" is then

> the melancholy by which a masculine gender is formed from the refusal to grieve the masculine as a possibility of love; a feminine gender is formed (taken on, assumed) through the incorporative fantasy by which the feminine is excluded as a possible object of love, an exclusion never grieved, but "preserved" through the heightening of feminine identification itself. . . . The straight man *becomes* (mimes, cites, appropriates, assumes the status of) the man he "never" loved and "never" grieved; the straight woman *becomes* the woman she "never" loved and "never" grieved.[12]

To suggest, as Butler does, that gender operates within an epistemological matrix of desire is to suggest that gender presupposes desire, that it is constituted by or as a result of desire. She asks rhetorically, "Does it follow that if one desires a woman, one is desiring from a masculine disposition, or is that disposition retroactively attributed to the desiring position as a way of retaining heterosexuality as the way of understanding the separateness or alterity that conditions desire?"[13] The answer is clearly the latter: if a heterosexual directing of desire is the normalized end, a retroactive attribution of masculinity to the desiring subject is in this case the means to that end. Desire, we might say, is here the beginning and the end of gender. The very content of masculinity and femininity is the performative maintenance, the stabilizing, of heterosexual identification. Within the heterosexual matrix, in other words, desire is not only constitutive of the performance of gender but one of this performance's enabling conditions, even its most crucial enabling condition. Žižek, claiming to identify an ambiguity in this same rhetorical question, choosing (unfairly, in my view) to read the question as not rhetorical at all, takes Butler's reading of melancholia to task for precisely this reason, for its conclusion that the normalization of heterosexual desire is more basic—or, as he puts it, more "primordial"—than gender. What "eludes the grasp of normative symbolization," Žižek responds, is not homosexual desire but what he calls in one place "the prohibition of incest" and what he calls in another place "sexual difference."[14]

The problem with Žižek critique, here again, is its Lacanian problematic. Žižek's terms here are even more resolutely ahistorical than Butler's: Butler's analysis at least insists that the very materiality of sexual difference itself has to be understood as time bound (an issue I will revisit). One question raised by Butler's argument that gender identification is constituted through this performative disavowal is indeed the question of how we are to understand, in historical terms, the relation between desire and gender—or, more specifically, the question of how to historicize the heterosexual matrix itself, the normalized regime of sexual knowledge within which this performance of gender operates. How, for example, to understand this instance of melancholic loss, this normalizing negotiation of desire and identification, in relation to the very different, historically specific instance of epistemological loss I considered in the previous chapter—not the loss of an object but the loss by the male body of the exclusive capacity for sexual desire, a capacity that centrally defined normative nineteenth-century physiological definitions of manhood?

The terms in which I defined manhood in chapter 1 were almost exclusively sexual: I referred there to a nineteenth-century, regulatory gender knowledge that represented male physiology as a closed "spermatic economy" of diffuse but limited sexual energy. Later in this chapter, it will be important to define manhood in less exclusively sexual terms. For the time being, however, recall that this "spermatic" energy was properly channeled into productive or procreative labor but could also be "wasted," channeled into nonprocreative, "counterproductive" sexual practices. As the late nineteenth century approached, this anxiety-producing energy was increasingly, less ambiguously valorized, a valorization that responded to a perceived threat of loss: to an intensifying concern that men were becoming increasingly feminized, domesticated, and that they therefore needed this energy if they would continue to survive, much less dominate. In the historian E. Anthony Rotundo's words, men began to fear "that civilization had so fully repressed their passions that their very manhood—their independence, their courage, their drive for mastery—was being suffocated."[15] This prospect of a general domestication of manhood was a reaction to what was perceived as women's encroachment into a properly manly public sphere, an encroachment manifested in numerous ways, from the increasing entrance of women into universities and the labor force to the suffrage and temperance movements. This reaction was typical of the discourse of progressivism perhaps most iconically embodied by Theodore Roosevelt.[16]

This increasingly cherished male passion was naturalized by a Darwinian, biological racism and inseparable from emergent imperial ambitions. "This country needs a war," Roosevelt declared in 1895, three years before the Spanish-American War—the inaugural violence of the imperial "American century"—would grant him his wish.[17] As the domestic frontier was closing, a national narrative of frontier expansion extended into a global one. The blood of manly American conquerors would be rejuvenated by the violent encounter with "primitive" peoples whose vigor had not been compromised by creeping, feminizing civilization. Building on the frontier image of the cowboy, the savage warrior who is also, paradoxically, an agent of civilization, this racialized, imperial progressivism valued the encounter with savagery as a necessary but temporary reversion, a Darwinian moment of regression that enhanced the aggressive qualities that protect men from civilization's domesticating excesses, even as those qualities ultimately serve civilization's cause. The strong impulse during this period to undermine the traditional influence of women on the education of boys and young men resulted not only in the founding of the Boy Scouts of America; Roosevelt's Boone and Crockett Club developed educational programs that endorsed hunting, for example, as a practice facilitating national, racial, and manly vigor, energy, and self-reliance.[18] And sports would instill the qualities of competitiveness ostensibly fundamental to building a strong nation.[19]

This physiologically articulated regime of sexual knowledge represents male bodies as operating according to an economy of desire, while female bodies operate according to an economy of reproduction. Male sexual energy is valuable from this perspective both for the energy it can contribute to what Roosevelt famously called the strenuous life and for its relevance to the future of the white race: male bodies are here represented as subjects of sexual desire, while female bodies—represented as *reproductive subjects*—are reduced to objects of sexual desire. "When men fear work or fear righteous war, when women fear motherhood," Roosevelt argued, "they tremble on the brink of doom; and well it is that they should vanish from the earth, where they are fit subjects for the scorn of all men and women who are themselves strong and brave and high-minded."[20] White Americans who rejected their assigned gender role were implicated in the possibility of race suicide; they were race traitors compromising the global mission for which they shared responsibility. Women who refused to carry children were, as far as Roosevelt was concerned, no less culpable than soldiers who shirked their duty in battle.[21]

How, then, was the threat of losing the very passion that constituted manhood gradually superseded by the performance of a masculinity that was also the performance of a lost homosexual object? How was one of these instances of epistemological loss displaced by the other? Here is one place where the terminological distinction between *manhood* and *masculinity* insisted on by scholars like Michael Kimmel, and to which I referred briefly in the previous chapter, becomes important. This distinction is simultaneously conceptual and historical: manhood is defined as an epistemological normalization of the male body characteristic of the nineteenth century; masculinity is its twentieth-century analogue. Manhood referred to an "inner quality,"[22] a capacity for independence, morality, and self-mastery that adult men were expected to have achieved— mastery of the body's diffuse sexual impulses especially, impulses thereby transcended—and that male adolescents were expected to learn as they matured, an education that in this respect might even be said to have defined manly maturity as such. The opposite of manhood, in these terms, was not womanhood but childhood. But if nineteenth-century manhood was defined internally, twentieth-century masculinity increasingly normalized the male body in terms of exteriorized "behavioral traits and attitudes," as Kimmel puts it.[23] Masculinity had to be performed; it was a physical demonstration, not a moral or ethical one. And what this performance held at bay, its opposite—and here Butler and Kimmel are in agreement—was not immaturity but femininity. Whereas the spermatic economy of manhood and the reproductive or nurturing economy of womanhood made men and women so irreducibly different that no standard of comparison between them was possible,[24] masculinity and femininity are defined wholly in relation to each other, bound together, as Butler would have it, in the very opposition between their accepted and prohibited objects of desire.

This shift from a physiological manhood to a performative masculinity was part of the shift, as I elaborated it in the previous chapter, from a regime of sexual knowledge that classifies bodies to a regime that partitions them, a shift that reifies sexual desire in that same partitioning. According to a residual physiological understanding of gender difference, for example, sexual "inverts" would certainly qualify as race traitors as well. At the turn of the century, as Siobhan Somerville has argued, scientific studies of the invert routinely reproduced the methodological and iconographic norms of racial science, especially its focus on ostensible anatomical anomalies. These studies espoused the Darwinian belief that more advanced species demonstrated higher levels of sexual differentiation. Inverts, therefore, were examples of biological and racial recidivism, throwbacks within a larger scheme of progress.[25] But if the links between racial science and sexual science continued well into the twentieth century (as scholars like Nancy Ordover have argued),[26] psychoanalytic paradigms also began to displace physiological ones—as a definition of the racially mixed *body,* for example, gave way, as Somerville argues, to a definition of interracial *desire,* an epistemology of miscegenation based on object choice rather than physiology.

Similarly and simultaneously, a physiological concept of inversion began to give way to what I think we need to call a performative one. What could it mean, in terms of this nineteenth-century view that men more or less have the market cornered on "passion," for a woman, or for a male invert, to be an agent of sexual desire? Women who were active sexual subjects—whether they desired a man or a woman—were comprehended in those terms as biologically ambiguous, as participating somehow in male physiology, while men who desired men were comprehended as participating somehow in female physiology—in terms, that is, of sexual objectification, sexual inertia, as the presumed passive partner in same-sex sexual practice, for instance. The very idea, however, that a sexual object like a woman (or like a man "trapped in a woman's body") could also actively desire necessarily began to insinuate an epistemological distinction between active desire and the male body; this idea seemed to make the corporeal origin and direction of desire, desire's "orientation," relatively autonomous vis-à-vis physiological gender distinction. As Chauncey suggests in his analysis of the emergence of heterosexual masculinity in the United States, and as I began to indicate in the previous chapter, urban male sexual types like the "fairy," while highly feminized, also seemed to be agents of desire—and thereby to indicate the performativity of that feminization, even of gender itself—as well as a relative unpredictability or irreducibility of desire vis-à-vis embodied gender difference. "The overtness of the fairy's sexual interest in men was . . . unsettling, because it raised the possibility of a sexual component in other men's interactions." The opening of this possibility—especially given the celebration of male bodies and passions advocated by figures like Roosevelt, perhaps—therefore "required a new policing of male intimacy and exclusion of sexual desire for other men."[27] The simultaneity of the overtly performative character of the fairy's femininity, on the one hand, and that figure's unmistakable sexual interest in men, on the other, raised the specter of a reified, universalized homoeroticism that could potentially implicate anyone. Once this figure of inversion, in other words, began to take on a performative rather than physiological character, it was increasingly less possible for any man, however masculine in appearance or behavior, to be seen touching another man or looking at another man without the potential attachment of stigma. The coexistence of residual and emergent ways of defining same-sex practice and its relation to subjectivity, moreover, was one context of the development of a performative ritualizing of masculine practice, a coexistence that captures the unevenness of the relative displacement of one by the other. What unfolds here again is an increasingly universalized, abstracted, reified sexual desire, a capacity for desire that begins to exceed the terms of any nineteenth-century classification of bodies.

But how was one to perform an "exclusion of sexual desire for other men"? What, exactly, could it mean to perform such a prohibition? The direction of desire, desire for an object of one gender and renunciation of desire for another gender, had somehow to be made corporeally manifest.

The injunction to avoid signs of effeminacy was also an injunction to perform something recognizable as masculinity. But whereas manhood had
been defined in terms of a physiological capacity for active desire independent of any particular object, the performance of masculinity meant
precisely the performance of an acceptable sexual object, an acceptable
directing or "orienting" of desire itself. Men now encountered an increasingly pervasive injunction to define themselves sexually in terms of "their
exclusive sexual interest in women," as Chauncey puts it.[28]

Whereas a physiological regime of sexual knowledge made the energy
of sexual desire a capacity of only the male gender, this new, emergent
regime of sexual knowledge seems to make gender secondary or dependent vis-à-vis desire. What Butler calls melancholic loss appears here to
presuppose an epistemological and historical loss to manhood of the exclusive capacity for sexual "passion." The male body's loss of this capacity
is a condition of possibility for the emergence of that sexual knowledge
regime centrally characterized by a heterosexual matrix. I intentionally
raise a question here that this study, limited as its focus is to the twentieth
century, can hardly answer adequately. But it seems important to raise
the question nonetheless, a question about what we might call an unacknowledged historical determination of Butler's rethinking of gender. To
what extent can the notion of gender performativity illuminate gender's
normalization in historical periods before the final years of the nineteenth
century? Masculinity and femininity, not manhood and womanhood, are
clearly Butler's terms. But we can still ask to what extent manhood and
womanhood can be understood as performative in Butler's sense. To what
extent, for example, are manhood and womanhood similarly theatrical,
similarly ritualized? Are they similarly repetitive, citational? Do they also
materialize, as Butler puts it, over time? The central point I would make
about gender norms as they operated in the United States before the beginning of the twentieth century is a relatively simple and limited one:
that any understanding of those norms that placed them within anything
resembling what Butler calls a heterosexual matrix would necessarily be
anachronistic. But then this raises questions that are not so simple: an effort,
say, to understand the operation of a gender norm in the early nineteenth
century as performative would also require some substantial reimagining
of the very meaning of "performative." What could the performance of
gender mean in a context historically prior to the epistemological positing

of heterosexuality, prior to gender's operation in the terms of a normalized heterosexual desire? What could the performance of gender mean if male and female bodies are not (yet) understood in terms of more or less equivalent capacities for sexual desire, much less melancholic loss?

One of the more prominent early-twentieth-century literary negotiations of this shifting regime of gender and sexual knowledge is *The Sun Also Rises*. The novel registers both of these instances of loss, suggesting their historical overlap and the unevenness of these developments, participating in the knowledge both of an emerging male homosexuality and of a residual, physiologically defined manhood and womanhood. It represents male homosexuality, first of all, in terms of an anxious, barely sustained contrast with male homosociality. Jake Barnes's status as a bullfighting aficionado, for instance, is deeply complicated for him by what can only be called homosexual panic. To be an aficionado is to participate in homosocial affection, to have a kind of passion that men who love bullfighting can only share with other men: when the novel's Spanish "natives" identify Jake as a "true" aficionado, he tells us, "There was this . . . embarrassed putting the hand on the shoulder. . . . Nearly always there was the actual touching. It seemed as though they wanted to touch you to make it certain."[29] Jake tries to share a similarly homosocial bond with his male cosmopolitan acquaintances, but this capacity is exactly what they and Jake have a sense of losing. Their escape into what they experience as an idealized, "primitive" Spanish landscape is also an escape from an emerging epistemology of homosexual desire, an escape that never quite succeeds. On the one hand, Jake enthusiastically experiences the homosocial affection he encounters in Spain in terms of his own national experience, in the residual terms of a nineteenth-century homosocial affection relatively free from the taint of homoeroticism. On the other hand, he and his cohort of expatriates cannot but remain painfully aware of the historical displacement and increasing unavailability of this epistemology of gender and desire: when his friend Bill Gorton remarks to Jake during one of their Spanish excursions, "You're a hell of a good guy, and I'm fonder of you than anybody on earth," he feels compelled to add, "I couldn't tell you that in New York. It'd mean I was a faggot."[30]

While a knowledge of male homosexuality is registered by the novel— if only in its male characters' attempts to escape this emerging knowledge, to establish some incipient version of what Eve Sedgwick called "the

privilege of unknowing"[31]—the text simultaneously fails to register anything we could call a heterosexual matrix. This inability manifests itself as
one of the fundamental questions about male-female sexual relations the
novel insistently raises but, within its historically conditioned epistemological limits, cannot answer: what does it mean for a female body to be a
subject of sexual desire, and what kind of loss to the male body is entailed
by the attribution of such a capacity to a female body? This question is
famously legible on the bodies of its two major characters: Jake Barnes and
Lady Brett Ashley. Brett, whose name obviously suggests gender ambiguity, frequently refers to herself as a "chap," while Jake describes her as
having "curves like the hull of a racing yacht" and, at the same time, hair
"brushed back like a boy's."[32] That Brett is both a woman and a desiring
subject is registered here in terms of an agonizing contradiction, a question about how to situate her body in relation to a dyadic conception of
males as desiring subjects and females as sexually inert objects, a question
beyond resolution within the available sexual terms.

And what is the cost of Brett's embodiment of desire to the series of
men with whom she finds herself involved? One such man is the bullfighter Pedro Romero. As Jake joins Brett in witnessing Romero's performance in the bullring, Romero is subject to Brett's gaze as well as Jake's,
gazes that explicitly share a capacity to objectify him sexually. Jake believes
Romero to be "the best-looking boy I have ever seen"; Brett, for her part,
could hardly agree more: "How I would love to see him get into those
clothes," she says. "He must use a shoehorn."[33] As Jake watches Romero
perform, he is clearly more concerned with the fact that Brett—with
whom Romero is at the moment sexually involved—watches him also:

> Everything of which [Romero] could control the locality he did in front of
> her all that afternoon. Never once did he look up. He made it stronger that
> way, and did it for himself, too, as well as for her. Because he did not look up
> to ask if it pleased he did it all for himself inside, and it strengthened him, and
> yet he did it for her, too. But he did not do it for her at any loss to himself.[34]

Jake's concern with whether Romero acknowledges Brett's gaze indicates
the extent to which he cannot imagine Romero's activity, as perceived by
Brett, in other than objectifying terms, terms that suggest a cost to Romero's
subjectivity. Not that Jake doesn't try: the repetitive, circular character of

this passage registers both a desire to imagine, and the difficulty of imagining, what it might mean for Romero to perform for Brett without "any loss to himself." The loss insinuated for Jake by this display is not a melancholic loss, the loss of a constitutive homosexual desire, but the loss of manhood as such, Romero's loss of his status as a sexually desiring subject. Performing "for her" and performing "for himself"—performing without looking up to acknowledge her gaze—are represented here as mutually exclusive. Jake seems both open to the possibility of reconciling these contradictory ways of performing and unable to comprehend what such a reconciliation would look like. If, presumably, it would look like a femininity that, within a heterosexual matrix, melancholically takes masculinity as object *of* desire without at the same time robbing masculinity of its capacity *to* desire, Jake's inability to register this possibility suggests the historical unavailability of that very matrix, the epistemological impossibility of heterosexual desire as such. If, as I am arguing, an epistemological stripping of the male body of the exclusive capacity for sexual desire is a condition of possibility for the heterosexual matrix, and therefore also for a masculine performance of what Chauncey calls "exclusive sexual interest in women," this performance is apparently not yet possible within the novel's terms. And it is not at all clear to Jake how Romero could reclaim the manhood that has appeared to slip away.

Jake himself, meanwhile, has his own sexual history with Brett, and the novel's most famous plot question is certainly the question of whether this history will or can resume. But this plot question also turns on this same, more fundamental epistemological question, now rendered as the concern with how to situate Jake's body along the sexual subject-object dyad. Jake and Brett are, indeed, inverted mirror images of each other in terms of the question of Brett's assumption of a desiring subjectivity and the costs to the male body of this assumption. If this question is embodied by Brett, it is registered in Jake's case in terms of a certain specter of disembodiment. If anything threatens to keep their sexual history from resuming, it is, of course, Jake's sexually debilitating but ambiguously defined war wound, a corporeal figure for the historically specific epistemological loss I am considering here. The precise nature of Jake's wound—is he anatomically damaged, or impotent but anatomically intact?—is never clarified. If Jake is clearly a subject, a status his position as the novel's first-person narrator may alone secure, it is less clear whether he is a desiring subject.

Perhaps he has been reduced to a sexually inert object. The violent, un-avoidably sexual opposition between the castrated steer and the uncas-trated bull in the bullfights that Jake witnesses loudly echoes his wound's ambiguous status: the novel never finally resolves our questions about whether Jake is a bull or a steer. Jake's desire has become an estranged pos-session, something that may or may not be lost, but which apparently *can* be. Does he want Brett, or does he want to want Brett?

His wound's ambiguous definition insinuates an irrevocable moment of woundedness into the historical shifting of sexual knowledge the novel negotiates. Male bodies lose the exclusive capacity for desire; they will re-trieve that capacity within a new, different regime of sexual knowledge. As both Brett's and Jake's gazes on Romero's body suggest, a body's perfor-mance of masculinity necessarily objectifies that body, constitutes it by way of the potentially desiring gaze of another. But within the terms of a heterosexual matrix, that objectification is no longer synonymous with a loss of manhood. The male body negotiates this inherent objectification within that emerging matrix by performing masculinity and all that such a performance entails: by insisting on that body's capacity for desire, by forestalling a homosexual objectification of that body through an insis-tent performance of "exclusive sexual interest in women"—by making that body impenetrable.

INTERPELLATION, KNOWLEDGE, CONSUMPTION; OR, LABOR WITHOUT CAPITAL

But this performance also signifies much more. Butler writes that "although heterosexuality operates in part through the stabilization of gender norms, gender designates a dense site of significations that contain and exceed the heterosexual matrix."[35] What might some of these broader significa-tions be? Her analysis of gender everywhere implies that the performance of gender is a form of labor: the compulsory labor of citation. And she states explicitly in her reading of Althusser in *The Psychic Life of Power* that the performance of subjectivity more generally is not only laborious but highly skilled. She in fact insists that skilled labor is the fundamen-tal material content of performative subjectivity as such. Butler's central effort in this essay is an immanent critique of the turn toward the law in Althusser's hailing metaphor; she argues that subject formation—the turn of the subject toward the law that interpellates that subject into the performative practices from which belief emerges—presupposes a desire for subjection to the law that hails, a "passionate attachment" to the law taking the form of guilt or conscience. An insistent guilt is here constitutive of the reiterative constitution of the subject: it is precisely this guilt that compels performative re-citation. Not only highlighting the role of conscience, of morality, in subject formation, but also explicitly distancing the dynamic of subjection from the reproduction of labor power—the routinely forgotten starting point of Althusser's analysis—Butler focuses instead on Althusser's argument that the corporeal mastery of certain skilled practices (like proper speech or religious ritual) is constitutive of subjection to ideology. She suggests, that is, that skill is the specific content of subjectivation. Performative subjectivity amounts here to a kind of corporeal mastery that constitutes submission to the law: "The lived simultaneity of submission as mastery, and mastery as submission, is the condition of possibility for the emergence of the subject." Skill, moreover, discloses the situatedness of subjection within the social: "The reproduction of social relations, the reproduction of skills, is the reproduction of subjection."[36] And crucially, "This performance is not simply *in accord* with these skills, for there is no subject prior to their performing; performing skills laboriously works the subject into its status as a social being." The subject doesn't work the skills; the skills work the subject: the content of subjectivity is a repetitive, citational skilled labor—"not simply to act according to a set of rules, but to embody rules in the course of action and to reproduce those rules in the embodied rituals of action."[37]

I want to underscore two points here. First, as I argued in the previous chapter, skill refers to nothing if not fully corporealized knowledge; skilled labor is by definition an immanently epistemological labor. Butler's essay in this respect insists that the performative is to be understood in epistemological terms. The performative citation of a norm is the performance of a certain knowledge only ever articulated in the course of that performance. Indeed, the normative character of the performance abides precisely in the knowledge embodied by, cited by, and constituting that performance. And this applies not just to the performative in general but to the performance of gender in particular: to engage the question of the legitimacy of bodies as a question of the intelligibility of bodies, for instance—as Butler repeatedly points out, the heterosexual matrix is a matrix of intelligibility—is to underscore the way in which the performance of gender is an epistemological as well as an ontological practice. And given that one of the Foucauldian lessons most basic to Butler's work is the inseparability of knowledge and power, one could go a step further and propose that Butler's focus is *primarily* epistemological rather than ontological, that her interest is less in ontology than in power/knowledge as it operates at the level of ontology. Butler has more recently suggested, for example, that social transformation, precisely because of power's entanglement with knowledge, requires a disruption of settled knowledges. Indeed power/knowledge, as she puts it, "dissimulates as ontology."[38]

The second point I would emphasize is that this relatively rare engagement with a figure firmly situated within the Marxist tradition suggests as strongly as any other instance in Butler's work the extent to which capital is not simply incidental to her analysis of the performative subject but simultaneously excluded from it and constitutive of it. For Marx, not only is the reproduction of labor everywhere mediated by capital; labor is itself a component of capital—specifically, "variable" capital. Labor is both opposed to capital and internal to it. But Butler maintains that "the reproduction of labor," Althusser's starting point, is not central here.[39] On the one hand, then, Butler indicates that the performative subject is constituted by skilled labor; on the other hand, her reading of Althusser isolates this laborious, performative subject from the reproduction of labor and thereby also from capital. The version of skilled labor we encounter in Butler's reading can then only be, from a Marxian perspective at least, some different, unexpected kind of skilled labor, skilled labor operating in some kind of vacuum. For both Althusser and Butler, in fact, interpellation entails a performance of skilled labor at some structural distance, we might say, from the direct employment of labor by capital. Althusser's starting point is the reproduction of the conditions of production. But in Butler's reading of Althusser, that distance is indeterminate. There is a long history of structuralist and poststructuralist readings of this most familiar of Althusser's essays that isolate the *interpellated subject* from capital, but Butler goes further: her reading of Althusser posits, in addition, *labor* without capital. The subject who has a complexly (even tortuously) mediated relation with capital in Althusser's analysis becomes here a laboring subject severed from its own reproduction, severed from capital, severed from the concrete social relations that constitute it.

I read this reading of Althusser as an invitation to rethink the relation between this skilled, performative subject and the horizon of capital elided from Butler's analysis of that subject. If the performative subject is held at an indeterminate distance from capital in this analysis, is there a useful way to read this distance as determinate, to read it as mediation? This is the point at which it becomes possible to avoid the kind of Marxian critique of Butler that concludes with the claim that her terms make capital "unspeakable," and to pursue instead a potentially more productive response. My remaining discussion in this chapter will try to suggest that if we think this skilled subject together with the gendered subject that we find elsewhere in Butler's work—and with the social circuit of capital she consistently abstracts from consideration—we can begin to see the way in which Butler's account of the gendered subject does not in fact preempt efforts to think that subject in relation to capital but, to the contrary, enables new ways of understanding this relation.

How, then, to further specify the skills that constitute subjectivity? Is it possible to distinguish between different social subject positions in terms of skill? Is there any such thing, in these terms, as a deskilled subject, or does an absence of skill prevent subjectivation as such? One way to concretize the performance of gender norms is perhaps to ask after their distribution. Does this normalizing, immanent corporeal knowledge operate consistently across the social field? If gender is always a performative skill, how might we begin to consider the nationally, racially, historically, and gender-specific distinctions and determinations of this skill? If gender norms are embodied knowledges, are these knowledges made more available to certain (potential) subjects than others?

To return to the specific time, place, and gender under consideration in this chapter, take the example of one of the earliest and most successful mass publications in the twentieth-century United States to interpellate a simultaneously gendered and consuming subject in terms of skills to be mastered. *Esquire* magazine's founding editor stated in early promotional material that the magazine would be "a new kind of magazine—one that will answer the question of What to do? What to eat, what to drink, what to wear, how to play, what to read—in short a magazine dedicated to the improvement of the new leisure."[40] The lead article in the magazine's inaugural issue, an interview with Nicholas Murray Butler, president of Columbia University, carried the unwieldy title "The New Leisure:

What It Means in Terms of the Opportunity to Learn the Art of Living."[41]
One of the magazine's burdens was to produce a consumer masculinity
sufficiently distanced from the close association of consumerism with femininity that persisted into the early twentieth century. It featured articles
explicitly masculinizing skills that ranged from etiquette to cooking to
home decor and gardening. It also featured the elaborate and overtly pedagogical detailing of techniques of laboring masculinity—how to hunt,
how to fish—in the series of columns or "letters" Hemingway wrote for
twenty-eight of the magazine's first thirty-three issues. (These columns
were in fact the origin of Hemingway's reputation as a sportsman, and
many of these letters would later be reprinted in periodicals from *Field
and Stream* to *Outdoor Life*.)[42] *Esquire*'s mission, in other words, was forthrightly and instrumentally pedagogical; it elaborated the means rather than
the end of masculinity, the how rather than the why, consistently articulating the performative practice of masculinity as a question of technical
competence. Displays of skilled masculine practice became objects of consumption in its pages, models to be emulated; embodied technical knowledge became the key commodity, the substance it sold. The performative,
skilled labor of masculinity is in this instance mediated by consumption
and unevenly distributed. Masculinity is here a performative norm made
available to those with sufficient purchasing power. The magazine began
publishing in the midst of accumulation crisis and devaluation, in 1933:
targeting affluent and middle-class men, *Esquire*'s debut represented an
effort to increase revenue by commodifying leisure time.[43]

Also mediating this instance of consumer interpellation was a certain
conservative social longing for a highly skilled laboring manhood in the
face of its ongoing disappearance, a response to a perceived domestication
of labor itself in the age of Taylorism. And working-class men were by
no means excluded from efforts to capitalize on this longing. Scholarship
on hard-boiled masculinity, for instance, has shown in detail that the seri-
alized hard-boiled fiction marketed largely to working-class men between
the wars featured protagonists who were explicitly identified as artisans,
and interpellated their readers as highly skilled masculine subjects—or at
least as subjects desiring the ability to obtain skilled work, work that would
grant them some measure of autonomy and thereby some measure of manliness. Pulp magazines like *Black Mask* promised opportunities to practice
an artisanal, manly labor even as those opportunities were relocated to the

moment of consumption; like *Esquire,* the pulps also had to negotiate established associations of consumption with femininity. *Black Mask* routinely featured advertisements that offered training in some kind of technical competence, from job training to bodybuilding to elocution lessons.[44] Masculinity was here too a skilled practice, a knowledge to be embodied. Erin Smith suggestively compares a typical passage from hard-boiled fiction with the time-motion studies employed in the service of scientific management: of a fight scene from Hammett's *The Maltese Falcon,* she comments that "such scenes functioned as instruction manuals for effective brawling."[45] And Christopher Breu has more recently characterized the practices of the hard-boiled masculine protagonist as void of affect, as instrumentalized, as demonstrating the ways in which hard-boiled fiction implicated itself in the very practices of scientific management it also critiqued.[46]

New "do-it-yourself" industries, meanwhile, emerged during this same period. Early in the century, as the suburbs grew, laborers working for Henry Ford began to house the automobiles they bought from their employer in garages they built and attached to their homes.[47] By the twenties and thirties, home maintenance and repair became another location for performances of masculinity. The earlier, short-lived arts and crafts movement, which began not only as an alternative to, but as a practical critique of, tedious, enervating new forms of office work, quickly took the form of leisure activity and thereby accommodated itself to capitalism's newest stage.[48] Similarly, new service industries—do-it-yourself books and magazines, power tools designed for home use—emerged during the twenties. As more and more men spent leisure time in the traditionally feminine space of the home, they reasserted direct, skillful, masculine control over the home's physical environment; consumption provided here for the creation of a distinctly masculine sphere inside the home. In Stephen Gebler's words, the "role for men in caring for their homes grew so palpably during interwar years that the house was transformed from a place *in* which to do things to a place *on* which to do things."[49]

Butler's reading of Althusser, considered in relation to such examples, begins to suggest an additional, gender-specific twist on the historically specific entanglement of knowledge and consumption I elaborated more generally in the previous chapter. There, in my discussion of the reification of desire within an emergent regime of sexual knowledge, I situated the body's subjection to that regime in relation to two developments in particular: an increasingly complex social division of labor and increasingly pervasive corporate efforts to normalize consumption—efforts that were indicative of an unevenly emergent, intensive regime of accumulation. I maintained that these broad socioeconomic developments produced new forms of social deskilling and made available new forms of knowledge. These forms of knowledge were at the same time compensations for the process of deskilling and products of this same process. Just as Taylorism expropriated what had been fully corporeal knowledges from laboring bodies, the broader social effects of the amplified productive capacity provided by Taylorism included a widespread social deskilling at a range of sites far beyond the shop floor, and in a range of emergent service industries especially. My primary example of subjectivity's constitution through the consumption of knowledge was psychoanalysis: in the clinic, a sexually deskilled subject is constituted, interpellated through a commodification of sexual expertise. The deskilled sexual subject's production is here coterminous with its subjection to a disembodied, reified, commodified knowledge.

If the buying and selling of a psychoanalytic knowledge of self made the body into a strategy of capital accumulation within an increasingly managed, disciplinary form of consumption, so did the performative normalization of the male body, during this period, as masculine, the emergent marketing of masculinity as a technique to be modeled, embodied, purchased. But in the latter case, knowledge is not simply sold to the subject; it is corporeally absorbed as skill. Consumption, interpellation, and this absorption of skill operate here in tandem. A dynamic division of labor, the emergence of service industries from psychoanalysis to do-it-yourself, and an increasingly regulatory consumption produced, I am suggesting, not only a broad disembodiment of knowledge but also new ways in which knowledge would be embodied, new ways in which skilled subjects would be formed.

Keeping in mind what I have argued is its historical specificity, I would even propose that the performative masculinity Butler identifies as a *regulatory norm* should be understood as one component of this emergent *mode of regulation*. Arjun Appadurai points out that consumption operates through "techniques of the body" and that it "must and does fall into the mode of repetition, of habituation"; consumption disciplines the body in a temporal fashion. Gender, for Butler, operates similarly: not only is gender materially immanent to the body, it is also defined by a temporality of repetition (a temporality that is itself significant for reasons I will consider below). Appadurai adds that "the techniques of the body . . . need to become social disciplines, parts of some habitus, free of artifice or external coercion, in order to take on their full power."[50] And Miranda Joseph, in her discussion of the performative as a dimension of production and consumption, makes an explicit connection between Bourdieu's concept of *habitus* and "what Butler calls *norms*."[51] Butler herself has indeed briefly suggested the resonance between the habitus and the performative—gesturing as it were "outward" from the bodily practices that are her focus toward the broader social field in relation to which we might begin to understand these practices. She has proposed that "the category of the 'social' . . . offers a perspective on embodiment, suggesting that knowledge, to the extent that it is embodied as habitus (Bourdieu), represents a sphere of performativity that no analysis of political articulation can do without."[52] More specifically, in her reading of Althusser, she proposes in an endnote that "Bourdieu's notion of the *habitus* might well be read as a reformulation of Althusser's notion of ideology," that "Bourdieu underscores the place of the body, its gestures, its stylistics, its unconscious 'knowingness' as the site for the reconstitution of a practical sense without which social reality could not be constituted."[53]

I bring up these momentary references to Bourdieu—and my own reference will be only slightly less momentary—because, in one of the key early texts of regulation theory, Alain Lipietz gestures just as briefly toward this same concept as he defines the mode of regulation any coherent accumulation regime requires: "The set of internalized rules and social procedures which incorporate social elements into individual behavior (and one might be able to mobilize Bourdieu's concept of habitus here) is referred to as a mode of regulation."[54] For Lipietz this reference to Bourdieu that, like Butler's, comes and goes so quickly also moves, as it were, in the opposite direction: "inward," toward the kinds of "on the ground" everyday practices that must be normalized if a regime of accumulation is to be sustained. Both Butler and Lipietz, then, gesture toward the possibility that the concept of habitus can be useful in elaborating—which is to say concretizing, further specifying in relation to what we might be tempted to call a social totality—what they mean, exactly, by regulation: by regulatory norms in the one case, and by a mode of regulation in the other. Returning then to what I proposed earlier were the historical limitations of Butler's theory of gender, limitations largely unregistered by that theory itself, I want to suggest that the regulatory norm of gender she theorizes instantiates a broader habitus we can specify: the mode of regulation that will ultimately secure an intensive regime of accumulation. One key aspect of this habitus I would highlight is precisely the broad social regulation of consumption at the level of everyday practices that centrally defined this emergent regime and provides the site at which a skilled masculinity is articulated. Each of these instances of regulation is constitutive of the other.

In the interest of ridding the idea of performativity of any voluntarist implications, Butler also explicitly distances it from consumerism.[55] But within this intensive management of social demand, consumption assumes a disciplinary character and can no more be associated with individuated voluntarism than can the performance of gender itself. Joseph, in a brief consideration of Butler's emphatic distinction between performativity and consumerism, rightly insists on consumption's status "as a highly constrained site of collective as well as individual subject constitution," adding that capital accumulation requires the "complicity" of discourses like gender and that the performative discourses that produce gender can operate at both moments in the production-consumption circuit.[56] I would complicate this important formulation by underscoring the historically specific character of this complicity, especially the way in which specific gender norms can, in specific historical situations, be relatively *displaced* within the production-consumption circuit as that circuit evolves—as in the present case, wherein the owners of capital begin more and more strategically to try and manage social consumption. That performative, disciplinary regulation of the gendered body as masculine here simultaneously subjects that body to, and instrumentalizes that body in the service of, an intensive regime of accumulation.

How, then, might we understand this constellation of consumption, knowledge, and gender embodiment in relation to Butler's insistence on the sedimentation of gender norms, her argument that the performance of gender "accumulates the force of authority through the repetition or citation of a prior, authoritative set of practices"?[57] What prior set of practices could this emergent masculinity have been citing? I ask this question because to the extent that an early-twentieth-century performative,

citational masculinity is regulated at the level of the body, this form of regulation contrasts strikingly with a nineteenth-century middle-class norm
of manhood, a norm articulated in a vexed relation with the body indeed,
as chapter 1 emphasized. Again, this norm of manhood defined itself both
with and against the tendencies of the body, against disruptive sexual energies that body nonetheless had a capacity to master and transcend. It also
defined itself very much against a range of others thereby reduced to their
bodies, in terms of the social autonomy that these radically corporealized
others, including women, slaves, Native Americans, and immigrants, ostensibly lacked. This especially meant independence vis-à-vis the corrosive,
atomizing chaos of industrialization: manly mastery of "the market," after
all, was hardly possible without having already learned not to squander
limited corporeal energy. Manhood *as such* is here articulated not only in
gender-specific but in racially specific terms. What I am calling middle-
class manhood, Dana Nelson calls national manhood, a dominant norm
of manhood that aspired in the nineteenth century to stabilize the chaos
of capitalist industrialization through an insistence on racial and gender
hierarchy.[58] This national manhood defined itself, for example, in terms
of a certain intellectual independence of the body—in terms of what Nelson identifies as a scientific, disembodied standpoint that was also a class-
specific, professionalized standpoint, a standpoint projecting dependence
and embodiment onto a range of racialized and gendered others. This
is what Nelson calls manhood's "altero-referentiality," the direction of its
rational, managerial gaze outward, toward social others whom it defined
in terms of the embodiment and dependence that are in this respect its
disavowed external supplements.[59]

But rather than being plagued by the body, white men seemed increasingly, as the century turned, to be defined by it. Again, Kimmel's distinction
between *manhood* and *masculinity* turns on the way in which masculinity
is exteriorized in the early decades of the century; masculinity is a norm
defined in terms of manifest and measurable traits and behaviors, in everything from success or failure in sports to the anxious search for bodily
or behavioral signs of homosexuality. This exteriorized masculinity, in
contrast with manhood, had an audience; it was the object as much as the
subject of an evaluating gaze, was indeed defined in terms of its own staged
body. Perhaps instead of a shift wherein manliness is increasingly exteriorized, as Kimmel puts it, we might say that the normative regulation of

manliness shifts from a position of transcendence to one of immanence vis-à-vis the body.

But it also seems important to point out nineteenth-century normalizations of manliness were not *everywhere* in contradiction with embodiment. If the early-twentieth-century regulatory norm of masculinity I have been considering is immanent to the body, so, apparently, was a norm of *working-class* manhood in the previous century, a norm just as corporeally epistemological, a norm constituted by the embodiment of a specific kind of technical knowledge: the embodied productive knowledge of the skilled laborer—first the preindustrial craftsman and increasingly, as the century progressed, the industrial craftsman. Embodied knowledge was precisely the way in which this laboring manhood tended to define manly aspirations to independence. The performance of this other, embodied manhood was centrally a performance of patriarchal autonomy, even or especially in the face of ever-intensifying threats to that autonomy posed by industrialization and deskilling. Skilled male laborers insisted on the inseparability of manhood, independence, and skill all the more tenaciously as industrial labor discipline became increasingly widespread, especially in the transition to a system of wage labor.[60] And this working-class norm was as gender and racially specific as its middle-class counterpart, industrialization's threat to laboring manhood only compounded in the context of the radical dependence, the utter lack of autonomy projected onto that same range of infantilized, racialized, and gendered others. The skill, the technical knowledge embodied by the craftsman, gave him independence vis-à-vis his foreman, but also vis-à-vis the disavowed, supplementary others working-class and middle-class manhood held in common. And as scholars like David Roediger point out, it became important for white male laborers to maintain a strong distinction between themselves and slaves as industrialization was reducing ever larger numbers of them to the form of dependence they began to call "wage slavery," and indeed "white slavery."[61] In this respect, it is putting it mildly to add that laboring manhood, like early-twentieth-century masculinity, was an unevenly distributed skill.

If the interpellation of the skilled masculine subject in the early century is mediated by an intensive managing of consumption, this interpellation can also hardly be understood in isolation from the way in which, during the same period, deskilling was still experienced as a threat to laboring manhood. Skilled workers could be displaced by newly arrived, unskilled and semiskilled immigrants, for example, to the extent that the expertise not merely possessed but embodied by those same skilled workers was increasingly expropriated by managers and engineers. And so if, as Butler's reading of Althusser insists, the performance of subjectivity is a form of skilled labor, skill nonetheless also had gender-specific meanings in the early-twentieth-century United States. If corporations' increasing need for clerical work threatened to feminize the workplace, a domestication of manly labor was also threatened in the emergence of a class distinction between scientifically knowledgeable managers on the one hand and de-skilled laborers on the other. As work became increasingly routinized, as a relatively chaotic, industrializing, and still to some extent entrepreneurial stage in U.S. capitalist development gave way to a corporate, systematically managed, bureaucratized one, aspirations to manly autonomy seemed increasingly less realistic. Men who were part of an emerging professional-managerial class found themselves engaged in sedentary rather than physical labor in a corporate office, while working-class men were, in Marx's metaphor, simultaneously being reduced to so many appendages of the scientifically managed factory. What these managers and laborers shared in common was an experience of work that seemed to threaten a loss of manhood itself. As indeed it did: a normalization of the male body in terms of manhood began to give way to something called masculinity, as corporate marketing efforts like the one that produced *Esquire* seized an opportunity. Consumption now intervened to constitute a manliness increasingly less in evidence at the moment of production. I would propose, then, that an additional component of what I earlier called the habitus mediating the regulatory norm of masculinity and the larger mode of regulation of which it is a part is this preexisting norm of manly, embodied, technical knowledge, now performatively cited as part of an emergent mode of regulation.

REPETITION AND REIFICATION

This new labor of masculinity offered during leisure hours, to white men with sufficient disposable income, a respite from a more tedious, routinized labor, the labor an increasingly bureaucratic capitalism required. Butler's representation of labor without capital is worth comparing, I think, with this one:

In a little while I had six [trout]. They were all about the same size. I laid them out, side by side, all their heads pointing the same way, and looked at them. They were beautifully colored and firm and hard from the cold water. It was a hot day, so I slit them all and shucked out the insides, gills and all, and tossed them over across the river. I took the trout ashore, washed them in the cold, smoothly heavy water above the dam, and then picked some ferns and packed them all in the bag, three trout on a layer of ferns, then another layer of ferns, then three more trout, and then covered them with ferns.[62]

One of the striking characteristics of this passage from *The Sun Also Rises* is the way it depicts the laboring subject's encounter with objective nature, an encounter so neat and tidy one is tempted to call it unnatural. Jake Barnes counts and arranges these fish with the meticulous attention of a retailer taking inventory, with a fetishistic attention to their surface and sensation. What Richard Godden has said about the trout pursued by another Hemingway protagonist, Nick Adams, we can also say about the trout secured in this passage: "There is something abstracted about the phenomenological innocence through which the fish is viewed."[63] These particular trout are ultimately interchangeable, any qualitative differences radically "shucked out" with the simple assertion that "they were all about the same size." Though Hemingway's famous aesthetic emphasis is on concrete, natural things and the avoidance of abstraction, in idealizing the things that constitute the natural landscape, his texts represent those things, paradoxically, as formal equivalents. And this representational tendency goes far beyond trout; as Godden puts it, "trout, bulls and white pebbles in a blue stream are equally, and almost interchangeably, opportunities for the creation of perfect and disembodied moments of isolate satisfaction."[64] Nature's concrete messiness, in other words, is "shucked out" less by Jake's labor than by the passage itself. What is at issue in this passage is then not only the performance of skilled masculine subjectivity but also the objective location of that performance. What kind if unnatural nature is this?

The countryside here becomes a sanctuary that is not merely "natural" but pristine, uncorrupted. Though such escapes from the tedium of de-skilled labor into nature constitute supposed returns to more simple, presumably pre- or extracapitalist forms of work and life, famously sparse descriptions like this one ultimately reify nature, producing a landscape of pure immediacy, a landscape of what we might call, following Lukács, a "second nature" that only purports to transcend the abstraction of labor capital enforces. And this second nature does indeed appear here to be what Lukács calls "frozen," a spatialized erasure of history itself, an erasure motivated by a desire for an existence that, ultimately, is not simply precapitalist but prelapsarian, in which the precapitalist becomes the prelapsarian. Repeated excursions into Spain here become rigorously reactionary efforts to stop historical movement as such, to trump historical distance with geographic distance, to escape into an imaginary geographic past. Such passages construct ahistorical sanctuaries from exchange value even as they carry historically specific exchange values of their own. They do what all commodities do: simultaneously constitute and obscure capitalist social relations. The space of unexploited, unalienated male labor they posit necessarily binds capital to itself, as its constitutive outside.

But if Lukács's characterization of the objective side of reification (an external world of false immediacy) is helpful in reading this passage, his characterization of the subjective side of reification (a subjective "second nature" that is itself a product of an objective "second nature") here begins to fail us, as it did in the previous chapter. This is a representation of labor that cannot adequately be grasped in terms of the state of passivity that reification, for Lukács, induces. If *History and Class Consciousness* and *The Sun Also Rises* agree at least that deskilled labor compels passivity, the labor performed in Hemingway's novel seems designed to escape that passivity. If the objects that directly result from the labor of shucking, tossing, and arranging have the sheen of commodities, fetishes, what this passage might appear to depict is a labored transformation of "natural" material into so many formal equivalents, but magically without the intervention of capital, a representation of labor that impossibly short-circuits that extraction of surplus value that makes the use values produced by labor interchangeable, abstract in the first place. But again, this immediacy is much more general and universal, defining the contours of this space itself: the trout, like the fetishized objects within that natural landscape generally, already *were* interchangeable, hence the equivalence that Godden rightly discerns between "trout, bulls, and white pebbles in a blue stream." The labor performed here would appear merely to "transform" abstractions into abstractions. This is a skilled performance of masculinity characterized not by transformative labor but by a purely, abstractly repetitive labor, a subjectivity constituted by skilled practice and by performative repetition.

So if we have, unmistakably, some kind of depiction not of passive "contemplation" but of active, skilled labor here, this is a recreational labor that has, in Marxian terms, no transformative capacity at all—which lacks the capacity that, for Marx, is concrete labor's single most defining characteristic. To the extent that we are uncritically persuaded by this representation of an escape from deskilled labor, this passage might appear to represent labor as the end in itself that Marx insists it should be, but which capital can never allow it to become.[65] But given this lack of transformative capacity, perhaps we should say instead that the performance of skilled labor is itself reified here, in the sense that labor as *means* is fetishized, that the instrumental character of labor assumes an autonomy vis-à-vis presumed ends to the point that any consideration of those ends (which are, for Marx, precisely material transformation) is suspended.[66] In Butler's sense, however, this labor is indeed productive: the end to which this performative labor is a means has become the reiterative constitution of masculinity itself. The objective of these repeated excursions into the idealized countryside is a practice of masculinity that *must* be repeated, and that defines the performative labor of masculinity in terms of an imaginary negation of alienated labor. If the labor of masculinity is a determinate practice here, we can at least propose that it is determined not by any transformative end in Marx's sense but, in Butler's terms, by the objective of producing the ontological illusion of a masculinity that exists prior to that reiterative practice itself.

This practice of masculinity indeed operates in the service of two different ends at least. What Butler characterizes as the ontological illusion of a masculinity that preexists its performance is here revealed to obscure both masculinity's performative, citational character and the way in which this regulatory norm positions that body as a strategy of accumulation. This norm of masculinity constitutively subjects the body so normalized to an unevenly emerging, historically specific, intensive regime of accumulation. To the extent that Taylorism makes skilled labor obsolete, a gender-specific practice of embodied technical knowledge—now "freed" from any socially recognizable objective but "sedimented," in Butler's terms, as an earlier, recognizable normalization of the laboring male body—remains to be invested by capital within a space of consumption. The novel from which this passage is taken does not merely represent the space within which this masculinity is performed; it is one component of a much larger, valuable constellation of texts and images, one fragment of the minor industry of iconic, early-twentieth-century masculinity that deserves the name "Hemingway" at least as much as any specific person does, this name being not merely a name, of course, but a brand name. Instead of merely representing this space, this novel instantiates it, participates in its constitution.

This masculinized body becomes a subject *of* technical knowledge precisely in becoming subject *to* technical knowledge, a performance of technical knowledge compelled by the historical sedimentation of laboring manhood, and both instrumentalized for the sake of accumulation and—mystified in a space of false immediacy—experienced as the simple content of masculinity itself. Here again, the subject does not work the skills; the skills work the subject. Kathi Weeks comments on Butler's account of the sedimentation of performative gender practices this way: "These practices, these repetitions, leave complex marks or traces which constitute something on the order of a second nature or a constructed, contingent necessity."[67] Similarly, I am suggesting that the performance of masculinity does indeed take the form of a subjective second nature, in Lukács's sense, that it presupposes an objective second nature marked off from the space of deskilled labor. What intervenes between this performance of skilled, masculine labor and the horizon of capital that goes unrecognized in both Butler's and Hemingway's representations of this performance is reification itself. These performances of a subjective second nature both obscure the horizon of capital and are constituted by it. Only in these terms can masculinity be understood as an instance of labor without capital.

Consider very briefly one more site of labor without capital: the increasingly commercialized, early-twentieth-century sports arena. The still largely male province of sports became around the turn of the century increasingly normalized and disciplined, increasingly capital intensive, and increasingly a site for the performance of an embodied and specialized technical knowledge. In a process that had gradually begun to get under way in the decades of accelerated industrialization following the Civil War, the practice of sports was ever more subject to bureaucratic regulation, technical specialization, marketing strategies, an emphasis on abstract statistics—to what Elliott Gorn, in his history of prizefighting, calls "a managerial ethos."[68] Until late in the nineteenth century, as historians of sport have emphasized, athletes were usually amateurs, and sports were controlled very loosely by the participants who organized them, with great regional variation and pervasive haphazardness in the enforcement of rules.[69] The gradual expropriation of this control by capital entailed an increasing standardization of rules and procedures and the organization of sporting events according to standardized time frames. "Increasingly, athletes were becoming subject to the dictates of owners and managers," Gorn points out. "Like factory whistles, boxing's new rhythms," for example, "mandated regular periods of work and rest."[70] The tendency of modern sports has been to fetishize the sports record, to quantify and measure every athletic feat.[71] The practice of sports manifested a trend toward greater athlete specialization and an emphasis on abstract statistics, or what we might call an entirely immanent subjection of specific sporting bodies to normalized and reified technical knowledges.[72]

Is this arena not also a haven from dreary routine, from an alienated labor actually experienced as such? A generation before Hemingway became a familiar name, even the myth of the frontier so basic to the manliness articulated by figures like Roosevelt was spatialized: staged in skillful, ritualized form in the circuslike spectacles of Buffalo Bill Cody. And after World War I, in Richard Slotkin's words, "commercial popular culture" would be the site at which the frontier myth "would be played out."[73] I have begun to move beyond this isolated performance of masculinity to what we may call its spatiotemporal coordinates. The hunting or fishing trip that allows weekend warriors with the time and money to escape the world of routinized, alienated labor takes them into an arena of false immediacy that is already itself a fully marketed, capital-intensive space, a space of objective "second nature," a space inseparable from the subjective second nature of the performance of masculinity itself. The moment of consumption here becomes the site for the articulation of a coherent definition of what it means to be a man, a definition presupposing and citing an earlier norm, that combination of physical labor and technical knowledge Taylorism was making increasingly obsolete, a norm incorporated into a different regime of accumulation and necessarily reshaped by a different, emerging mode of regulation. An emergent norm of masculinity performatively reconciles what Taylorism had dissociated at the moment of production. Spaces of consumption become the aggregate arena in which masculinity is put on display, quantified, measured, the site of a relief from deskilling that is also a highly mediated product of deskilling.

Laboring, embodied nineteenth-century manhood was, of course, already a gender norm mediated by a temporality of capital accumulation. The skilled laborer possessed knowledge that the managers of the industrial factory did not: a central aspect of the manly autonomy that skill made possible here, as labor historians like David Montgomery point out, is the control that industrial artisans exerted over the production process. Before Taylorism craftsmen were, even within industrialization, substantially self-directing at their tasks, their skill giving them the opportunity to exercise broad discretion in their own rhythms of work and in those of their assistants.[74] In Marx's terms, the technical basis of production remained to some extent subjective; it had not yet become fully objective. A norm of manhood was here constituted by the laboring male body's ability to control the pace, the temporality of the production process in the face of managerial efforts to increase the rate of surplus value extraction. Nineteenth-century labor struggles over deskilling were then also struggles over who would fundamentally control this temporality. And what Taylorism represents in this respect is a pivotal defeat of the industrial craftsman's manly efforts—efforts manifested collectively as well as individually—to control the intensity with which the body is used as a strategy of accumulation.

In the relative displacement of the skilled labor of manhood by the skilled labor of masculinity, then, capital's employment of the male body as an accumulation strategy assumes a fundamentally different temporality as well, a temporality I characterized in the previous chapter, drawing on the work of Moishe Postone, as a relatively abstract temporality. Postone emphasizes that one of the key forms taken by capital's mediation of subjectivity is temporal: as I mentioned in chapter 1, what Postone calls "concrete time" is dependent on events, a function of events, while "abstract time" is uniform, homogeneous, independent of events. A concrete temporality is measured *by* activity, while an abstract temporality is a measure *for* activity.[75] To be a subject both *of* and *to* technical knowledge is in this case also to be subject to an increasingly abstract temporality of accumulation, to be constituted as a masculine subject in that very subjection to capital. Time remains, for instance, relatively concrete within the practice of industrial craftsmanship, a function of that practice, dependent on that practice. The manhood of industrial craftsmanship embodies and performs resistance to any erosion of this state of affairs.

Resistance to an intensified extraction of surplus value in this way also constitutes a highly mediated resistance to the increasing social pervasiveness and depth of the commodity form itself, resistance to the ongoing reification of social relations—and therefore also to an intensification in the general social abstraction of time: abstract time becomes increasingly pervasive and dominant precisely insofar as the commodity form becomes increasingly pervasive and dominant. Scientific management, a technological innovation that was also a disciplinary weapon in class struggle, reduced, like earlier innovations, the amount of socially necessary labor time to produce the same output. Through a shift in the temporality of the labor process, scientific management dramatically increased productivity and thereby the rate of surplus value—an increase that ultimately required in turn that increasingly coordinated management of demand characterizing a newly intensive regime of accumulation. In the historical narrative unfolded by the first volume of *Capital,* as the technological basis of production becomes increasingly objective rather than subjective, at precisely the point at which the laborer becomes the appendage of large-scale machinery, workers direct rage at that machinery.[76] In this historically subsequent example of the reduction of the laborer to a mere appendage, the more sophisticated disciplinary weapon of consumption intervenes to compensate, to make available new embodiments of technical knowledge citing old embodiments of technical knowledge.

The laborer's loss of control over the rhythm of work is socially bound up with a more strict separation between time spent working and time spent not working. The performance of masculinity is in this respect measured by, made dependent on, time, by and on the clock's determination of the temporality of sports, for instance—but also more generally in the fact that commodified, disposable leisure time is a product of the abstraction of social labor, is constituted by its antithesis to labor time, is measured by the clock in its very opposition to the time of work. Masculinity is performed within what Georg Simmel called, in his influential discussion of the modern metropolis, that "firm, fixed framework of time which transcends all subjective elements."[77] Leisure space—the unnatural nature of Jake Barnes's fishing expedition, the sports arena, that space increasingly marked off from production—is here also leisure time. In the ostensibly distinct social space of consumption in which masculinity is performed, the space of labor "without" capital, a space marked off from and opposing the space of routinized work, time itself nonetheless becomes space, becomes precisely what time becomes in Lukács's famous characterization of the deskilled factory; it becomes uniform space, it becomes masculinity's abstract, determinate frame.[78] Time becomes what Postone calls "a uniform sort of time" that "constitutes an apparently absolute frame for motion."[79]

Or in the terms employed by the Frankfurt school, we might say that an emergent, corporeally epistemological norm of masculinity takes the form of a gender-specific instantiation of a more fully instrumentalized knowledge—which is to say, the performative embodiment of an emergent instrumental reason. Not yet a mere appendage of the factory, skilled, laboring manhood experiences itself as the active, technical basis of production, as actively mediating the means and ends of production. But increasingly obsolete techniques of gender-coded, skilled practice give way to a gendered performance mystifying ends altogether, a performance constituted by the reiteration of pure, reified means. Like Jake's excursions into Spain, masculinity reconciles technical knowledge and physical labor within an abstract space compelling the abstract temporality Butler calls performative ritualization. From its historical emergence in the early twentieth century, I am proposing, the performative norm of masculinity instantiates what Postone calls the "abstract form of compulsion" enforced by the abstract temporality of capital.[80] Just as the space of performative masculinity abstracts time, so does that performance itself. The performance and its location, subjective and objective instances of second nature, are mutually constitutive.

In the historical shift from a norm of embodied, laboring manhood to a norm of embodied, laboring masculinity, then, the performative normalization of the male body is displaced from a position of independence to a position of dependence vis-à-vis the increasingly abstract temporality of accumulation. The performative norm of skilled, laboring manhood was cited *as resistance to* increases in the intensity with which the body would be deployed as an accumulation strategy. This very performance of embodied knowledge, however, is subsequently cited as masculinity, a citation in which, by contrast, the male body is performatively normalized *consistently and simultaneously with* capital's employment of that body as an accumulation strategy. The relatively concrete temporality of manhood *is measured by* manhood; the relatively abstract temporality of masculinity *is a measure for* masculinity. Labor without capital is then only labor differently mediated by capital, if anything more mystifyingly mediated by capital and thereby more rigorously subject to it. Labor *without* capital is only labor *within* the broader social horizon of capital opened up by the leisure space-time of intensive, normalized consumption. And if masculinity is in this way subject to the temporality of capital, this ultimately means that social labor—not just the implicitly individuated subject who performs and is performed—produces this norm. I argued in the previous chapter that psychoanalysis, another product of social labor, participates in the social reification of desire precisely in attributing to sexuality a temporality of its own, an abstract temporality that is independent of desire, a temporality of symptomatic repetition that defines desire. The performative, historically specific norm of masculinity also instantiates this increasingly reified social temporality.

BUTLER AND ABSTRACTION

And it is precisely Butler's rethinking of gender that enables such an understanding of masculinity's mediation by the temporality of capital. It was the emphasis on temporality with which *Gender Trouble* so dramatically displaced the appearance of a stable ground for gender politics: gender here ceases to be a stable political ground precisely to the extent that it is centrally defined by an internal and temporal discontinuity. These familiar words from *Gender Trouble* bear repeating: "Gender is an identity tenuously constituted in time, instituted in an exterior space through *a stylized repetition of acts.* . . . This formulation moves the conception of gender off the ground of a substantial model of identity to one that requires a conception of gender as a constituted *social temporality.*" One of Butler's great early innovations was her emphasis on what she called the "gendered corporealization of time."[81]

But I have also tried to suggest the way in which the temporality Butler attributes to gender is itself already spatialized. If Butler's notion of performative gender is especially useful in understanding the operation of gender norms in relation to an increasingly reified early-twentieth-century temporality—and I have tried here, with the example of masculinity, to

suggest some of the ways in which it is very useful indeed in this respect—
what does this same capacity suggest about the social and historical limits
of that notion itself? If the performative normalization of masculinity
operates within a history of social reification and, specifically, within an
abstract temporality that history opens up, this raises the question of the
extent to which her analysis participates in that reification, in that temporality—in, for instance, a certain kind of methodological "immediacy" as
Lukács defines that term, in the limit of her scrutiny to the discursive surface of the body itself and of its normalization, its discursive "materialization," over time.[82] Butler's focus, for instance, is less on history than on the
"historicity" of discourse—as *Bodies that Matter* emphasizes in an endnote:

> The historicity of discourse implies the way in which history is constitutive
> of discourse itself. It is not simply that discourses are located *in* histories,
> but that they have their own constitutive historical character. Historicity
> is a term which directly implies the constitutive character of history in dis-
> cursive practice, that is, a condition in which a "practice" could not exist
> apart from the sedimentation of conventions by which it is produced and
> becomes legible.[83]

Butler is forthrightly more interested in the historical character of discourse
than in the way historically specific discourses are impacted, inflected, and
reshaped by social determinants irreducible to the specific discourse in
question. The representation of performativity in terms of pure contingency is one symptom of this larger abstraction of broader socioeconomic
determinants. We encounter in Butler's work on gender "a contingency
that admits no necessity, . . . a kind of absolute contingency," as Kathi
Weeks has put it: "It would often seem that in order for the subject to
maintain its indeterminacy, it is rendered underdetermined." Weeks, like
the other critics of Butler's work I cited at the beginning of this chapter,
notes the absence from Butler's analysis of a "larger institutional framework":[84] the horizon of the discursive is the ultimate horizon of that analysis, an analysis that effectively identifies the social with the discursive,
thereby abstracting both. Butler argues that the sedimentation of conventions determining the body's practical, gendered materialization is itself
constituted by repetition of an embodied practice, leaving out any consideration of qualitative, historically specific determinants of or differences

between the one and the other, between the sedimentation determining the practices and the practices producing the sedimentation. Temporality in her analysis is a highly abstract affair: any consideration of qualitative, historically specific differentiations between one embodied citation and another—or of quantitative differentiation *giving way* to qualitative differentiation—is suspended.

In another endnote to *Bodies That Matter,* an especially intriguing one, Butler underscores the similarities between Marx's theoretical terms and her own. She emphasizes that for Marx also, matter cannot simply be understood as the empirically given, that in the terms of historical materialism, matter is by definition temporal: "The object *materializes* to the extent that it is a site of *temporal transformation*." Being is always becoming; transformative activity is "constitutive of materiality itself."[85] Here I want to underscore both the strong resonance of Butler's analysis with Marx's rejection of naive empiricism and the importance, in this context, of making a distinction on which Marx, but not Butler, insists, the distinction between the temporal and the historical. For Marx, materiality is not merely temporal but social and historical. And disaggregating the temporal from the historical is precisely what makes it possible to theorize gender in relation to capital's ongoing abstraction of time.

But it is important to underscore again that the abstract temporality of gender norms does not necessarily imply repetition pure and simple. Butler insists on the "complex historicity" of gender norms, that their capacity for sedimentation is no more powerful than their capacity for differentiation. Not only is it the case that "reiterations are never simply replicas of the same"; the possibility of agency, of performing a norm differently, is itself a "function" of those norms' inherent "*inefficacy,* and so the question of subversion, of *working the weakness in the norm,* becomes a matter of inhabiting the practices of its rearticulation."[86] How then do this historicity, this labor of desedimentation, this performative "working," come about? For Butler, these are both facilitated and constrained by repetition itself and immanent to the discourse cited itself—fully determined, in other words, by that discourse. On the one hand, Butler's analysis preempts the question of broader social and historical determinations—multiple determinations, overdeterminations—of this discursive historicity/temporality. On the other hand, reference to the limitations of her analysis make it all the more necessary to emphasize also the potential of that analysis to contribute to an effort to think gender and sexual desire in Marxian terms. In the context of the present argument that the reification of desire compels a reification of gender, the power of Butler's analysis lies especially in what it has the capacity to reveal about the complex relation between desire and the normalizing embodiment of gender, its rigorous and unprecedented scrutiny of this relation. This scrutiny is ultimately inseparable from what, in the present context, we might reasonably call the "false" immediacy of her analysis, an analysis that forthrightly refuses to conceptualize anything resembling a social totality, which offers a powerful analysis of gender normalization instead, indeed can offer that analysis only because of that same refusal. Butler's analysis makes possible an understanding of how the performance of masculinity both facilitates a normalization of heterosexual desire and can subvert the normalization of heterosexual desire. But I would add again that this account of gender can be read as a suggestive, richly legible symptom of reification's "false" immediacy, can be employed within a critique of gender's complex entanglement with capital precisely to the extent that reification is understood as a central mediating category. In particular, Butler's insistence that gender must be understood temporally raises a host of questions about the ways in which gender can and should be understood in relation to the various historically conditioned, evolving, increasingly abstract temporalities capital imposes.

Butler has more recently considered the extent to which norms are *inherently* abstract. Here she seems to posit a stark opposition between abstraction and practical activity: specifically, she suggests that one has to make a choice between understanding norms in terms of action, or in terms of abstraction. Citing Mary Poovey's contention that norms are measurements, means of generating common standards, and therefore abstract and quantitative by definition, Butler rejects such a view, endorsing instead Pierre Macherey's argument that norms are forms of action.[87] But to the extent that activity is immanent to capital, activity is also immanent to objective forms of abstraction. If we are to think capital and performative gender as mutually constitutive, and if we are to think this relation in historically specific terms, gender norms have to be understood as both practical and abstract. Abstract performative norms do not cease to be activity; they become differently mediated activity. Abstract norms of gender consist, for example, of weaknesses that can be worked. One final sense of labor without capital: labor mediated by capital is by no means labor reducible to the predations of capital. Against Lukács's stark opposition between reified, passive subjectivity and concrete, active praxis—an opposition that Butler's more recent distinction between abstraction and action comes surprisingly close to endorsing—we should take seriously, for example, Andrew Parker's contention that performativity must be understood as internal to and constitutive of praxis, "as an enabling condition [for praxis] rather than a fall into secondariness."[88] If for Lukács the laborer in a scientifically managed factory "is reduced to the mechanical repetition of a specialised set of actions,"[89] the male body normalized by masculinity is "reduced" to a repetition not quite so mechanical. Concretizing Butler's theory of gender has here required concretizing the concept of reification as well, a social dynamic irreducible to subjective passivity. As I will contend in chapter 4, which will return to the question of masculinity as a performative norm, and specifically to the labor of working its constitutive weaknesses, reification is a condition of possibility for practices less predictable than typical Marxian deployments of this concept might be expected to allow.

In the familiar words of Fredric Jameson (and rather like Jake Barnes's war wound, if I can be indulged in a bad joke), history is what hurts.[90] The stripping of manhood of its exclusive ownership of autonomous sexual energy, the stripping of manhood of its technical and practical skill: these historically specific losses, woundings, are pivotal and inseparable. The form of reification called masculinity creates conditions of possibility for new forms of activity within that "immediate" horizon of gender and sexual discourse and practice to which Butler so productively limits her attention, and with potential consequences far beyond it. Butler insists, again, both on the compulsion to cite preexisting gender norms and on the historical mobility of those same norms, on gender's capacity, in particular, to exceed the heterosexual matrix. "To the extent that gender is an assignment," she argues, "it is an assignment which is never quite carried out according to expectation." The reified citation of masculinity "both constrains and enables [its] reworking."[91] How then would the performance of a masculinity that also normalizes heterosexual desire make resistance to that same normalization possible? In particular, how could that sexual objectification of masculinity by masculinity that is a heteronormalizing masculinity's constitutive outside be "reworked" within the very terms of that norm? What other possibilities of performative masculine labor does this instance of reification open up? One of my objectives in chapter 4 will be to historicize and concretize the working of this homosexual weakness both within its own terms and within the specific mode of regulation mediating those terms. The heterosexual matrix's constitutive exclusion of masculine desire for the masculine, a sexual objectification of the masculine by the masculine, is an exclusion which, later, a collective, gay male formation would "work," a disavowed and defining component of masculinity that formation would tenaciously avow.

First, however, chapter 3 initiates this shift of perspective away from the normalization of bodies as subjects and toward the critical and political capacities of the subjectivities so produced. Beginning a change of perspective from reification per se to praxis—to reification's dialectical other, to the praxis that Lukács calls the aspiration to totality—chapter 3 considers the work of the only major participant in the Marxian dialectic of reification and totality who also made a dramatic impact on political consciousness in the United States.

chapter 3

REIFICATION AS LIBERATION:
THEORY, PRACTICE, AND MARCUSE

In his essay "The Affirmative Character of Culture" (1937), Herbert Marcuse proposed—in an almost offhand manner, and without addressing the implications of this claim for any larger tradition of Marxist thought—that "in suffering the most extreme reification man triumphs over reification," insisting that this triumph would be erotic in nature.[1] In Marcuse's relatively early work, especially in the work written before his influence within the New Left, he employed the concept of reification in a strikingly new way. Marcuse's eroticization of this concept would take its most sustained theoretical form in *Eros and Civilization* and would ultimately be inseparable from his conceptual and explicitly political effort to radicalize psychoanalysis. Both before and during his sustained scrutiny of Freud's more revolutionary intimations, Marcuse would, first of all, consistently link capital's estrangement of labor power to repression: what he called a reification of the body, under the interdependent regimes of what the Frankfurt school called instrumental reason and of what Marcuse called genital supremacy, required the restriction of eroticism to the genital area of the body. But he insisted at the same time that only by polymorphously re-eroticizing the body—erotically objectifying it, reifying it, turning it into a thing, into a very different kind of instrument—could the former type of reification be negated.

Lukács, as I argued in chapter 1, and despite his own claims to the contrary, had formulated the concept of reification in fundamentally quantitative, cumulative terms: with the expansion of capitalism came a quantitative increase in reification's pervasiveness and depth. Reification denoted for Lukács a social and historical dynamic to which total negation was the only viable response. By the time Marcuse was writing, the Frankfurt school had articulated this concept in terms of a similarly quantitative increase in the pervasiveness and depth of an instrumental reason driven by purely pragmatic, technical interests and concerned with the efficiency of means to predetermined ends. An earlier, critical, Enlightenment reason had devolved into a totalitarian reason that was the driving force behind what Marcuse called the "comfortable, smooth, reasonable democratic unfreedom which prevails in advanced industrial civilization."[2] Reification as instrumental reason had so saturated social consciousness and the social psyche that neither proletarian consciousness nor, indeed, social consciousness as such could any longer be a site of critique, much less historical optimism. This emphasis on the instrumental, on the technical, was here inseparable from a rejection of Lukács's emphasis on consciousness and of his narrative of the proletarian, identical subject-object of history, the teleological agent of reification's overcoming as such.

But Marcuse's negotiation of Lukács's formative theory of reification is also more complex than the Frankfurt school's reframing of reification tends to suggest: in his early work, the concept carries the insidious, mystifying implications it carried in Lukács—the reification to be triumphed over—as well as more positive, liberatory, erotic implications—the reification to be suffered through as a means to this triumph. On the one hand, Marcuse's aspiration to totality exemplified the epistemological capacity that Lukács attributed to proletarian consciousness. On the other hand, in an age in which instrumental reason had, as he saw it, wholly compromised any subjective capacity for negation, negation had to be located as dialectically as Lukács had located it, but in some other place. Marcuse found this place outside subjectivity, in the sensuous, erotic, revolutionary instrumentalization of the body. To a limited extent—and I will specify these limitations as the chapter proceeds—Marcuse's early work reconceptualizes reification as I reconceptualize it in this book: as a concept that has to be understood not only in terms of consciousness but also in terms of the body. For Marcuse instrumental reason has so thoroughly pervaded social life—not just work but leisure, not just production but consumption—that a nonrepression of primal sexuality, an extreme sexual reification of the body, is an indispensable precondition for any negation of reification's mystifying effects. In attributing this dual capacity to reification, as I intend to show, Marcuse begins to formulate this concept in terms of a potentially *qualitative* historical process, a process with complex, multiple forms of social and historical effectivity. A rethinking of reification that prioritizes its objective rather than its subjective moment, a potentially radical divergence from the dialectic of reification and totality this book examines, begins to take shape here.

But in Marcuse's work this divergence *only* begins, begins and then takes an emphatic step back. Within a decade of *Eros and Civilization*'s publication—at the very moment when what Marcuse viewed as potential revolutionary agents, potential substitutes or spurs for what he and his Frankfurt school comrades viewed as a fully assimilated, hopelessly compromised working class, were manifesting themselves in practice (youth movements, dispossessed people of color, insurrectional guerrilla armies in other parts of the world)—Marcuse abandoned what was, finally, a more or less exclusively figural, speculative, impractical emphasis on the liberatory potential of the sexual reification of the body. This abandonment becomes deeply ironic when one considers the collective effort, simultaneous with this backing away, to translate Marcuse's erotic speculations into political action by at least one strain of New Left activism, the gay liberation movement.

The arguments of *Eros and Civilization* are easy to construe as quaint, especially given the time that has passed since the Foucauldian critique of Freud (and, indeed, of Marcuse).[3] Though close examination of key passages from Marcuse's corpus, especially *Eros and Civilization*, will make up a substantial portion of my analysis in this chapter, his relevance to the present attempt at a queer reading of the Marxian dialectic of reification and totality will have at least as much do with situating his arguments in relation to certain contemporaneous historical developments. The distinctive erotics of reification he formulates, first of all, bring into view a dialectical and historical relation between an influential and hugely phobic postwar clinical psychoanalytic establishment, and the gay liberation movement as it took shape in the immediate wake of Stonewall. Marcuse's work mediates the conceptual vocabularies of these politically opposed formations, vocabularies strikingly consistent with one another, even as critiques of clinical psychoanalysis were from the beginning central to the broader social critique gay liberation developed. The form taken by gay liberation was determined by complex and in many ways contradictory relationships with formations including the women's, antiwar, and Black Power movements and contemporaneous insurrectionary nationalism all over the globe. But this chapter will emphasize the ways in which the Freudian vocabulary on which Marcuse drew had a central impact on the early vocabulary of gay liberation, in the context of Freudianism's influence on U.S. social and political discourse more generally during this period. Chapter 1 contended that a broad social reification of sexual desire unfolds around the beginning of the twentieth century and that psychoanalytic discourse exemplified this development. This chapter will focus on Marcuse's employment of that same discourse. Marcuse's reading of the social totality his work aspired to comprehend, his reading of a fully instrumentalized totality that seemed to neutralize any capacity for critical leverage, is not necessarily difficult to read against a Fordist background, given what is sometimes posited as that regime of accumulation's relative socioeconomic and cultural uniformity. Fordism and its crisis in the late sixties and early seventies will be the key background for my discussion of this same period in chapter 4. Here I focus instead on the implications of Marcuse's Freudian framing of the dialectic of reification and totality.

BEAUTIFUL THINGS

Marcuse's framing of reification in terms of a liberation of the sexual body begins, again, in his pre-Freudian phase, in his politically charged analyses of eroticism in the late thirties. In "The Affirmative Character of Culture," for example, he distinguishes between a bourgeois imperative—"marketing the body as an instrument of labor"—and a bourgeois taboo—marketing it "as an instrument of pleasure"—arguing that, while both forms of reification objectify the body, the taboo negates the imperative. Contending that the prohibition of pleasure is a condition of bourgeois freedom, he articulates bourgeois sexual hypocrisy in these terms: "For the poor, hiring oneself out to work in a factory became a moral duty, while hiring out one's own body as a means to pleasure was depravity and 'prostitution.' . . . Insofar as the body becomes a commodity as a manifestation or bearer of the sexual function, this occurs subject to general contempt." Contempt is the response, moreover, not only to "prostitution but [to] all production of pleasure that does not occur for reasons of 'social hygiene' in the service of

reproduction." These objectified, pleasurable, "demoralized" practices, however, "provide . . . an anticipatory memory. When the body has completely
become an object, a beautiful thing, it can foreshadow a new happiness.
In suffering the most extreme reification man triumphs over reification."[4]

This connection between remembering and foreshadowing is of central
importance in Marcuse's ongoing eroticization of reification, and especially in the critique of existentialism in general and *Being and Nothingness*
in particular he published eleven years after "The Affirmative Character
of Culture," and seven years before *Eros and Civilization.*[5] This extended
essay-review was in part a continuing exploration of the implications of
this more positive, liberatory form of reification, representing a stage in
the development of his rethinking of the concept that links his relatively
offhand remarks in the late thirties with its more central place in the elaborate, influential rethinking of Freud's metapsychology *Eros and Civilization* would subsequently undertake. For the moment, Marcuse considers,
in existential rather than psychoanalytic terms, the relationship between
the body and the ego. He criticizes Sartre for hypostatizing the opposition between freedom and enslavement. Politically speaking, Marcuse sees
Sartre's argument as quietism in the guise of radicalism. In urging human
beings to embrace their potentials for conscious action in the world (being-
for-itself) and to resist their potential for passive, thinglike existence (being-
in-itself) Sartre rationalizes and justifies, in Marcuse's view, the bourgeois
demand to work, to produce, to participate in what *Eros and Civilization*
would call that "performance principle" that distinguished midcentury
capitalism from its earlier stages.

The one component of Sartre's argument Marcuse finds useful is what
Sartre has to say about sexuality—remarks that, Marcuse insists, are the
weak link in Sartre's analysis, the component that ultimately contradicts
and undermines the rest of it. Marcuse contends that for Sartre, "le désir"—
which is "essentially 'le désir sexuel'"—becomes the negation of all activity, all "performance," that in the experience of sexual desire, the human
subject becomes thinglike, given over to pleasure in its own body.[6] Marcuse thus concludes that "enslavement and repression are cancelled" as
"the 'désir sexuel' reveals its object as stripped of all the attitudes, gestures,
and affiliations which make it a standardized instrument, reveals the 'body
as flesh' and thereby 'as fascinating revelation of facticity.'" In sexually
objectifying itself, in abandoning productive activity and giving itself over

to the passive experience of pleasure, the ego becomes conscious of the material substance of its own body. Marcuse's critique of Sartre entails a certain setting of Sartre on his feet: he locates a promise of liberation from the realm of necessity in being-in-itself rather than being-for-itself, inverting Sartre's privileging of the latter over the former. "Reification itself thus turns into liberation," and this by way of a return to a more natural state of "facticity," a regressive liberation from the performance principle.[7]

This regressive return, in other words, anticipates a less oppressive, less instrumentalized future, intimates a qualitative transformation of the subject-object dynamic instantiated and enforced by the performance principle. Sartre's "image of fulfillment and satisfaction is . . . in the fascination of [the body's] being an object (for itself and for others)."[8] Of paramount importance here is Marcuse's emphasis on the passive object over the active subject: on the one hand, these parenthetical "others" are implicitly active subjects, active objectifiers of the ego's body (and may well be objects themselves). On the other hand, he avoids overtly endorsing active subjectivity of any kind, especially insofar as the performance principle requires precisely that active, struggling subjectivity "for itself" that Sartre sanctions. What Marcuse represents as the *passively* self-eroticizing body, then, challenges as far as he is concerned the very regime of instrumental rationality that has so hopelessly, exploitatively estranged subject *from* object, and in particular instrumental reason's exploitative hierarchizing of subject over object, its drive to dominate nature and the world. "The fundamental change in the existential structure caused by the 'désir sexuel' affects not only the individuals concerned but also their (objective) world. The 'désir sexuel' has, according to Sartre, a genuinely cognitive function: it reveals the (objective) world in a new form." Marcuse concludes that "the 'attitude désirante' thus releases the objective world as well as the Ego from domination and manipulation, cancels their 'instrumentality,' and, in doing so, reveals their own pure presence."[9] It promises a oneness of subject with object, of humans with nature. No longer an instrument of production, the body is instrumentalized into a "subject-object of pleasure," as *Eros and Civilization* would later put it, a moment of instrumentalization promising a transcendence of instrumentalization as such.[10] Only by passing through objectification, Marcuse suggests, does the body again become a free, noninstrumentalized subject—only in suffering the most extreme reification does it triumph over reification.

Thus does Sartre—in providing an inadvertent glimpse of a realm of freedom beyond that realm of necessity he elsewhere hypostatizes—finally contradict and undermine his own project:

> The "attitude désirante" thus reveals (the possibility of) a world in which the individual is in complete harmony with the whole, a world which is at the same time the very negation of that which gave the Ego freedom only to enforce its free submission to necessity. With the indication of this form of the "réalité humaine," Existentialism cancels its own fundamental conception.[11]

The gendered pronouns—"when *man* becomes a thing, . . . *his* free activity becomes complete inertia"[12]—are themselves, moreover, a key to the way Marcuse will later develop this rethinking of reification. Not merely the erotic, but the male homoerotic connotations of this positive form of reification are registered in the emphasis on passivity. Marcuse quotes Sartre: "It is . . . as reverberation of my flesh that I seize the objects in the world. This means that I make myself passive in relationship to them. . . . My perception is not utilization of an object and not the transcending of the present with a view to a goal. To perceive an object, in the attitude of desire, is to caress myself with it."[13] Both Sartre's and Marcuse's universalizing of the category *man* and its gendered pronouns above is pivotal: they implicitly represent this sexual passivity in terms of a male, homoerotic objectification of the body. In *Eros and Civilization,* the male homoerotic character of this dynamic will become explicit.

PSYCHOANALYZING THE SOCIAL, HOMOSEXUALIZING THE SOCIAL

But before turning to *Eros and Civilization*'s psychoanalytic translation of this existential way of relating body to ego, I want to specify a broader social horizon against which, and in terms of which, Marcuse's later rethinking of reification will proceed. By the fifties, homophile movements like the Mattachine Society had rejected their communist roots and, in contrast with the later gay liberation movement, were employing increasingly assimilationist political tactics. Increasingly made up of middle-class professionals with a great deal financially to lose, they began portraying themselves as an oppressed minority largely analogous to national, religious, and other ethnic groups, a minority therefore deserving of basic equality under the law.[14] At the same time, homosexuality played a privileged part in the imagining of social radicalism in the work of figures as divergent in political outlook as Marcuse, Allen Ginsberg, and Paul Goodman. Marcuse and Goodman, for instance, sought ways of intervening critically in a society they saw as being fundamentally without opposition, a society Goodman would pejoratively call "organized" and Marcuse would call "one-dimensional."[15] The discourses they produced, which were driven by anarchist and Marxian-Freudian perspectives, respectively, attributed an unprecedented political homogeneity to postwar social life in the United States, characterizing it in terms of a draconian neutralization of those radical forms of politics that had seemed more consequential earlier in the century. We can begin to understand the divergence between these representations of homosexuality in terms, first of all, of the persistent incoherence Eve Sedgwick attributes to twentieth-century definitions of homosexuality, the opposition between "minoritizing" and "universalizing" understandings of the term—in this case an opposition between an assimilationist, minoritizing emphasis on winning basic civil rights and a more radical, universalizing argument for the subversive character of homosexuality, an argument for its status as a direct challenge to the very terms in which civil rights would be granted, an affront to a bourgeois, "repressive" state. If the relatively militant character of the early gay liberation movement was influenced not only by a broad context of increasing social radicalism but also negatively by the conservatism of organizations like Mattachine, this movement was at the same time influenced positively by figures like Marcuse. Gay liberation was in this respect dialectically overdetermined by these earlier, polarized representations of homosexuality, by this political, historically and nationally specific operation of minoritizing and universalizing forms of sexual knowledge.

These developments unfolded against a wider politicization of homosexuality in Freudian terms during this period. In contesting arguments that homosexuals were in any meaningful way radically different from heterosexuals, for example, the homophile movements opposed especially the practically ubiquitous psychoanalytic argument during this period that homosexuals were ill and maladjusted, and to that extent defined themselves negatively in relation to it. But the widespread interest in Freud's ideas among U.S. intellectuals after World War II was itself dramatically split along political lines. The conservative character of psychoanalysis during this period was in part an aspect of its medicalization. Paul Robinson noted in 1969 that "by the 1940s . . . psychoanalysis had become a branch of the medical profession, and the typical practicing psychoanalyst carefully distinguished the discrete precepts and techniques of his therapeutic science from the ambitious metahistorical adventures in which Freud had indulged."[16] Similarly, this period in the history of U.S. clinical psychoanalysis was centrally characterized by an intensely moralizing tone and an alignment with mainstream, conservative social norms. This took the specific, hugely consequential clinical form of an increasingly adaptational focus on the "total personality," a tendency to deinstinctualize the determinants of what was viewed as deviant sexual practice:[17] homosexuality, the new argument went, was the product of unhealthy family environments rather than fundamental intrapsychic dynamics.

This movement "outward," from the instincts to interpersonal relations and the "whole personality," had deeply conservative implications. Contrary to what it might have promised in terms of a more sociologically critical psychoanalysis, this movement in fact fetishized both the personality and the society in which that personality was located by naturalizing the latter, by emphasizing the importance of the personality's adjustment to the society in which it found itself rather than, say, that society's radical adjustment to what suffering personalities might demand of it. For figures like Adorno and Marcuse, this revisionist isolation of the personality from basic intrapsychic dynamics also isolated it from the social and historical as such. Adorno emphasized, in direct opposition to this revisionism, the radical implications of Freud's "ambitious metahistorical adventures," especially the access to what Adorno understood as the genuinely social and historical thinking, in an era of positivist, ahistorical thinking, promised by what he called, in a paper delivered in 1946, the "inner history" of the libido: "Concretely, the denunciation of Freud's so-called instinctivism amounts to the denial that culture, by enforcing restrictions on libidinal and particularly on destructive drives, is instrumental in bringing about repressions, guilt feelings, and need for self-punishment."[18]

Almost ten years later, in the "Critique of Neo-Freudian Revisionism" included as an appendix to *Eros and Civilization*, Marcuse more fully explored and more explicitly situated in relation to a pervasive instrumental reason the reactionary character of this ongoing clinical revisionism. With this postwar emphasis on interpersonal relations, for Marcuse, "psychoanalytic theory turns into ideology: the 'personality' and its creative potentialities are resurrected in the face of a reality which has all but eliminated the conditions for the personality and its fulfillment" (*Eros and Civilization,* 240). Like Adorno, Marcuse identifies the neorevisionists' "expurgating [of] the instinctual dynamic" as the linchpin of their conservatism: "Whereas Freud, focusing on the vicissitudes of the primary instincts, discovered society in the most concealed layer of the genus and individual man," Freudian revisionism failed "to comprehend what these institutions and relations have done to the personality that they are supposed to fulfill" (240–41). Consequently, "the weakening of the psychoanalytic conception, and especially of the theory of sexuality, must lead to a weakening of the sociological critique and to a reduction of the social substance of psychoanalysis" (243). This development was, moreover, the product of objective historical circumstances: "In a repressive society, individual happiness and productive development are in contradiction to society; if they are defined as values to be realized within this society, they themselves become repressive" (245).

Like the more anarchistic Goodman, whose work highlighted the confrontation between the state power comprised in "the organized society" and "homosexual subversion," Marcuse represented homosexuality as a privileged instance of subversion of the regime of the indissociable reproductive and performance principles, a crucial metonym for the polymorphous sexuality of which he advocated the liberation. Pervasive instrumentalization of subjectivity, of what Lukács called consciousness and what Marcuse called the ego, could be negated by way of what that same instrumental reason made historically possible: a sexual instrumentalization of the body. Rejecting any emphasis on the "whole personality" and in fact paying scant attention to the ego at all, Marcuse dialectically embraced the psychoanalytic configuration of unrepressed homosexuality as a direct threat to bourgeois, instrumental "progress," reversing the conservative Freudian narrative from infantile polymorphous sexuality to the mature repression that progress requires, and advocating instead a transformative trajectory from that historically specific, instrumental form of social repression "back" to polymorphous sexuality. A critique of bourgeois narratives of progress seemed implicit in psychoanalytically defined regression, a concept understood here to partake, again, of genuinely historical thinking.

What I want to emphasize, first of all, is a near saturation of political discourse on homosexuality by psychoanalytic discourse during this period, a pervasive articulation of competing, minoritizing and universalizing definitions in its terms. The rejection of psychoanalysis was not merely incidental even to homophile political formation. Even these movements were, again, compelled to contest a pervasive psychopathologizing of homosexuality, to define themselves in negative relation to it. The conservative medicalization of psychoanalysis during this period dialectically gives rise in this respect to at least two recognizably opposing discourses: Marcuse's universalizing, utopian radicalization of psychoanalysis, on the one hand, and the minoritization of homosexuality by the homophile movements, who rejected political radicalism as emphatically as they rejected psychoanalysis, on the other.

But this horizon of Freudian representation has to be broadened yet further; it would ultimately implicate the U.S. government as well. The clinical emphasis on the ego gave rise during this period to a conservative universalization of homosexuality strikingly similar to that of radicals like Marcuse, a universalization contesting minoritizing homophile arguments even more directly. While homophile movements insisted on minority status, the government began to represent homosexuality as an invisible, insidious, and socially pervasive threat to the social order itself and drew centrally on this same Freudian revisionism to do so. If homosexuals were represented as especially vulnerable to "communist influence" precisely because they were fundamentally unhealthy, maladjusted, and weak, this was a small step away from representing homosexuality in terms every bit as fluid, as uncontainable, as communism itself. Cold War–era political and juridical discourse sought to delegitimate whatever critical purchase Marxism may have had by emphasizing, very much in line with the psychoanalytic revisionism of this period, the individuated experience of social relations, as opposed to those relations themselves. Influential figures extended the conservatism of clinical psychoanalysis by suggesting that people who were attracted to radical political movements were maladjusted, thereby fueling the closetedness of both communism and homosexuality by linking both with psychopathology. Arthur Schlesinger suggested, for example, that homosexuals and communists alike were invariably "lonely and frustrated people."[19]

But this political discourse that seemed to individuate properly social questions like communism—and the instances of specifically juridical discourse through which it was mobilized, such as the Senate's 1950 characterization of homosexuals as a national security risk—also paradoxically and ineluctably partook of a universalizing logic whereby homosexuality, like communism itself, constituted a potentially uncontainable force fundamentally subversive of the nation as such. That Senate report has become an easy document to mock; but it also seems important for this very reason to read the document as a reminder of what the homophile movements were up against. Appealing directly to "a number of eminent physicians and psychiatrists," the report expressed grave concern that, according to these "experts," "there are no outward characteristics or physical traits that are positive as identifying marks of sex perversion"—which meant that perversion, or at least the disposition toward it, was potentially invisible. Many of these perverted human causes for governmental concern appeared, in fact, to lead normal lives, which was especially worrisome given that their perversions made them "susceptible to the blandishments of the foreign espionage agent." Because, as the report anxiously emphasizes, it is not possible to determine with any accuracy the number of homosexuals employed within the government (the only known cases are those that have been discovered as a result of arrest or other form of disclosure) and because "one homosexual can pollute a Government office," the report calls for a dramatic intensification of efforts to ferret out the walking homosexual threats lurking potentially everywhere.[20] It harshly criticizes government agencies that have not worked hard enough to "get these people out of government," accusing them of "fail[ing] to take a realistic view of the problem of sex perversion" and calling for a much more thorough investigation of suspected or reported cases.[21]

Politically driven universalizations of homosexuality, from Marcuse and from the U.S. Senate, in this respect held in common the view that homosexuality represented a direct threat to state power. And both Marcuse and the Senate developed these views in response to the clinical revisionism of the period: in the one case, as an explicit critique of that revisionism, and in the other, as a conclusion anxiously drawn from its claims. As Robert Corber has pointed out, moreover, the medical evidence of homosexuality's insidious invisibility that was marshaled by the government "acknowledged the resistance of sexuality to containment through representation." It therefore "called into question the fixity of male and female *heterosexual* identities."[22] The state's reliance on psychoanalytic discourse thus began inadvertently to add government legitimation to a universalizing logic implicating heterosexuality and homosexuality alike. If the immediate goal of this reactionary brand of universalization was the containment of the specter of homosexuality, its ultimate, utopian goal—like that of state attempts to "contain communism"—was its elimination: the universalization, that is, of heterosexuality. Indeed, both revolutionary and reactionary versions of the psychoanalytic model—framed in relation to the state, as a critique of that state's enforcement of "repression," on the one hand, and as a defense of the state's internal stability, on the other—suggested that both homosexuality and heterosexuality were potentially universal components of experience, homosexuality articulating a resistance to a universalized heterosexuality, heterosexuality articulating a fear of universalized homosexuality. The extent to which Marcuse and the U.S. government commonly invoked a universalizing sexual logic is not without relevance to Marcuse's complex relation to the gay liberation movement, as I will argue later. But for the moment I simply want to underscore the way in which Marcuse's and the U.S. government's respective representations of homosexuality were mirror images of each other. If, for Marcuse, clinical revisionism deradicalizes the implications of Freud's work, the state might be seen here to reradicalize those implications—even in opposition to the "expert" revisionism on which it drew—by invoking an invisible homosexuality that threatens to corrupt the state, and by extension the nation itself, from within.[23]

ANTICIPATORY MEMORY

After the critique of Sartre, Marcuse's focus on the reification of the body increasingly located this broader "battle of universalizations" on the body itself: the theoretical transition from this critique to *Eros and Civilization*, that is, entailed a translation of Marcuse's distinctive use of the concept of reification, as well as the more general subject/object dynamic framing that concept, into psychoanalytic terms. Here the reification of the body promising transcendence of instrumental reason's enforcement of the subject's domination over the object was framed by a certain Freudian understanding of the liberating force of repressed, polymorphous impulses. And here again Marcuse and the Senate were strikingly on the same page, even as their objectives were opposed. The Senate explicitly endorsed the medical view that "indulgence in sexually perverted practices indicates a personality which has failed to reach sexual maturity."[24] Both Marcuse and the Senate framed homosexual threat in terms of a perverse, sexual disruption of "mature" subjectivity.

But for Marcuse, the instincts denote memory: his emphasis on memory constituted a psychoanalytic attempt to reclaim, again, some critical comprehension of history. The linchpin of this embodied, liberating force is the "affinity between phantasy" and what Marcuse in *Eros and Civilization* explicitly calls "the perversions": "In its refusal to accept as final the limitations imposed upon freedom and happiness by the reality principle, in its refusal to forget what *can be,* lies the critical function of phantasy" (146, 149). Relapse, memory, phantasy: psychoanalysis provides *Eros and Civilization* with a ready-made narrative frame in which to reformulate the link between reification and social transformation more tentatively glossed in earlier texts. As Marcuse puts it in his penultimate chapter, under the regime that radically dissociated "possessive private relations" from "possessive societal relations," the latter constituted a realm in which the body is fully instrumentalized through labor, while by contrast

the full force of civilized morality was mobilized against the use of the body as a mere object, means, instrument of pleasure; such reification was tabooed and remained the ill-reputed privilege of whores, degenerates, and perverts. . . . With the emergence of a non-repressive reality principle, with the abolition of the surplus-repression necessitated by the performance principle, this process would be reversed. In the societal relations, reification would be reduced as the division of labor became reoriented on the gratification of freely developing individual needs; whereas, in the libidinal relations, the taboo on the reification of the body would be lessened. No longer used as a full-time instrument of labor, the body would be resexualized. The regression involved in this spread of the libido would first manifest itself in a reactivation of all erotogenic zones and, consequently, in a resurgence of pregenital polymorphous sexuality and in a decline of genital supremacy. The body in its entirety would become an object of cathexis, a thing to be enjoyed—an instrument of pleasure. This change in the value and scope of libidinal relations would lead to a disintegration of the institutions in which the private interpersonal relations have been organized, particularly the monogamic and patriarchal family. (200–201)

But by the time *Eros and Civilization* was published, any number of real social threats to the "monogamic and patriarchal family" were several decades old. What Marcuse identifies as a relatively recent, "bourgeois" domestication of the sexual instincts would come closer to describing what the previous chapters have characterized as a nineteenth-century regime of sexual knowledge firmly situated within an extensive regime of accumulation, an epistemology representing the body in terms of its productive and reproductive capacities. Transposing nineteenth-century taboos into the postwar period, this passage fails to register the way in which a mid-twentieth-century sexual order is already a product, say, of first-wave feminism, or of the commodification of gender and desire that kicked into high gear earlier in the century. And if, in the years following the publication of *Eros and Civilization,* Marcuse managed to acknowledge capitalism's well-entrenched instrumentalization of desire, that acknowledgment became unambiguously pessimistic. In *One-Dimensional Man* eroticism would carry no revolutionary import whatsoever, the relatively fair fight Marcuse depicts in the passage just quoted, between instrumentalities of pleasure and "surplus repression," morphing into a fight so fixed that it's no fight at all, "repressive desublimation" becoming the only form of sexual instrumentality Marcuse recognizes.

I will return to the larger implications of this shift in tone; for the moment I want to emphasize, in spite of my stated reservations, that this passage is Marcuse's most forceful statement of reification's transformative power, its power to negate and supersede the estrangement, under the regime of instrumental reason and the performance principle, of the public and private realms, the realms of labor and pleasure, "man" and "nature," subject and object. One of the reasons for the relative optimism of *Eros and Civilization* is Marcuse's belief (in striking contrast to *One-Dimensional Man*) that increasing technological rationality creates, again, certain conditions of possibility for liberation—instrumental rationality making possible a liberating instrumentalization of the sexual body, for instance— that what Marcuse calls the "established reality principle" is historically conditioned and limited (129), that many of Freud's most fundamental assumptions about history and culture no longer hold:

In Freud's theory, freedom from repression is a matter of the unconscious, of the subhistorical and even subhuman *past*, of primal biological and mental processes; consequently, the idea of a non-repressive reality principle is a matter of retrogression. That such a principle could itself become a historical reality, a matter of developing consciousness, that the images of phantasy could refer to the unconquered *future* of mankind rather than to its (badly) conquered past—all this seemed to Freud at best a nice utopia. (147)

But this ongoing opening of opportunities for liberation was the very thing that required not a constant degree of social repression but an increasing degree of "surplus repression" and especially an instrumentalized, individuated definition of happiness that was itself repressive. What Marcuse identifies as regression "would still be a reversal of the process of civilization, a subversion of culture—but *after* culture had done its work and created the mankind and the world that could be free. It would still be 'regression'—but in the light of mature consciousness and guided by a new rationality" (198). *Eros and Civilization* is nothing if not an exercise in narrative construction, an exercise in transforming an increasingly conservative Freudianism into a radically historical Freudianism. It remains a brilliant use of Freud's metapsychology to link memory with a future beyond the realm of necessity, to imagine qualitative historical change during an era in which historical, utopian thinking had been, it seemed, trumped by that ahistorical, positivist thinking of which the clinical emphasis on the "whole personality" was only one example.

While this manipulation of Freudianism has been widely acknowledged as a source of *Eros and Civilization*'s conceptual originality, the book's psychoanalytically formulated emphasis on the transformative power of reification has barely been noted. Martin Jay, for instance, emphasizes the revolutionary implications of memory in Marcuse's thought, connecting memory to "dereification" and asserting that "it was not really until Georg Lukács introduced idea of reification in *History and Class Consciousness* that the emancipatory potential of memory was tapped by a Marxist thinker of note. . . . The concept of dereification implied a certain type of remembering, for what had to be recaptured were the human origins of a social world that had been mystified under capitalism as a kind of 'second nature.'"[25] But again reification takes on two contradictory meanings in Marcuse. He does indeed use the term to designate a quantitative historical increase in mystification, now identified with a quantitative historical increase in repression. But the term now also designates the polymorphous embodiment of memory, the negation of this same increase. For the Marcuse of *Eros and Civilization,* the radical reformulation of the concepts of an ostensibly conservative metapsychology is indissociable from a radical reformulation of the concept of reification itself.

At the same time, anticipatory memory is a memory of "human origins" as fundamental for Marcuse as it was for Lukács, as Jay rightly points out. And this framing of the sexual objectification of the body in terms of memory, in terms of the body's radical capacity for regression, for "immaturity," ultimately assimilates sexual objectification to that same historical schema that frames the reification of consciousness posited by Lukács—an assimilation that, within the terms of this schema, finally trumps Marcuse's rethinking of reification, subordinates an eroticized reification as a mere transitory stop on the dialectical path to what both he and Lukács ultimately prioritize, a negation of reification as such. Both Lukács's and Marcuse's conceptions of history presuppose an ultimate, dialectical reconciliation of subject and object; both envision some fully human, organic, dereified future that is identical with some fully human, organic, prereified past; and both ultimately identify reification with dehumanization. I emphasized in chapter 1 that what can now be seen as the heteronormativity of *History and Class Consciousness* was a product of its identification of reification with dehumanization; *Eros and Civilization,* and Marcuse's larger rethinking of reification in sexual terms, begins here to look every bit as heteronormative. That proletarian subject-object of history in Lukács—now, for Marcuse, reduced by instrumental reason to a mere proletarian subject, a fully instrumentalized subject evacuated of any radical historical capacity—is transformed, as I mentioned earlier, into what *Eros and Civilization* calls a "subject-object of pleasure," a subject-object carrying that capacity Marcuse now believes the proletarian subject to lack. For Lukács, the subject breaks the spell of reification by overcoming its own objectification at the hands of capital. For Marcuse, the object overcomes its fully instrumentalized subjectivity and ultimately social instrumentalization as such. A teleologically posited, catalytic subject-object in Lukács ultimately assumes, in Marcuse, a different, startlingly eroticized form. His radical eroticizing of the narrative of decline elaborated by Lukács, which in this respect diverges so dramatically from *History and Class Consciousness,* is in another respect just another version of the same narrative.

We encounter in Marcuse a radical eroticization of the reification/totality dialectic itself. Marcuse's rethinking of reification, and the aspiration to totality *Eros and Civilization* performs, are similarly and indissociably Freudian. Polymorphous, perverted pleasure is an affront to the social order because that social order is already comprehended in Freudian terms, in terms of a reigning reality principle. What is ironic, again, is this aspiration's logical consistency with the U.S. government's aspiration to totalize heterosexuality, as it were, from above. But what is then in Lukács a *subjective, active* negation of the reification of subject-object relations becomes in Marcuse an *objective, passive* negation of the same. And this strange, provocative emphasis on passive negation, passive overcoming, an emphasis that within traditional Marxian or Hegelian-Marxian terms is counterintuitive to say the least, finally constitutes an unreconciled contradiction within Marcuse's own analysis and is symptomatic of the depth of his pessimism regarding the depth of instrumental reason itself. I argue in the next section that Marcuse's later remarks about *Eros and Civilization* themselves indicate as much.

Incorporating psychoanalysis into Marxism and reconceptualizing the instrumentalization of consciousness as the instrumentalization of the ego, Marcuse locates negation in those primal somatic impulses that same instrumentalized ego definitionally excludes. On the one hand, whether it is consciousness or the ego that is instrumentalized is of less importance in the present context than that Marcuse gives up on what he views as a totally instrumentalized subjectivity altogether. On the other hand, these somatic impulses are reframed in revolutionary terms. *Eros and Civilization*'s emphasis on the radical implications of sexual objectification would have a social and historical effectivity that would exceed its Freudian and Lukácsian presuppositions.

As I suggested in my discussion of Marcuse's response to Sartre, Marcuse implicitly rejects as politically quietist, as already in harmony with the performance principle, any homosexual subject's instrumentalization of another, objectified body. His emphasis on an (implicitly male, homoerotic) passivity is, again, a response to the subject's domination over the object characteristic for him, as for his Frankfurt school colleagues, of instrumental reason. The sexual objectification of the body by another subject would appear to partake, in Marcuse's terms, of that same coercive, "dehumanizing" domination of subject over object identical with the "performance principle." This is why resistance to instrumental reason is, for

Marcuse, to be located wholly within the (passive) object. Marcuse's refusal to consider subjectivity could not be recapitulated by a movement
endeavoring to establish a political subjectivity that is also a sexually radical subjectivity, by a collective formation also aspiring to legitimate the
homosexual objectification of bodies. A radical formation centrally influenced by his emphasis on the liberatory implications of sexual objectification would at the same time be faced with the question of how to mobilize
those implications politically, how to translate them into historically situated practice.

MARCUSE AND GAY LIBERATION; OR,
THEORY AND PRACTICE

When Marcuse finally gets around to elaborating the specific power of the
only catalysts of historical change that *Eros and Civilization* specifies—the
"perversions"—the register of his argument shifts in a subtle but significant way. The mythic figures Marcuse uses to envision a specifically homoerotic negation of the contemporaneous reality principle are Orpheus and
Narcissus, whom he represents primarily in terms of their striking contrast with Prometheus, representative of instrumental reason, the struggle
to control and exploit nature. Identifying the reality principle with "pro-
ductiveness" and the pleasure principle with "receptiveness" (12), Marcuse
asserts that Orpheus and Narcissus represent a passive, receptive relation
to the natural world and the ultimate reunification of man with the nature
he had subjugated: "Trees and animals respond to Orpheus' language; the
spring and the forest respond to Narcissus' desire. This Orphic and Narcissistic Eros awakens and liberates potentialities that are real in things animate
and inanimate, in organic and inorganic nature—real but in the un-erotic
reality suppressed" (165). As a result of this liberation, "the Orphic and
Narcissistic experience of the world negates that which sustains the world
of the performance principle. The opposition between man and nature,
subject and object, is overcome" (166). Further, Marcuse explicitly registers
Orpheus's love for "young boys": "Like Narcissus, he rejects the normal
Eros, not for an ascetic ideal, but for a fuller Eros. Like Narcissus, he pro-
tests against the repressive order of procreative sexuality. The Orphic and
Narcissistic Eros is to the end the negation of this order—the Great Refusal" (171). Here, where Marcuse draws on the explicitly mythological

vocabulary that is foundational for the "science" of psychoanalysis itself, he also makes explicit the symbolic character of his emphasis on the "perversions." Homosexuality, which constitutes for Marcuse a kind of "regression," offers an anticipatory image of, a *figure for,* a new reality principle beyond the realm of necessity. Homosexuality holds out a kind of metonymic promise of a fuller, unifying extension of Eros into nature. "In the world symbolized by the culture-hero Prometheus, [the Orphic and Narcissistic Eros] is the negation of *all* order; but in this negation Orpheus and Narcissus reveal a new reality, with an order of its own, governed by different principles" (171).

Marcuse is ultimately more interested in utopian, speculative figures of perversion than he is in real perverts. He reminds us that "Plato blames Orpheus for his 'softness' (he was only a harp-player), which was duly punished by the gods—as was Narcissus' refusal to 'participate.' Before the reality as it is, they stand condemned: they rejected the required sublimation" (209). This reminder, however, should remind us also that at the very moment Marcuse was writing these words, the U.S. government was condemning gays and communist sympathizers for their "softness" as well. It is an ironic lapse, for this text, of memory: *Eros and Civilization* seems unaware—completely and we might even say blissfully so—of this real-life, contemporaneous, governmental implementation of blame. Like the state he otherwise opposed, Marcuse's text conceptually displaces real people by universalized, uncontainable figural perversions. Whatever one thinks of the politics of the homophile movements, for instance—and to say nothing of the labor resistance that also took place during this ostensibly one-dimensional period—their very existence discloses the blindnesses, and the undialectical character, of Marcuse's claim in *One-Dimensional Man* that this period provided "no ground on which theory and practice, thought and action meet."[26]

And in spite of itself, *Eros and Civilization* ultimately represents homosexual liberation and proletarian liberation as wholly incommensurate, if not contradictory, political imperatives. In the book's final pages, Marcuse takes care to point out that "remembrance is no real weapon unless it is translated into historical action" (233). But he never gets around to elaborating how the memory-driven reification of sexuality he elaborates would manifest itself in practice. "Where Freud's instinctual theory is designed to explain the structure of real and existent mental phenomena," as Fredric

Jameson has put it, "Marcuse's use of that theory has a more speculative and hypothetical cast"[27]—precisely because he begins by turning the Freudian narrative around, "revers[ing] the direction of progress," as he put it in the "Political Preface" to the 1966 edition of *Eros and Civilization* (xi), because the wholly integrated, organic past is here identical to the wholly integrated, organic future. And as Marcuse insisted in the first edition, "We use Freud's anthropological speculation only in this sense: for its *symbolic* value. The archaic events that the hypothesis stipulates may forever be beyond the realm of anthropological verification; the alleged consequences of these events are historical facts" (60). In this respect, *Eros and Civilization* constitutes a thoroughly immaterial and ahistorical critique of material and historical realities. Marcuse's most sustained attempt to imagine the role of (homo)eroticism in social revolution, to explore the political implications of homoeroticism in particular, is largely "symbolic."

I stress this because a struggle to transform this figuration into something material, practical, and historical is one way of reading the early gay liberation movement: if Marcuse's influence on and involvement with the New Left was in part consciously cultivated by him, the influence of *Eros and Civilization* on the gay liberation movement that emerged roughly fifteen years after its publication was a use to which Marcuse could scarcely have imagined, much less intended, his arguments being put. To situate *Eros and Civilization* in relation to the larger history of Marcuse's political engagement is in this respect illuminating. The book was published in 1955, and while radical politics during the mid-fifties were never as neutralized as the Frankfurt school critique of instrumental reason suggests, it is equally undeniable that the U.S. political landscape of this year looks relatively tame in contrast to the historic level of radical activity in the years following the 1964 publication of *One-Dimensional Man*. The latter was, along with the controversial and widely read 1965 "Repressive Tolerance" essay,[28] the first of Marcuse's texts to have an unmistakable influence on the New Left—primarily because of the way they diagnosed contemporary society's seemingly endless capacity to neutralize resistance.[29] *One-Dimensional Man* was the most despairing political diagnosis Marcuse would produce; it is indeed ironic that it was published just as the youth movement began to develop momentum, that this was the text that, more than any other, put Marcuse on the New Left's map. The "Repressive Tolerance" essay he published only a year later became widely controversial for its advocacy not merely of resistance but of revolutionary violence. Indeed, the dramatically changing political situation apparently made the pessimism of *One-Dimensional Man* disappear almost overnight, sending Marcuse on what Douglas Kellner has called a "desperate" search for new agents of social change, agents that could potentially goad what Marcuse viewed as a relatively prosperous, apolitical working class into action.[30]

Eros and Civilization, in other words—historically separated from the revolutionary enthusiasm of Marcuse's involvement in the New Left by the valley of despair manifested in *One-Dimensional Man*—holds a very different theoretical and political relationship with New Left politics than do most of his other major texts, which were published a decade or more later. Paul Breines emphasizes that it was only the "spreading influence" of *One-Dimensional Man* that "led to new and renewed study of *Eros and Civilization*" within the New Left.[31] This way of contextualizing *Eros and Civilization* is confirmed by a series of subsequent gestures on Marcuse's part that can be seen as revisions, even rejections of the earlier argument, including the shift in tone, to which I have already referred, of *One-Dimensional Man*—where, for example, he reverted to a more predictable use of the concept of reification. Against the contrast I have elaborated between conservative and revolutionary instrumentalizations of the laboring and sexual bodies, respectively, in *One-Dimensional Man* he asserted without qualification that "to exist as an instrument, as a thing" is "the pure form of servitude."[32]

His "desperate" search for new agents of social change after 1964 was, moreover, a search for practical rather than symbolic ones. For all its pessimism, *One-Dimensional Man* briefly and tentatively concludes, for example, by locating the only possible source of revolutionary negation in a radicalized version of the emerging civil rights movement, in "the substratum of the outcasts and outsiders, the exploited and persecuted of other races and other colors, the unemployed and unemployable."[33] In *An Essay on Liberation*, Marcuse would explore the political implications of the student movement and sixties youth culture more generally and intimate the possibility of an alliance between this domestic movement and foreign, insurgent guerrilla armies.[34] In *Counterrevolution and Revolt*, written as capitalism's long Fordist midcentury boom was finally, visibly running out of steam, he would even espouse renewed hope for the participation of an increasingly anxious, besieged working class in a "United Front."[35]

But Marcuse's most telling autocritique of the narrative he constructed in *Eros and Civilization* was certainly the "Political Preface" he included in the 1966 edition, eleven years after the book's original publication. Here he emphasizes that *Eros and Civilization*'s erotic emphasis had really been his way of stressing the political importance of the life instincts more generally. "Can we speak of a juncture between the erotic and political dimension?" he asks (as if the first edition had not already answered that question in the affirmative) (xxi). "Today the fight for life, the fight for Eros, is the *political* fight" (xxv, original italics). Marcuse deemphasizes, in other words, any more direct political implications his original argument might have had: "'Polymorphous sexuality' was the term I used to indicate that the new direction of progress would depend completely on the opportunity to activate repressed or arrested *organic,* biological needs" (xv, original italics). His connection between decade-old theory and contemporary practice here is that between the forces of Eros and emerging contemporary political movements, as if to suggest a connection between the "regression" he had idealized and the "instinctual" revolt of these movements—that of insurgent guerilla armies in other regions of the globe, for example:

> In the revolt of the backward peoples, the rich societies meet, in an elemental and brutal form, not only a social revolt in the traditional sense, but also an instinctual revolt—biological hatred. The spread of guerilla warfare at the height of the technological century is a symbolic event: the energy of the human body rebels against intolerable repression and throws itself against the engines of repression. (xix)

Here we see a foreshadowing, in fact, of the harmonizing of foreign and domestic fronts of protest Marcuse would advocate at length in *An Essay on Liberation:* "instinctual" revolt turns out to be the common denominator linking internal and external sites of resistance. His most sustained articulation in the "Preface" is indeed that between the force of Eros and domestic youth movements. Here, as in *An Essay on Liberation,* "regression" signifies a valorized immaturity:

> In and against the deadly efficient organization of the affluent society, not only radical protest, but even the attempt to formulate, to articulate, to give word to protest assume a childlike, ridiculous immaturity. Thus it is

ridiculous and perhaps "logical" that the Free Speech movement at Berkeley terminated in the row caused by the appearance of a sign with the four-letter word. It is perhaps equally ridiculous and right to see deeper signifi-cance in the buttons worn by some of the demonstrators (among them infants) against the slaughter in Vietnam: MAKE LOVE, NOT WAR. (xxi)

"'By nature,'" he concludes, "the young are in the forefront of those who live and fight for Eros against Death" (xxv). If *Eros and Civilization* was the theory, the "Political Preface" was the applied theory. The "per-versions" turn out to be the one agent of utopian negation Marcuse emphasized over his long career, the sole alternative to a compromised proletariat, which is not merely theoretical but purely figural, purely spec-ulative, articulated in exclusively idealist terms, not incidentally dissociated from but precisely in lieu of political practice: presupposing its contem-poraneous impossibility, presupposing the mutual exclusivity of the fig-ural and the practical and in this respect contradicting the practical. In the larger context of Marcuse's oeuvre, *Eros and Civilization*'s symbolic regis-ter produces simultaneously an articulation of "perversions" as figures of negation, and an implicit concession of the impossibility of that nega-tion. In attempting to assimilate proletarian and sexual forms of revolu-tion on a purely speculative level, Marcuse ultimately posits their relation as contradictory.

The ostensibly significant shift in tone from *Eros and Civilization* to *One-Dimensional Man* is in this respect little more than the making explicit of an already implicit pessimism. If increasing technological rationality con-stitutes (theoretically?) a condition of possibility for erotic liberation in *Eros and Civilization*, there is an emphatic retreat from *any* emphasis on the political implications of eroticism in *One-Dimensional Man*, where the pessimism about technological rationality's complete saturation of the psyche is so profound that a kind of nostalgic puritanism rears its head:

Compare lovemaking in a meadow and in an automobile, on a lover's walk outside the town walls and on a Manhattan street. In the former cases, the environment partakes of and invites libidinal cathexis and tends to be eroticized. Libido transcends beyond the immediate erotogenic zones—a process of nonrepressive sublimation. In contrast, a mechanized environ-ment seems to block such self-transcendence of the libido. Impelled in the striving to extend the field of erotic gratification, libido becomes less "poly-morphous," less capable of eroticism beyond localized sexuality, and the *latter* is intensified.[36]

For the Marcuse of *Eros and Civilization,* "Eros signifies a quantitative and qualitative aggrandizement of sexuality" (205). Unlike the socially ex-pansive "nonrepressive sublimation" of Eros with which Marcuse links the homoerotic in that text (but which has become more or less unattainable in *One-Dimensional Man*), "localized sexuality" constitutes a mere repres-sive containment of eroticism, "repressive desublimation." Mere *sexuality* is repressive, the properly *erotic* is not. *One-Dimensional Man* conveys a qualified nostalgia for a preindustrial, pretechnological, preurban land-scape: "This romantic pre-technical world was permeated with misery, toil, and filth," Marcuse admits, but at least "there was a 'landscape,' a medium of libidinal experience which no longer exists."[37] Here reification denotes, exclusively, the cumulative, practically unbreakable historical force of technology. If in *Eros and Civilization* the force of homosexuality, "the perversions," prefigures a reality principle beyond the realm of necessity, in *One-Dimensional Man,* where no such "beyond" is imaginable, repres-sive desublimation signifies an instrumentalized, subjective individuation of eroticism that merely contains threats to the established system. And if the optimism one finds in Marcuse's work through 1955 is consistently inseparable from his redefining of reification, here we get a reversion to a more Lukácsian view of reification, but a reversion in which even Lukács's teleologically formulated hope evaporates—an unambiguously, undialec-tically quantitative definition of reification that no longer has anything to do with connecting past and future, with anticipatory memory. Marcuse has at this point consigned the force of Eros unambiguously to the past.[38]

The ongoing space of origin of homosexual subjectivity and of the polit-ical formations articulating it, meanwhile, has consistently been within the "town walls." And notwithstanding differences in tone between *Eros and Civilization* and *One-Dimensional Man,* neither of these texts espouses any belief in those mere real-life homosexual subjects who inhabit a "mecha-nized environment" and whom Marcuse's work would therefore consign to the category of repressive desublimation. Eros, after all, is indissociable from procreation, even in Marcuse. While on the one hand critiquing the *injunction* to procreate under the regime of the performance principle, and approvingly citing the *Symposium*'s assertion that "the road to 'higher culture' leads through the true love of boys," Marcuse simultaneously and uncritically locates in Eros a synthesis of "spiritual" with "corporeal" pro-creation, ultimately allowing Freud's original association of Eros with the biological "life instincts" to stand (*Eros and Civilization,* 211). But for this reason it is all the more important to emphasize *Eros and Civilization*'s influence on the gay liberation movement. This text is routinely identified as one of only a handful of theoretical and programmatic texts—several of which were rediscovered, and including texts by Goodman as well as Wilhelm Reich—that influenced not only the New Left in general but gay liberation in particular.[39] Like these other texts, it provided a vision of lib-eration—a refusal of repressive tolerance—that fueled and corroborated a New Left–influenced militancy that distinguished gay liberation from the relative conservatism of the homophile movements. Only in a context of widespread activism did gay liberation take seriously this text that had pre-supposed a universally reactionary postwar political landscape.

For Marcuse, would gay liberation, especially given its origin within the town walls, constitute repressive desublimation, and perhaps its more overtly political equivalent, "repressive tolerance"? For its own part, gay lib-eration defined itself, in a Marcusean vein, very much against this sort of tolerance, contending that homosexuality could in no way be integrated into the existing order of things ("Two, four, six, eight—Smash the family, smash the state").[40] Gay liberation's objectives also invoked a universaliz-ing sexual logic even as they also shared in common with Marcuse a tren-chant critique of clinical Freudian revisionism.[41] Martha Shelley certainly demanded far more than liberal tolerance in her widely cited early formu-lation of gay liberation's aims, "Gay Is Good." Here Shelley insisted that the very existence of homosexuals threatened the most basic organizing structures of family and society, structures she called "citadels of repres-sion." Crucially, she framed gay liberation's aims in terms of a movement beyond majority/minority understandings of the relation between hetero-sexuality and homosexuality, insisting that gays repress their heterosexual-ity as radically as straights repress their homosexuality. "We are one with you," she boldly insists; "to understand us," you must "becom[e] one of us." "We are the extrusions," as she put it, "of your unconscious mind."[42] This freeing of gays and straights from analogous forms of repression was also a central theme in Carl Wittman's influential "Gay Manifesto."[43] And the

Red Butterfly collective responded to Wittman's document by trying to un-
pack the simultaneous connection and differentiation he makes between
personal and social forms of liberation. They emphasize that no personal
liberation can unfold outside of fundamental reorganizations of social relations, taking an explicitly socialist position and emphasizing, with Shelley,
that personal repression and social repression are inseparable. Their statement concludes by citing the same words from Marcuse's "Political Preface"
cited earlier, that the "fight for Eros, the fight for life, is the political fight."[44]

And in 1971, in one of the most important early programmatic statements
of gay liberation's aims—and certainly one of its most explicitly Marcusean statements—Dennis Altman wrote that "liberation implies more than
the mere absence of oppression. . . . To achieve liberation, as Marcuse
has pointed out in another context, will demand a new morality and a
revived notion of 'human nature.'" As in the statements of Shelley, Red
Butterfly, and to a lesser extent Wittman, gay liberation was here an aspiration to totality articulated in Freudian terms. Indeed, Altman's program
for the development of gay liberation can be summed up by the Marcusean imperative he espouses, "to transform sexuality into eroticism." Altman
characterized repressive tolerance as a manifestation of "greater apparent
freedom but a freedom manipulated into acceptable channels. Thus most
of the Western World has abolished legal restrictions against homosexuality
while maintaining social prejudices."[45] This formation tended to endorse
Marcuse's suggestion that the "tolerance" homophile organizations sought
would be "repressive" in that it would individuate and thereby neutralize
the revolutionary negation promised by the "perversions."

But one cannot simply call the active attempt of gay politics to secure
(not merely to prefigure) a more free, less heteronormative world "erotic"
in Marcuse's sense while simultaneously designating urban gay formations
merely "locally" sexual. If critiques of the gay ghetto were also central to
gay liberation's statements and aims—in the statements by Altman and
Red Butterfly, for example—this movement also performed, like more
recent variations on queer politics, a refusal to settle for merely local gay
space, an imperative to push the boundaries of what constituted gay space
at any given historical moment.[46] For a proverbial wrench to throw into the
Marcusean machinery I have tried to describe here—especially the absolute distinction between a localized sexuality and a universalized eroticism
gay liberation both articulated and struggled against—one need look no

farther than the spilling over of the Stonewall riots from the bar itself into
Christopher Street and beyond, a "beyond" epitomizing this boundary-
pushing, simultaneously spatial and historical imperative. This instance
of radical resistance that was sparked from within the commodified, local
space of a bar in Greenwich Village is an objectively historical (and increasingly, since gay liberation, *also* symbolic) event that challenges Marcuse's
distinction between the erotic and the sexual. This spatial and historical
spilling is then both like and unlike the hydraulic force of polymorphous
desire itself: undeniably influenced by Marcuse's utopian speculations, the
early gay liberation movement can be understood both in terms of the
limitations of what a collective homosexual subject can accomplish from
within its own historically specific limitations and in terms of a radical,
simultaneous pushing of those limitations—or, in a more Marxian parlance, in terms both of the history it makes and the historically specific
constraints that keep it from making that history just as it pleases. From
this vantage, part of the movement's struggle is to negotiate Marcuse's
influence, to translate the speculative into the practical, and especially to
translate revolutionary impulses located exclusively in the object into a
form of collective political subjectivity. In a deconstructive and psychoanalytic register, Matt Bell has recently argued that gay liberation repeated
rather than broke with the pervasive fifties representation of homosexuality as a ubiquitous, spectral threat. Arguing that gay liberation represents
"an ironic repetition of the governing narrative mechanics that it meant
to subvert," Bell takes issue with narratives of gay liberation that represent
Stonewall as a radical repudiation of fifties homophobia.[47] He examines
the way in which these spectral threats, not legible on human bodies, were
given corporeal form by those bodies moving out of the closets and into
the streets. Rather than adjudicating between a narrative of break and a
narrative of repetition, I would emphasize instead the way in which gay
liberation simultaneously broke with *and* repeated that earlier articulation
of threat invoked by Marcuse and by the state, striving to embody the
universalizing implications of perversion in subjective and collective form.
This movement's negotiation of *Eros and Civilization*'s influence gave it a
certain social, historical, practical efficacy utterly out of Marcuse's hands.

   The connections I have tried to historicize between clinical psychoanalysis, *Eros and Civilization,* and the gay liberation movement register what
chapter 1 contended was the unpredictable social and historical effectivity

of the reification of sexual desire psychoanalytic discourse instantiates. Chapter 1 situated the historical emergence of psychoanalytic discourse in relation to the uneven, contingent emergence of Taylorism and an intensive regime of accumulation. By the postwar period, with the relatively stabilized metamorphosis of these two closely related developments into a pervasive, large-scale Fordism, a similarly pervasive shift takes place with a wide-spread framing of social political questions in psychoanalytic terms. For apologists for the social order—including the U.S. government, as well as the conservative psychoanalytic establishment that government found itself consulting—"therapeutic" approaches are advocated as a means of helping civilization's discontents adjust to the social order rather than change it. From a more radical perspective—articulated by figures like Marcuse, Reich, and Adorno—psychoanalytic categories seem especially promising tools for theorizing widespread social conformity as well as the preconditions for breaking that conformity. In his "Critique of Neo-Freudian Revisionism," Marcuse suggests that this period throws into unprecedented relief the "discrepancy" between theory and therapy: "While psychoanalytic theory recognizes that the sickness of the individual is ultimately caused and sustained by the sickness of his civilization, psychoanalytic therapy aims at curing the individual so that he can continue to function as part of a sick civilization without surrendering to it altogether." But for Marcuse, this qualified refusal to surrender was negligible: "The difference between mental health and neurosis lies only in the degree and effectiveness of resignation"—indeed, "therapy is a course in resignation" (*Eros and Civilization,* 246). At the same time, I have also tried to suggest the ways in which psychoanalytic theory became for Marcuse its own kind of course in resignation, became itself symptomatic of a conviction of the impossibility of gaining any practical leverage on what he viewed as a homogeneously instrumentalized social totality.[48]

When we move from the level of sexual epistemology that Sedgwick characterizes in terms of a universalizing/minoritizing definitional incoherence to the question of how this epistemology was articulated in political terms during this same period, what Sedgwick deconstructively posits as incoherence begins to assume the form of a political dialectic. As capitalist social relations erode older forms of social and political hierarchy, confronting them with commodity relations and their similarly abstract, bourgeois-democratic political analogue—abstract, equivalent citizens—

forms of social hierarchy that the bourgeois revolutions ultimately refused to address, hierarchies of gender and race, for example, eventually come into palpable contradiction with this bourgeois identification of equality with equivalence. Étienne Balibar identifies the revolutionary articulation of this abstract citizen in the eighteenth and nineteenth centuries with a "purely negative" political proposition that has profoundly contradictory and dynamic historical effects, most crucially an ongoing dialectic between equality and freedom: a materially and institutionally irreversible principle of "equaliberty" inherent in "the ideological space opened by the revolutionary proposition."[49] In this ideological space, equality and freedom are identical, the absence of one necessarily denoting the absence of the other. Not only is the freedom on which the bourgeois revolutions were ostensibly based only partially, problematically achievable in the absence of genuine equality; these contradictions have themselves played a role in determining, in opening up a certain terrain for, subsequent political struggles. The principle of equaliberty is thus "the anchoring point for the series of claims that . . . begin to base upon it their claims for the rights of women, of workers, of colonized 'races'"—and, I would add, stigmatized sexualities—"to be incorporated into citizenship." But this set of interpellative contradictions has not merely served to assimilate subordinate groups into the order of citizenship; a dialectic, rather, is established between a tendency to assimilate into that order, and an opposing tendency to reject that order as hopelessly constraining and exclusionary. By equating equality with freedom, the bourgeois revolutions introduce "an indefinite oscillation, . . . a structural equivocation between two obviously antinomical forms of 'politics,'" what Balibar calls "an *insurrectional politics* and a *constitutional politics*. Or if one prefers, a politics of permanent, uninterrupted revolution, and a politics of the state as institutional order."[50]

The reified political category of the citizen structures both the positive and negative political responses to the state in each of the psychoanalytically conditioned midcentury articulations of homosexual politics I have posited: respectively, a *constitutional* articulation of minoritized sexual subjectivity and rights claims that constitutively rejects psychoanalysis, which defines itself, again, in negative relation to psychoanalysis (the homophile movements); and an *insurrectional* articulation of a universalized, polymorphous eroticism and a rejection of the logic of rights (*Eros and Civilization*, gay liberation). What I referred to earlier, moreover, as gay liberation's historical embeddedness and limitation, on the one hand, and simultaneous radical impulse to push that limitation, on the other, can be understood in Balibar's terms, in terms of the "permanent tension" between that formation's historically specific, determinate conditions and what Balibar calls the "hyperbolic universality" of its insurrectional impulse.[51]

This constitutional/insurrectional dialectic underscores the limits of Marcuse's psychoanalytic articulation of sexual politics, especially the limits imposed by his pessimistic unwillingness to engage questions of subjectivity in any sustained way, the same pessimism that motivated the Frankfurt school's turn to Freud in the first place. Universalized desire, in Sedgwick's general epistemological terms or in Marcuse's more narrowly Freudian ones, is opposed to the terms of subjectivity as such. Just as the ego is the component of psychoanalytic discourse that gets lost in the war between pleasure principle and performance principle that is Marcuse's focus, so *Eros and Civilization*'s theoretical momentum preempts any recognition of whatever practical purchase subjectivity can be said to have in the mid-twentieth-century United States. I suggested that Marcuse anachronistically transposes into the mid-twentieth century sexual taboos more appropriately identified with the nineteenth century. I now want to add that Marcuse's text also fails to acknowledge the extent to which what he theorizes as an objectifying reification of the eroticized body has already taken place in practice. Decades before the publication of *Eros and Civilization,* the use of the body as an instrument of pleasure, as a pleasurable means rather than a productive end, had already been institutionalized within that sexual knowledge regime Foucault elaborates, in the epistemological categories of heterosexual and homosexual subjectivity, subjectivities defined in terms of object choice, which posit gendered bodies as objects of pleasure and desire. It is significant, I think, that *Eros and Civilization* uses terms like "perversions" and "homosexuality" to signify subversive utopian fantasies but never uses the noun form of "homosexual": subjective categories based on object choice—queer egos, real live homos— are erased in Marcuse's transposition of nineteenth-century taboos, only to return later under the more pessimistic heading of "repressive desublimation." Indeed, the contradiction between a universalized desire irreducible to subjective categories and the subjective "orienting" of that desire is visible in the theoretical differences that distinguish *Eros and Civilization* from *One-Dimensional Man,* texts that characterize reified eroticism as

REIFICATION AS LIBERATION

hydraulically revolutionary objectification and individuated, neutralized subjectification, respectively. In Marcuse's ultimate prioritizing of reification's total overthrow, in his elision of reification's objective historical effects, he ultimately prioritizes, with Lukács, reification's subjective moment as well, in spite of an initial movement in a different direction. If Marcuse stopped short of the implications of this earlier emphasis on the liberatory potential of the sexually objectified body, gay liberation endeavored to take additional steps he would not.

Both insurrectional and constitutional forms of politics are necessarily articulations of political subjectivity—the insurrectional in terms of a radical collective subject, the constitutional in terms of the citizen-subject of individual rights. If gay liberation appropriated the revolutionary erotic implications of universalized desire—directly from Marcuse, indirectly from Freud, and against the assimilationist tendencies of the minoritizing homophile movements—this was necessarily a critical appropriation on the part of a formation that could challenge sexual minoritization and political individuation only by way of a collective, historically situated, insurrectional subjectivity. I remarked earlier that if the clinical psychoanalytic focus on the ego, on the "whole personality," was for Marcuse a kind of resignation to the existing, instrumentalized order of things, Marcuse's own universalizing, psychoanalytic speculations were ultimately themselves symptomatic of a certain resignation. Gay liberation's collective appropriation of Marcuse's emphasis on erotic liberation is in this respect a refusal both of mere tolerance and of more than one kind of resignation.

Marcuse speculatively connects past with future, teleologically posits the anticipation of future by the past, within the terms of what chapter 1 identified as that psychoanalytic reification of desire that attributes an abstract temporality to desire, which defines desire in terms of a temporal opposition between a constitutively repressed ego and the polymorphous impulses that disrupt the ego's boundaries. This psychoanalytic reification of desire defines desire itself in terms of that temporality. Necessarily appropriating the abstract temporality of psychoanalysis along with its radical intimations, Marcuse assimilates history itself to the psychoanalytic temporality of desire. He formulates the polymorphous overwhelming of the body by eroticism as a *reification* of the body. But this way of theorizing the body's reification has as a condition of possibility what chapter 1 identified as a historically specific reification of the economy of desire basic to a nineteenth-century knowledge of the male body, psychoanaly-sis's disarticulation of sexual energy from its spermatic "containment," a disarticulation any such overwhelming must presuppose. Rather than historicizing psychoanalytic discourse, Marcuse conceptualizes historical thinking itself in psychoanalytic terms, obscuring reification's complex objective effectivity in the process.

Reification is in this respect a condition of possibility for at least three historically specific developments I have tried to identify: the abstract, psychoanalytic temporality in terms of which *Eros and Civilization* recon-ceives history; the epistemological positing of homosexual subjectivity *Eros and Civilization* ignores; and the political representation of that sub-jectivity in both constitutional and insurrectional terms. All three of these effects of reification helped constitute the situation of the gay liberation movement. Reification must here again be seen as a social and historical force with multiple and divergent objective repercussions, a force that un-deniably effects historically specific instances of mystification but cannot be exhaustively understood as a form of mystification. Indeed, the histor-ical situation I have delineated for *Eros and Civilization* indicates radically divergent forms of effectivity: reification as a condition of possibility for that text's rethinking of reification is mystified by the text itself, by the abstract temporality in which it participates, while reification also in mul-tiple ways conditioned gay liberation's practical, politically radical appro-priation of this same text. The following chapter will further consider the way in which a sexual and political form of subjectivity that opposes com-pulsory heterosexuality takes shape during this same period. But here the articulation of sexual objectification with political subjectivity will pick up where the previous chapter left off: with the question of masculinity, with the way in which gay men in the late sixties and early seventies articulated collective subjectivity within the terms of the politically promising sexual objectification of the body that Marcuse advocated, and within the terms of that masculine, performative normalization of the male body I situated within capitalist social relations in chapter 2.

Chapter 1 emphasized history's irreducibility to the unifying dialectic that has tended to frame reification as a concept. As in my analysis of Lukács, here again it has been my intention to read a specific elaboration of the reification/totality dialectic in terms of its historical conditions. I have tried to subject Marcuse's rethinking of this concept to a certain kind of historical, antiheteronormative scrutiny, to elucidate in dialectical terms the limitations of a tenaciously dialectical argument. To read *Eros and Civilization* in relation to a broader, contemporaneous reading of the social as such in psychoanalytic terms, and in terms of certain political uses to which this text was subsequently put, is to discern an ongoing historical and politically radical participation in the reification of sexual desire. This text constitutes a historically conditioned link between this century-old history of reified desire and what arguably remains the most pivotal movement against compulsory heterosexuality the United States has yet witnessed. While reification is neither a form of liberation nor liberation's teleologically posited, anticipatory promise, it does open certain conjunctural, historically specific conditions of possibility for liberation and in fact had already opened them long before Marcuse rethought reification so strikingly. Marcuse eventually retracted the connection he had made between reification and liberation. But it was already out there.

chapter 4

CLOSING A HETEROSEXUAL FRONTIER:
MIDNIGHT COWBOY
AS NATIONAL ALLEGORY

If a single American cultural theorist continues prominently to carry the mantle of *History and Class Consciousness,* it is certainly Fredric Jameson, who, like Lukács, reads narrative in the terms of an aspiration to totality. His interpretive practice is centrally a practice of allegorical analysis, allegory as a mode of reading rather than writing, a hermeneutic to which he has, at various moments, attached different names, perhaps most notably "transcoding" and "cognitive mapping."[1] Though I do not want to understate the difference between these two practices—a difference that to a great extent turns on the difference between modernism and postmodernism, as Jameson historicizes those terms—each of the names given to the hermeneutic he develops refers to a specific variation on the critical practice of totality thinking, an interpretive movement outward that articulates relays between distinct levels of a text, levels that ultimately refer to a series of increasingly broad and increasingly mediated social and historical horizons. Within this general schema, for example, the narrative representation of private or socially local phenomena allegorizes broader, ultimately global socioeconomic and historical processes. Focusing on the same historical period that I considered, from a different angle, in the previous chapter, this chapter reads the film *Midnight Cowboy* both with and against the terms of this interpretive grid.

The New York premiere of *Midnight Cowboy* took place a month before the Stonewall uprising catalyzed the gay liberation movement, and a few years into a national legitimation crisis manifested most prominently, perhaps, in the counterculture and in broad opposition to the war in Vietnam. The relation between these contemporaneous developments can be understood in any number of different ways—in the influence of national liberation struggles like the one unfolding in Vietnam on the self-understanding of the gay liberation movement, for example. This chapter situates *Midnight Cowboy* against a national horizon that is ultimately distinct from either of these developments but closely related to both of them: the contemporaneous legitimation crisis of a national, Fordist mode of regulation, a crisis evident not only in the forms of social rebellion that marked "the sixties" but also in the increasing, mass-mediated national visibility during the sixties of an "underground" formation of gay men. My discussion will consider the way in which this formation was consolidated within a Fordist mode of regulation, and the way in which its increasing visibility in the sixties was indicative of that mode of regulation's eventual crisis.

I begin here by picking up on a line of analysis initiated in chapter 2. There I argued that the historical content of the performative normalization of masculinity was best understood as a certain kind of skilled labor located at the moment of consumption rather than production, a regulatory, embodied, gender-specific technical knowledge operating as part of an emergent, intensive regime of accumulation's unevenly developing mode of regulation. I also argued, following Butler, that homosexual desire is both constitutive of this normalized masculinity and excluded from it, and that what Butler calls the "weakness" in this heteronormalizing citation of masculinity, male homosexual desire itself, would subsequently be "worked" by a historically specific gay male formation. This subsequent working of the weakness in the norm of masculinity—among gay male liberationists but also within a more general, national gay male formation that begins to congeal and eventually emerges, in the sixties, into national media visibility—will be my focus in the first section of this chapter. This collective working of masculinity's weakness is not incidental to, but is itself constitutive, I will contend, of this emergent formation.

Regulation theory characterizes Fordism, the corporate and governmental consolidation of U.S. capitalism that secured vigorous, unprecedented rates of accumulation after World War II, most fundamentally in terms of a systemic, unprecedented coordination of mass consumption with mass production. The consumption of highly standardized goods was broadly normalized during this period. A social compact between capital and labor kept wages relatively high and secured a widespread socialization of workers into a national consumption norm that kept profits strong for roughly a generation. Unions achieved a high degree of purchasing power for the workers they represented, at the cost of reining in more radical aspirations. Government intervention was fundamental to Fordism's success in achieving high levels of accumulation (hence the alternative term "Fordism-Keynesianism"). State intervention in the economy, from monetary policy to tax-subsidized development of a welfare state, also fueled consumption, as did major changes in the geography of accumulation itself, notably the broad suburbanization that fueled private spending on automobiles and public spending on the infrastructure this new geography required. The most important facet, for my purposes, of this complex stage in U.S. economic development is Fordism's state-subsidized normalizing of consumption and the simultaneously national and global implications of the accumulation crisis that began in the late sixties.

Read in relation to these two contexts, I contend, *Midnight Cowboy* takes the form of a national allegory—one that opens up the opportunity for rethinking the role of sexuality, and of the nation-state, in Jameson's interpretive practice. The film's most crucial allegorical level, for my purposes, is what I will call its narrative *deterritorialization* of the cowboy: a shuttling of this distinctly American image of both masculinity and nationalism out of the frontier and into the big city. The film's protagonist is would-be heterosexual gigolo Joe Buck, whose hustling persona— a naive, self-commodifying emulation of John Wayne and other Western film stars—produces only poverty after he makes his way from rural Texas to New York City to seek his fortune. Joe quickly discovers, to his dismay, the cowboy image's largely exclusive appeal to gay men in this new, radically unfamiliar space. For Joe, the city is a brutally disorienting and homosexualizing environment, an environment in which he finds himself destitute in very short order. In ways I will make clear, drawing as much on contextual analysis as on textual analysis, this narrative of deterritorialization figures Fordism's legitimation crisis as well as its crisis of profitability. I conclude the chapter by considering the way in which this particular national allegory sheds a different light on Jameson's hermeneutic.

WORKING THE WEAKNESS

When he picks up his pay before departing for New York, and fresh into a brand new cowboy outfit, Joe tells a fellow dishwasher—who, like other coworkers, wonders what Joe is doing "in that getup"—about the new career he's going to New York to pursue. While New York women are "begging for it, paying for it too," Joe insists, most New York men are "tutti fruttis." Joe's bus trek from Texas to New York points this cowboy eastward instead of westward but shares with the cowboy's traditional westward movement implications that are historical as well as geographic. In particular, this narrative inversion already begins to disrupt a certain sedimented heterosexualization of this same commodified figure. Joe sits on the bus listening to a radio talk show, hearing women describe their ideal man: one woman remarks that her "ideal man is Gary Cooper—but he's dead." The bus ride from semirural Texas (where, the film suggests, some possibility of unproblematically heterosexualizing the cowboy remains) to Manhattan (where, apparently, no such possibility remains) leaves this presumably heterosexualized commodity behind and replaces it with a new, urbanized version, appropriated and homosexually objectified. Joe attaches a poster of Paul Newman sexily posed as "Hud" to the wall of his New York hotel room; this image serves precisely to underscore his lack of a certain kind of urban sexual sophistication, his adherence, which is somehow a product of his background "on the range," to an image of masculinity the orientation of which, he will soon discover, has become increasingly ambiguous, slippery. If the death of a solidly heterosexual masculinity represented by Gary Cooper and articulated in the course of Joe's bus ride frames the distance between Texas and New York as both geographic and historical, we have little reason to wonder—once a very confused Joe begins to recognize the homosexual objectification, in Manhattan, of his masculine costume—at the fragility even of his iconic, primary point of heterosexual reference. To the challenge from his new partner in crime, Ratso Rizzo, that "no rich lady with any class at all buys that cowboy crap anymore," that "that's faggot stuff," Joe's defensively sputtered response invokes John Wayne: "You're gonna tell me he's a fag?" This narrative of deterritorialization figures a process ongoing through, and indicative of, the Fordist era: the consolidation of a relatively dispersed network of homosexual men into a collective, national formation.

Fordism has frequently been understood in terms of a relatively homogeneous production-consumption circuit, a circuit organized around highly standardized commodities; this is especially the case when Fordism is viewed from the perspective of a post-Fordism that internally differentiates this circuit into a range of niche markets. Michel Aglietta notes that, within Fordism, consumption needed to be "rendered uniform."[2] This uniformity is in significant ways ruptured from within and from very early on, in U.S. capital's unprecedented interpellation of teenagers as a target market during this period, for example, a rupture to which I will return. But for the moment I am interested in what a relative uniformity of production and consumption would not accommodate during this period, in exclusions that constituted this uniformity itself. In the wake of what Allan Bérubé has represented as a national "coming out" of gays and lesbians during World War II,[3] a gay male formation took shape in part within a postwar circuit of commodification sometimes figured as an underground, a circuit phobically marginalized in relation to Fordism's expansion of the scale of distribution—marginalized by censorship crusades as well as by government and police tactics, for example, which seemed designed to keep homosexuals isolated from one another, to keep any collective gay formation from developing in the first place, as John D'Emilio was among the first to document.[4] In this respect, the state's managing of a Fordist mode of regulation included a certain effort to enforce social uniformity through anxieties about national security, anxieties about keeping the national body safe from homosexual enemies within—even as those enemies were also constantly invoked, in the form, for example, of the specter of a universalized homosexual threat I considered in the previous chapter.

But then, in the sixties, instances of a growing representation in mainstream media not merely of a dispersed homosexual network but of a relatively consolidated gay formation included everything from reactionary, anxious *New York Times* articles with titles like "Growth of Overt Homosexuality Provokes Wide Concern" to major, simultaneously sympathetic and stigmatizing theatrical and film productions like *The Boys in the Band* (play 1968, film 1970).[5] An increasingly visible gay male population is also evident within the narrative of *Midnight Cowboy*. This film registered with unprecedented prominence a certain homosexualization not merely of the frontier hero but of masculinity itself, which had been under way within this underground network since at least World War II. Indeed, it figures the emergence of this formation, an increasingly visible, collective challenge to compulsory heterosexuality, in terms of a crisis of gender performance, in its representation of the contingency and fragility of masculinity's capacity to normalize heterosexual desire. I will consider the way in which this working operated in a few distinct but closely related contexts before circling back to the film to discuss how it brings these horizons together.

In the face of the typical fifties representation of the homosexual in terms of a narcissistic, preening femininity, a working of what Butler would call masculinity's constitutive contingency and fragility can be discerned within the circulation of those marginally disseminated gay pictorials of the fifties (*Physique Pictorial* is perhaps the best-known example) that featured photographs and paintings of male bodies, often in little more than posing straps. When there was more than a posing strap, the objects of desire displayed in these pages were often explicitly masculinized, not only by highlighting where possible a particular model's rebelliousness (even in some cases his history of trouble with the law) but also by dressing them in just enough of the garb of cowboys or sailors, for example, to signify a simultaneously iconic and homosexualized masculinity. If this working of a weakness appears to take place at the level of the commodity, this circulation of commodities helped consolidate an underground gay network; this working also worked against the social dispersal and isolation of homosexuals that government tactics strove to enforce. Thomas Waugh, in his groundbreaking analysis of what he calls this underground "physique milieu," remarks that "the era of consumerism into which Western society had gradually awakened now seemed to embrace even its most invisible and disenfranchised minority." As he points out, the pictorials included readers' columns and pen pal addresses. He emphasizes the extent to which this marginal circuit of commodification was central to a consolidation of national gay male networks during and after World War II:

> The flourishing physique cultural network . . . could become a safe and nurturing institutional shelter for deviant cultural transformation, including a distribution system that enabled anonymous two-way communication among consumers and producers (and horizontally among consumers), and a proliferation of inexpensive image-making technology accessible to amateurs as well as small-scale artisans, all outside of state control.[6]

Waugh goes on to emphasize the ideological distance between physique culture and the assimilationist politics increasingly espoused by groups like the Mattachine Society during the period. Gay men read about gay politics "in the timid unvisual pages of *One* and *Mattachine Review,* but got their rocks off with the physique magazines. . . . The homosexual rights movement, respectable and 'out,' and the commercial gay cultural network, raunchy and in the closet, treated each other with frosty disdain."[7] But Waugh also emphasizes that the gay male activism of the early seventies was at the same time directly facilitated by this pervasive national circulation of commodified, homoerotic images of male bodies: the "exponential expansion" of this circulation "constitutes the most significant gay cultural achievement during the formative quarter century following World War II," both "evidence of and cultural cement for this important sexual/ cultural minority"; "however furtive, however unconscious, however masturbatory, using pictures was an act of belonging to a community composed of producers, models, and, most important, other consumers."[8]

Christopher Nealon emphasizes the uncertainties informing this circulation of images—uncertainties from the perspective of government officials, and from the perspective of the consumers of these images. Uncertainty, Nealon suggests, operated here in two opposing directions that seemed merely to invert each other: for government officials, uncertainty about who exactly was consuming these images reinforced anxieties about homosexuality's invisible, national pervasiveness, while for consumers, this same circulation seemed to hold out the promise of a larger horizon of gay sociality.[9] I maintained in chapter 3 that gay liberation was influenced negatively by the homophile movements and the clinical psychoanalytic establishment, and positively by a widespread representation, which drew on radicalized Freudian logics, of homosexuality as a potentially explosive enemy within. To complicate further the social and historical overdetermination of this later, more radical movement, we can add that if gay liberation provided an overt sense of collectivity, this underground network linking producers and consumers of images, a network that expanded quickly in the course of the fifties, had helped provide that covert sense of collectivity that was one of gay liberation's conditions of possibility.

But it is important to emphasize that the specific "era of consumerism" under consideration here, far from "embrac[ing]" this "invisible and disenfranchised minority," was also marked by determined efforts to mitigate the social threat this minority ostensibly posed. One of the obvious characteristics of this underground circulation was its radical marginality to Fordist distribution networks. On the one hand, this underground did seem to insinuate itself into mainstream channels of distribution. The pictorials appeared on newsstands, for example, but these were certainly risky places to purchase them. Waugh cites one instance of a mother suing

Physique Pictorial, April 1961. Copyright athleticmodelguild.com.

a newsstand for "corrupting" her son.[10] But even the pictorials served primarily as catalogs for photographs that, Waugh emphasizes, were a much more significant source of income. And while the more profitable distribution of photos took advantage of the U.S. postal service as a channel of distribution, local and state authorities also tried to prevent this distribution. Waugh notes that such efforts even led some vendors to sell the

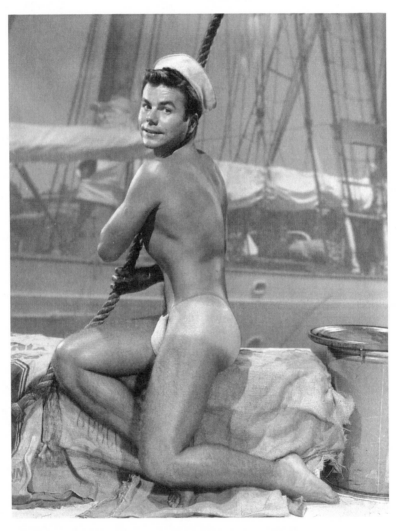

Physique Pictorial, Spring 1955. Copyright athleticmodelguild.com.

photos from motel rooms instead. And potentially even more relevant than channels of distribution here are the ways in which these images were produced. These were exceedingly low-tech forms of production, which Waugh characterizes as isolated and artisanal. Photographs were often processed by hand, for example, because the use of photo labs could open producers to harassment. The authorities appear to have succeeded in marginalizing this

Physique Pictorial, July 1962. Copyright athleticmodelguild.com.

circulation of images until at least 1962, when the Supreme Court ruled that the distribution of such materials was constitutional, a development that opened up this production-consumption circuit to corporate encroachment.[11] What I would emphasize is the marginality of these underground networks to Fordist mass consumption, a marginality enforced in the interests of maintaining what we might understand as a certain moral "uniformity" of production and consumption.

How are we to understand this consolidation of an underground network in relation to this working of a weakness in the norm of masculinity, and *in spite of* the state's ongoing efforts to enforce this uniformity? In masculinizing its objects of desire, this network actively wreaked havoc with the presumed heterosexuality of masculinity itself. An opposing and more typical reading of gay male culture's appropriation of masculinity represents this appropriation as little more than an uncritical recapitulation of straight ideals that undermines the struggle against compulsory heterosexuality. From this perspective, all the imaginative constraint and rigidity suggested by the word "straight" are merely recapitulated by those who should be resisting it. Waugh himself insists on such a reading, positing a certain mutual exclusivity between male homosexuality on the one hand and such performances of masculinity on the other, contending that the latter valorize "nongayness." The pictorials disseminated an iconography not of "our bodies, but of *theirs*," as he puts it, portraying not a genuinely underground form of gay sociality but "the mainstream of homosocial normalcy."[12] But the assumption that such appropriation is uncritical understates the extent to which homosexual desire is not only *excluded from* but also *constitutive of* masculinity in the first place. Within the heterosexual matrix, as Butler argues, what is lost as sexual object is retained as identification: masculine identification presupposes the exclusion of desire for a masculine object. But this exclusion is never stable and must be performed, reiterated, indefinitely.

Doesn't this underground network, in this respect, work to embody a desire for masculinity that need not retroactively feminize the desiring subject, to challenge the historically sedimented heterosexual terms of masculinity's corporeal normalization? Isn't this marginal production and consumption of images a form of subversive social labor? Given, as Nealon emphasizes, the uncertainty about who was consuming these images, it seems impossible just to assume that the consumers of these images

desired "nongayness," especially inasmuch as the same circulation of commodities began to put isolated gay men in contact with each other. This
underground network, I am suggesting, collectively works the sexual objectification of masculinity by masculinity that is heterosexual masculinity's
constitutive outside. And this working is collective precisely insofar as it
operates within a network of isolated men whom this very circulation
begins to make less isolated. And is this subversive homosexual labor not
also a labor of imagining a beyond, as Nealon suggests, to that same social
isolation? If a performative, heteronormalizing masculinity evolved within
a fitfully developing, intensive regime of accumulation between the wars,
as part of this regime's emergent mode of regulation, here we encounter a
performative homosexualizing of masculinity within a commodity circuit
vigorously marginalized within Fordism, the regime of accumulation that
had among its conditions of possibility these earlier, regulatory efforts. Or
perhaps it would be more accurate to say that this circuit operates both
within a Fordist mode of regulation and outside it. The performative heterosexualizing of masculinity considered in chapter 2 is as internal to this
mode of regulation as this later, performative homosexualizing of masculinity is external to it. Indeed, the vigorous state tactics in trying to preempt
any genuine socialization of homosexuals—efforts to mitigate the circulation of these images, efforts like the routine police raids on gay bars—suggest that we might understand this marginal circuit, this collective labor
of homosexualizing masculinity, to be not merely heterosexual masculinity's constitutive outside but a constitutive outside of a uniformity not only
of sexual morality but of production and consumption, a provocation for
the ongoing enforcement not only of a Cold War–era "national security"
but of a Fordist mode of regulation.

Actively participating in but also pictorially figuring the later emergence
of a gay formation into broader national visibility is another photograph,
this one not marginal to, but at the center of, Fordist distribution. This
photograph consumes the two opening pages of an important article called
"Homosexuality in America," which appeared in 1964 in that mainstream
periodical par excellence, *Life*. The photograph soberly acknowledges the
emergence into the mainstream light of day of a "sad and often sordid
world," indeed performs an illumination of what it thereby represents as
having previously been invisible. Shot inside a gay bar, its broad margins
are pitch-black darkness while shadowy, dimly lit male figures in barely

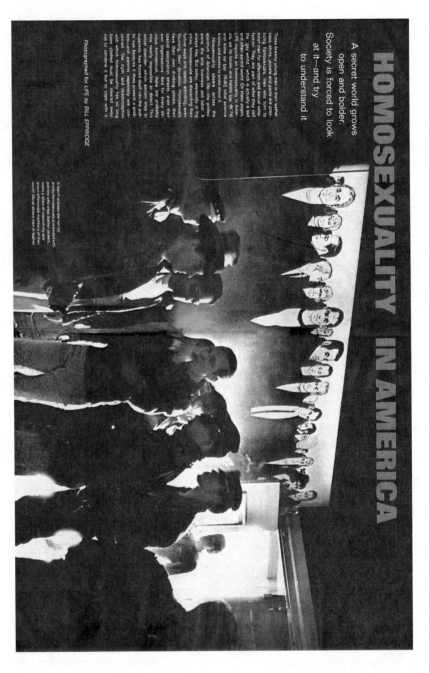

Life, June 26, 1964. Photograph copyright Bill Eppridge. All rights reserved.

discernible biker gear and cowboy hats huddle in its center, the only light faintly emanating from another room through an open door. "A secret world grows open and bolder," *Life* declared. "Society is forced to look at it—and try to understand it." As the caption at the bottom of the photograph indicates, part of what was being illuminated here was a different performance of masculinity, a kind of collective gay pressuring of the norm of masculinity: "A San Francisco bar run for and by homosexuals is crowded with patrons who wear leather jackets, make a show of masculinity and scorn effeminate members of their world." Indicative of *Life*'s ambivalence about how much of this "show" it was willing to illuminate is the caption's added clarification of the image itself: "Mural shows men in leather."[13]

In an examination of the larger article of which this image is a part, Lee Edelman focuses on homosexuality and its relation to U.S. national identity in the fifties and sixties, rightly pointing out that the larger feature in *Life* is characterized by an inability to see male homosexuality as anything other than masculinity's opposite (as the words "make a show of masculinity" already suggest). But Edelman also deconstructs these effeminizing figurations of homosexuality, arguing that these figurations inevitably disclose "a category subverting alterity within the conceptual framework of masculinity itself."[14] This is also what this image does, presumably in spite of *Life*'s editorial intentions. If this ostensible scorning of effeminacy would suggest an uncritical appropriation of masculinity, this is also explicitly a site of desire for masculinity, a desire that does not appear from the image, at least, to retroactively feminize the subject who desires. The photograph, that is, figures the emerging visibility of that same formation in terms of a simultaneous homosexual identification with *and* desire for masculinity. It would appear to deconstruct the very opposition between desire and identification maintained by the heterosexual matrix of gender.

But it might be more accurate to say that the photo figures historically specific struggles against the normalization of heterosexuality or, more accurately yet, the negotiation of masculine identification itself within those struggles. As Edelman's analysis makes abundantly clear, one would not want to overstate the insight of *Life*'s claim that these men "make a show of masculinity and scorn effeminate members of their world." But one also would not want to understate a "scorning" of effeminacy undeniably evident within certain regions of this emerging formation, especially when one considers its insistent, phobic feminization within a Fordist "consensus" well over a decade old by the time this photograph is published. Whatever kind of masculine identification is depicted here would be indicative of a highly fraught negotiation of masculine identification itself during this period.

Masculinity was controversial, to say the least, within an emergent New Left, for example, and certainly within gay liberation. New Left discourse tended to maintain a strong association between radical activism and masculine identification, an association that led some male activists within gay liberation to distance themselves from what they viewed as a soft, effeminate focus on desire and pleasure. For others, a refusal to identify with masculinity seemed an entirely logical response to associations, also operative within the New Left, between masculinity and militarism. This last impulse was further reinforced by the generational tensions between gay liberation and its homophile elders, who had tended to struggle exclusively on the terrain of legal rights, including the right to serve in the military. For gay men, the gendered connotations of radicalism itself were in this respect controversial (and not exclusively as a result of masculinity's role in the enforcement of heterosexuality): did gay male radicalism require one to identify with masculinity, or to refuse such an identification?

The strong association of a politically radical, revolutionary identification with masculinity drew heavily on the masculinizing (and antihomosexual) discourse of activists including Eldridge Cleaver, Jerry Rubin, and Abbie Hoffman, a discourse that sometimes went so far as to portray the U.S. military itself as an enclave of macho homosexuals.[15] Even given a striking and famous exception to this tendency, the statement in August 1970 by Huey Newton encouraging members of the Black Panther Party to support women's liberation and gay liberation, the stigmatizing of homosexuality as inherently demasculinizing had a tendency to influence gay liberation discourse in such a way that homosexual desire and pleasure were understood to be, at best, politically inconsequential.[16] In response to what he viewed as homophile quietism, for example, the activist (and close associate of Abbie Hoffman) Jim Fouratt asserted, "No matter what you do in bed, if you're not a man out of it, you're going to get screwed up. Be proud of what you are man! And if it takes riots or even guns to show them what we are, that's the only language the pigs understand!"[17] Some gay liberationists also feminized their elders, the "mere liberals" within homophile organizations, as "a bunch of middle-class, uptight, bitchy old queens."[18] The homophile Society for Individual Rights was mocked as "sissies in revolt": "At best, . . . [SIR] will remain a private dancing club unless some teeth are put into those busy gums."[19] The use of the phrase "private dancing club" should moreover remind us of that ideological separation of gay politics from erotic consumption Waugh underscores. These words suggest the degree to which that impulse to cordon off consumption from activism, and to associate desire and pleasure with the former, is recapitulated within gay liberation, even as an underground circuit of homoerotic production and consumption was basic to the consolidation of that national sense of gay male collectivity that made the movement possible.

In any case, it is hard to square this strong masculine identification and attendant feminization of homosexual desire and pleasure with an equally evident alternative strategy: opposing male homosexuality to masculinity in such a way that homosexuality is privileged over masculinity—and this in an age when, if you were straight, pretending to be gay was a familiar approach to trying to avoid the draft. If a refusal of masculine identification opposed the logic by which the military could be portrayed as an enclave of macho homosexuals, it was also logically consistent with a widespread reactionary tendency to homosexualize activist (or at least countercultural) "hippies" and "longhairs." David Suran, in a discussion that situates gay liberation in relation to antiwar activism specifically, distinguishes between the more politicized who, in rejecting militarism, also rejected norms of masculinity, and the less politicized who embraced those norms. Suran quotes the activist Jim Rankin: "We gay (powerless) males must of necessity of our condition be anti-war, and anti-imperialist. We are already a conquered territory."[20] Other subgroups within gay liberation—the Effeminists, for example—rejected what they viewed as the obsession with masculinity within gay culture, identifying masculinity as a fundamental component of the social structure they wanted to overturn. The Flaming Faggots insisted they were actually far to the left of macho revolutionaries, while with the Street Transvestites Action Revolutionaries, as Kissack puts it, "the paradox of the 'street-fighting' queer revolutionary was brought to its logical extreme."[21]

This opposition internal to gay male liberationist practice—whether or not to identify with masculinity—exemplifies that negotiation of the opposition between sexual desire and gender identification enforced by the heterosexual matrix. This radical collective negotiates that matrix from within its own sedimented terms. And I would emphasize that the performative subject is here no longer the implicitly individuated subject of Butler's theory of gender, but a collective subject: working the weakness in the norm of masculinity becomes in this case a fundamentally collective performance, complete with the contentiousness internal to that collective. This specific example of collective practice in this way raises the question, at least implicitly or incipiently, of what kind of relation between desire and identification might obtain outside the heterosexual matrix—even as these competing articulations of gender in relation to radicalism share the assumption that sexual desire and gender identification are opposed, and in this way participate in the terms of that same matrix. We might say that heterosexuality is here denaturalized or defamiliarized *as* a question. If the weakness in the performance of a heteronormalizing masculinity is, again, precisely male homosexual desire's simultaneous constitution of and exclusion from that norm, a collective, gay male liberationist practice discloses a certain fragility or volatility within the performance of masculinity itself—the same fragility or volatility figured by the image from *Life* magazine, and disclosed by that marginal circulation of homoeroticized male bodies that served ultimately to facilitate the emergence of that same liberationist practice.

John Wayne, who won his only Academy Award (for *True Grit*) the same evening *Midnight Cowboy* won for Best Picture, joked that evening, according to the London *Times* journalist Michael Leapman, that "I work with my clothes on. I have to. Horses are rough on your legs." Leapman identified anxiety about the schism between Hollywood's "old conservatism" and its "new permissiveness" as the reason for this remark.[22] But here Wayne also distances his own body from sexual objectification by associating it with labor, suggesting that this distancing is dependent on the performance of labor. But the collective working of masculinity's constitutive homosexual weakness is itself just that—working—and a labor just as skilled: an embodied knowledge of masculinity's heterosexual performance joined with a critical knowledge of compulsory heterosexuality itself. Skilled labor here persists as masculinity's content, as a performative and epistemological avowal of masculinity's constitutive homosexual outside.[23]

To begin to think through *Midnight Cowboy*'s relation to this collective homosexualizing of masculinity, then, we also have to clarify its relation to this intensive regime of accumulation itself, to think about a broader national horizon within which these collective workings of masculinity's weakness unfolded. We can begin by returning to the figuration of a mid-century gay male formation as an underground. Underground film was a simultaneous early site of a performative homosexualization of the costumes of masculinity, in Kenneth Anger's *Fireworks* (1947) and *Scorpio Rising* (1963), for example. Meanwhile Joe Dallesandro, who was introduced to a covert nation of gay men in *Physique Pictorial,* went on, as this covert nation became less covert, to feature in a number of films produced or directed by Andy Warhol—among them *Lonesome Cowboys* (which was released only a few months before *Midnight Cowboy*)—and to become the most homoerotically admired of Warhol's "superstars." *Midnight Cowboy* comes strikingly close to acknowledging its dependence on and participation in these underground developments in its orgiastic party sequence; Joe Buck is invited when Viva, another superstar, approaches him in a coffee shop and confronts him, in Warholian fashion, with a camera. Warhol himself later indicated that *Midnight Cowboy* marked, for him, "a crucial turning point" in the history of film, precisely because it made the distinction between the underground and the mainstream less emphatic:

I had the same jealous feeling thinking about *Midnight Cowboy* that I had had when I saw *Hair* [on Broadway] and realized that people with money were taking the subject matter of the underground, counterculture life and giving it a good, slick, commercial treatment. What we'd had to offer—originally, I mean—was a new, freer content and a look at real people, and even though our films weren't technically polished, right up through '67 the underground was one of the only places people could hear about forbidden subjects and see realistic scenes of modern life. But now that Hollywood—and Broadway, too—was dealing with those same subjects, things were getting a little confused: before, the choice had been like between black and white, and now it was like between black and gray. I realized that with both Hollywood and the underground making films about male hustlers—even though the two treatments couldn't have been more different—it took away a real drawing card from the underground, because people would rather go see the treatment that *looked* better. . . . I kept feeling, "They're moving into our territory."[24]

But who was moving into whose "territory," exactly? If *Midnight Cowboy* was by no means a direct product of the underground, it wasn't unambiguously "mainstream" either, but rather a site at which the distinction between underground and mainstream was destabilized, as the young, hip, countercultural audience to which the film explicitly appealed became an ever more prominent aspect of national life, and as contradictions evident in the film's distribution indicate. It was not only among the first major Hollywood releases to receive an X rating, but also—as the trailer advertising its twenty-fifth anniversary rerelease proudly declared—"the only 'X' rated film to win an Academy Award for Best Picture." In terms of any rigorous opposition of underground to mainstream, in other words, *Midnight Cowboy* is perhaps best understood as oxymoronic.[25] If it is in one sense located within what Warhol refers to as mainstream "territory," it also questions the boundaries of that territory, now compromised by the discursive inroads of the counterculture itself and by the emerging interpellation of the counterculture as a target market.[26] As the differentiation of a relatively invisible underground from a social-cultural mainstream is giving way to an overt confrontation between a counterculture and Nixon's "silent majority," the very frontier between these territories here also begins to blur, having indeed already begun to blur with revelations like *Life*'s pictorial exposure of a "secret world."

The film's status as a symptom of this eroding or at least radically shifting distinction between an underground and a mainstream can I think be understood in terms of what Martyn J. Lee, appropriating a formulation from Daniel Bell, calls Fordism's "cultural contradictions." Bell's influential thesis about post–World War II capitalism is that this new stage of capitalist development pulls the population in contradictory directions, the central incompatibility being the one between capitalism's traditional ethic of conservative, ascetic self-denial—an ideological principle designed to ensure the reinvestment of profit—and a relatively hedonistic, consumerist disposition, an impulse toward immediate gratification. As Lee emphasizes, hedonism is a central aspect of Fordism's mode of regulation: "Capitalism is actively required to endorse and foster a generally hedonistic, spendthrift and throw-away ethic in order to operationalize a greater acceleration of commodity and value turnovers that is implied in the principle of mass consumption."[27]

And youth, specifically teenagers, were a key focal point for this new regulation of mass consumption, "the most prominent materialization," as Lee sees it, "of the new mass-consumption ethic." To secure necessary levels of social consumption required by an accelerated mass production, one of the central innovations of the Fordist mode of regulation was to enfranchise youth with "material and symbolic resources," to interpellate the teenager as a consumer. These resources, however, easily became resources with which to challenge the enforced uniformity of Fordism, the tedium of life in suburbia, for example, a social "consensus" that youth identified with their parents as much as with the government or the economy. The increasingly pervasive distribution of commodities marketed to teenagers, "ripe for use as symbolic markers of a new subcultural status," provided a potentially powerful way to maintain an ideological distance from the values of an older generation.[28] If Fordism was on the one hand relatively uniform, it also facilitated the development of counterhegemonic formations, especially through the limited empowerment the extension of consumption to youth entailed. The politically radical or countercultural movements of the late sixties and the legitimation crisis to which they both responded and contributed, overdetermined as these movements were in a range of ways, were to this extent also a manifestation of contradictions in the mode of regulation. Responding to the enforced consensus of Fordism they experienced to a large extent in generational terms ("don't trust anyone over thirty"), these movements had a practical if obviously limited form of consumer empowerment within Fordism as a condition of possibility.

If Fordism's dialectical facilitation of the activism of the late sixties entailed its inclusion of youth in mass consumption, these were of course largely white, suburban youth. Fordism's legitimation crisis was also the product of the exclusion of any number of social groups, including those who would ultimately participate in that activism. Discontent with Fordism's cultural homogeneity was all the more evident for the high expectations fueled by its productive and distributive capacities, especially since race, ethnicity, gender, and sexuality so frequently determined who benefited and who did not. And whatever benefits or limited forms of empowerment might have been extended to subordinated segments of the population through the expansion of consumption were qualitatively different and brutally uneven. The suburban, capital-intensive "feminine mystique" was as different from the violent exploitation, dispossession, and policing of black populations consigned to burgeoning ghettos, as these were from an underground circulation of homoerotic images. Indeed, one especially striking divergence here is the way in which this circulation helped to consolidate dispersed, isolated homosexuals, while black militancy emerged not from population dispersal but from its opposite, a population concentrated in inner cities and violently policed as whites fled to the suburbs. The point I would underscore is that the consolidation of an increasingly less underground gay male network that took shape outside the circuits of Fordist uniformity was one dimension of the more general contradictions of the Fordist period, including the consumer enfranchisement of a generation that would ultimately rebel, the product of a mode of regulation that could police homosexuality only by constantly invoking it. And to the extent that Fordist mass consumption was, above all, an attempt to secure a broad and sustained accumulation of capital, and to the extent that the same mass consumption contributed to the legitimation crises of the sixties, it is worth emphasizing that these were properly social contradictions rather than exclusively "cultural" ones, especially since Lee's analysis tends to presuppose a distinction between the two.

By the time Joe arrives in New York City, a collective working of the weakness in the norm of masculinity is well under way. Masculinity itself is no longer so naturally straight, its constitutive, denaturalizing homosexual outside having become harder to disavow. In *The Boys in the Band,* a male hustler dressed as a cowboy is presented to a gay man, by his gay friends, as a birthday gift; in *Midnight Cowboy,* too, the frontier hero is reduced to a commodified boy toy. Joe's outfit, those trappings of a national and heterosexual masculinity, begins, like the sailor and similar images, to have increasingly queer connotations. The film is in this respect symptomatic of Fordist contradictions already apparent by 1969. Its active participation in blurring the very distinction between mainstream and underground includes, for example, its Oscar-winning participation in the increasing media visibility of gay men. It illuminates, with *Life,* a "sad and often sordid world." But its narrative of deterritorialization, its encoding of historical distance as geographic distance that is also a narrative elaboration of the ever more sexually volatile character of masculinity's heteronormalizing performance, has at the same time an allegorical relation to that emerging visibility, especially as that visibility took the form, as I have suggested, of a challenge to the terms of that same performance.

Joe is confident he has chosen the right costume, but begins to experience that costume's performative fragility once he arrives in New York and finds himself face to face with a cowboy-hungry network of men. Even as Joe's male customers are the stereotypical, sad, isolated perverts of a Fordist homophobic imaginary, this particular costume's broad appeal also insinuates something beyond the limits of that imaginary. The costume seems to appeal not just to this homosexual or to that homosexual but to an entire "demographic," we might say, to "every Jackie on Forty-second Street," as Ratso memorably puts it, to an entire niche market that seems as actively to *disrupt* the costume's heterosexual signification as to *demand* such a signification. This appeal offensively insinuates for Joe that even John Wayne may be a fag, insinuates that "category subverting alterity within the conceptual framework of masculinity itself" to which Edelman refers. What is disruptive here is precisely the film's raising of the very question of this costume's sexual signification, its refusal to resolve this question. The film invokes a homosexual network that it never directly depicts, the network that actively thwarts Joe's intention for his costume. The film's disruption of the representational parameters of heterosexual masculinity might even be said to figure a homosexual challenge to a more broadly defined national consensus, to Fordist, mass-cultural uniformity itself, inasmuch as homosexuality is, again, a constitutive outside not just of a performatively normalized masculinity but of the very mode of regulation that performative norm helps constitute.

But any disruption within this film of national norms we can identify with Fordism remains just as ambiguous as the film's disruption of masculinity's heterosexual regulation. After Joe experiences more than a little difficulty earning income from female clients, women eventually seem prepared to pay for his services. But just as *Midnight Cowboy* begins to flirt with the possibility of a heterosexual redemption of the cowboy, just as Joe finally begins to have some success hustling women, Joe's (homoerotic?) commitment to Ratso, whose health begins rapidly to deteriorate, compels him to leave the city. The last time we see his costume, he deposits it in a garbage can, concluding that "there's gotta be an easier way to make a living than that." The film is symptomatic of the contradictions of Fordism in this way as well: even as it appears to homosexualize the cowboy, it simultaneously and just as clearly reiterates the normalization of heterosexuality by trashing the outfit along with the stigmatized desire it has begun to signify. Cowboys, sailors, construction workers: by the late seventies the Village People, named for gay Greenwich Village, were nothing if not a hypostatizing, pop-cultural pantheon of these sexually ambiguous icons of masculinity, whose appeal to gay and straight audiences alike depended on and exploited that very ambiguity. But in the late sixties, emerging narratives of the sexual underground were perhaps easier to read in terms of a persistent—or at least residual—national aspiration to uniformity. *Midnight Cowboy* shocked viewers and has been praised as "a milestone in the mature and responsible treatment of sexuality, particularly the self-contained world of the homosexual, in the American commercial cinema."[29] But the film also associates homosexuality with self-loathing and, thanks to one of Joe's recurrent flashbacks, rape. Among Ratso's many enemies, meanwhile, is a swishy figure identified (by Ratso) only as "faggot." And though the film focuses on an emerging love between two male characters, it also seems to presuppose audience resistance, endorsing sexual phobias by just as consistently distracting its audience's attention from the precise character of that love. As Vito Russo pointed out in *The Celluloid Closet*, gay stereotypes deployed in the film's background seem intended to distract the audience from considering the nature of the male relationship in the foreground.[30]

Michael Moon helps us answer this question of why the nonsexual character of this relationship might have needed emphasizing. In a discussion of *Midnight Cowboy* that reads the film in terms of a performance of masculinity and national identity as these were being refigured in the course of the sixties, Moon suggests that the relation between Joe and Ratso is indeed a homoerotic and "perverse" one. He takes issue with two major tendencies in published analyses of the film: heteronormalizing readings that interpret Joe's and Ratso's relationship as fundamentally nonsexual, and queer readings that take the film to task for its ostensible endorsement of gay-hating violence. These two ways of reading the film are not, of course, inconsistent with each other; the significant difference is in whether they approve or disapprove of the heteronormativity they impute to it. But Moon argues instead that the film's violence can be understood as undermining any presumed opposition between pleasure and pain and that the film is not simply about a homoerotic relationship but about "the anguish of two men trying to establish a meaningful S-M relationship despite their both being Ms in relation to each other." This brilliant response to arguments that *Midnight Cowboy* is heteronormative simultaneously and forthrightly emphasizes its own status as a reading against the grain, emphasizes just how obliquely or confusingly represented the erotic aspects of that relationship are: Moon suggests that the film is not "in control" of its own representational codes, that its "success at representing a range of sexualities" is "notable, if only partial."[31]

I am less interested in adjudicating the question of how heteronormative the film is or is not than in the way this very interpretive uncertainty begins to illuminate the film's figuration of an even broader interpretive horizon. Moon remarks of the film's ending, where Joe mourns the death of Ratso, that "in the years since the film's appearance, many commentators have taken this ending as yet another act of ritual mourning of the death of straight-white-American-male 'innocence' in the face of successive waves of black, antiwar, feminist, and gay and lesbian political activism"; for Moon, the film "suggests something much more complicated, and much more perverse, about its protagonists and the masses of men they represent."[32] By the same token, the film also deploys the cowboy as figure in a more complicated fashion than I have thus far been suggesting. The volatile sexual connotations of the cowboy could just as easily represent *both* an increasingly visible, subversive gay male formation *and* the film's, and the culture's, efforts to neutralize that subversiveness. The film unfolds a homosexual fall from national/heterosexual greatness, perhaps: what is to keep it from being read in those heteronormalizing terms articulated by the Eldridge Cleavers and Abbie Hoffmans of the sixties, for instance—as a deeply, even violently gay-hating critique of, say, imperial interventions in Southeast Asia, interventions widely represented in terms of cowboy and frontier imagery? If this homosexualizing performance of masculinity, this working of masculinity's homosexual weakness is, from a gay male perspective, an active *transvaluation* of masculinity—a transvaluation the film enacts—that same transvaluation is just as surely, from the heteronormalizing national perspective the film also actively endorses—and as the ultimate fate of Joe's costume, the film's central trope of a performative masculinity, clearly indicates—a *devaluation*. But what, exactly, is being devalued here? As I propose in the next section, this narrative of deterritorialization also allegorizes the devaluation of the Fordist regime of accumulation itself, a devaluation with global implications.

DEVALUATION

Given the devaluation of masculinity within certain segments of the counterculture and the sixties political Left, a tendency also to devalue the cowboy within these same formations is hardly surprising. In the context of this allegorical reading of the film, it is worth remembering that the cowboy was already a highly charged image during this period, increasingly used to figure—and justify—the U.S. "mission" in Vietnam. Joe's naive, uncritical assumption of the cowboy persona also has to be understood in relation to this more widespread allegorical use of a discourse of "Cowboys and Indians." Richard Slotkin points out that by 1967 "American troops would be describing Vietnam as 'Indian country' and search-and-destroy missions as a game of 'Cowboys and Indians'; and Kennedy's ambassador to Vietnam would justify a massive military escalation by citing the necessity of moving the 'Indians' away from the 'fort' so that the 'settlers' could plant 'corn.'" Additional, vivid examples cited by Slotkin of the militaristic deployment of the cowboy figure—both at home and abroad—to give meaning to U.S. intervention in Southeast Asia include historian Samuel Eliot Morison's 1965 comment about the 1958 French withdrawal from Algeria: "It was as if the Tecumseh Confederacy of 1811 had succeeded in forcing all white Americans to return to Britain." A notice posted in a U.S. military war room in Hawaii, meanwhile, had a heading that read "Injun Fightin' 1759. Counter-Insurgency 1962."[33] We might then situate *Midnight Cowboy* in relation to a filmic subgenre developing by the midsixties that should perhaps be called the antiestablishment Western and included films like *The Wild Bunch* (1969) and *Little Big Man* (1970). These films did not merely revise the film Western's conventions—a process steadily ongoing from at least the early fifties—but, in the context of an increasingly unpopular war, called its fundamental imperial ethos into question.

Joe Buck idealizes this same image, *Midnight Cowboy* indeed underscoring that image's anachronism for the young audience it targeted precisely through Joe's passionate, comically uncritical attachment to it. Identifying with Western heroes like Gary Cooper, Paul Newman's Hud, and especially John Wayne—but utterly disoriented by an intimidating New York City "frontier," confronting that landscape in a manner quite unlike the typically stone-faced, silent, brave Western hero—Joe is hilariously, even hysterically loquacious. More akin to the polite, fundamentally decent John Wayne of *Stagecoach* (1939), say, than to the dangerous, destructive John Wayne of *The Searchers* (1956)—or more precisely an amusing exaggeration of the former—Joe makes a hopelessly outdated cowboy at a moment when even the volatile Wayne of latter film has itself already begun to give way to the hardened, embittered antiheroes of *The Wild Bunch* or Sergio Leone's *A Fistful of Dollars* (1964), for example.[34]

But *Midnight Cowboy* is in no obvious way a Western at all, and Joe's outdated heroes are themselves, just as obviously, commodities: the film's constant references to Wayne, Cooper, and Newman, to say nothing of the mass-produced costume Joe wears to emulate his idols, explicitly represent them as such. *Midnight Cowboy* frames the cowboy as a specifically cinematic, mass-cultural, standardized image from the outset. Even as the cowboy carries wildly different political inflections in the United States during this period—think of the difference, for example, between the hawkish John Wayne and the rebellious, "antiestablishment" Paul Newman of *Hud* or *The Left Handed Gun*—for *Midnight Cowboy* all cowboys are equivalent, relevant for Joe precisely insofar as they interchangeably represent an unambiguously heterosexual masculinity. *Midnight Cowboy*'s release and distribution was indeed contemporaneous with the waning of what is typically understood to have been the golden age of the cinematic Western—which is to say, Fordism's golden age. The genre was a staple of Hollywood production from the early fifties to the late sixties, its popularity at a historic high. This was the apex of the incorporation of the cowboy figure into mass consumption, the era of the so-called A-list Western, a trend encouraged by the critical success of films like *Stagecoach* and *Red River* (1948), as well as by the increasing appropriation of the genre by the cinema's new competitor, television, which made the traditional B Westerns less and less profitable for the film industry.[35] I would add that the antiestablishment Western itself was a product not only of the Vietnam conflict but also, if less directly, of the hegemonic uniformity of Fordism and its subsequent legitimation crisis in the sixties, inasmuch as even the movement against the war has to be understood in relation to the activism of those empowered by Fordism's incorporation of youth into mass consumption, and those excluded from the Fordist consensus.

Midnight Cowboy is then about many things, and one of those things is Fordism itself. Even the film's response to Wayne, who embodied as much

as any celebrity the explicit association of the Vietnam War with the cowboy, positions him less as a hawk than as an increasingly devalued commodity. Most of the film's direct references to Wayne, whose strong support for
the war was firmly established by 1969, serve to challenge the cowboy's
presumed heterosexuality. But very early on the film makes a direct if fleet-
ing reference to Wayne's first directorial effort, *The Alamo* (1960).[36] Before
Midnight Cowboy's opening credits are even complete, we see Joe making
his way to the restaurant where he washes dishes, to say goodbye and collect his pay. The camera briefly follows him past an old movie theater
functionally transformed into a used furniture store by elderly men who
sit on secondhand chairs and, like Joe, wear cowboy hats. Still dangling
from the marquee are most but not all of the letters that once invited spec-
tators in to see a Western that is clearly no longer playing:

J HN   AYNE THE A AMO

If this sad invitation suggests, in 1969, the anachrony of Wayne's jingoism,
it also suggests a devaluation of the Fordist Western itself.

   And even before we see Joe pass this old theater, the film's opening
sequence suggests his immersion from childhood to adulthood in mass
commodification. As the film begins, the screen fades from black to white
as the sound track fades in the stock cinematic sounds of "cowboys and
Indians" on galloping horses. As the camera pulls back, it reveals the white
screen of the film we are watching to be a screen within the film, reflect-
ing bright Texas sunlight, the screen of the Big Tex Drive-In. As the sound
of galloping gives way to Joe's voice, singing the famous "Get along little
dogies" refrain, the drive-in is revealed to serve also as the preadolescent
Joe's playground: on a strip of grass between the screen and the expanse
of parking spaces, a young Joe rocks a rocking horse as the camera continues its retreat. As if to underscore the opening shot's intimated reduction of Joe's identity to an interpellation into mass consumption, the film
cuts immediately to a close-up of an adult Joe in the shower, still singing
the same refrain and already on the verge of departure for New York. We
then see him put on a brand new cowboy outfit the film first displays, still
in its box, on the bed in his motel room. Seconds later he emerges from
his room in his new costume and carrying a suitcase, and only then do the
opening titles and theme music begin.

Midnight Cowboy's cinematic interpellation of the spectator is less important here than its representation of the cinematic interpellation of Joe: this brief preliminary sequence suggests in the course of a few seconds Joe's sustained and unproblematic interpellation by the Fordist Western, without even the benefit, apparently, of some form of familial, "private" mediation. (The film is elliptical at best about Joe's childhood: another dense early sequence of fragmentary, rapid-editing shots suggests that Joe was at one point handed over to his grandmother and subsequently raised by her. That we see him showering and dressing in a motel, moreover, only underscores his rootlessness.) Joe's status as a native Texan makes his costume no less a costume, and if his real name actually sounds more like a cowboy nickname—in addition to making him sound, already, like a hustler, as Michael Moon points out[37]—the costume is, similarly, both artificial and the only sustained identification of Joe the film offers. It is as though it doesn't even occur to Joe to self-commodify except in the most predictable, standardized way, and why would it? The film's opening moments represent Joe as a kind of tabula rasa, not unlike the white drive-in screen that signifies nothing until celluloid-filtered light is projected onto it. Or we might say that his costume wraps him in the mass-cultural packaging that then becomes his only substance.

And if anything here underscores the Fordist setting of this interpellation, it is the film's opening landscape, the drive-in itself. Drive-ins were at the height of their popularity and profitability during the Fordist period, and in this respect they dramatically bucked a major trend as, with the emergence of television, total movie attendance was in decline.[38] This popularity was most obviously a testament to the centrality of the automobile to the Fordist mode of regulation. Fordism was fueled in large part by the mass production and consumption of durables, and perhaps by the automobile more than anything else, a commodity basic to the stimulation of demand required for mass consumption in more ways than one: huge quantities of surplus capital and labor were absorbed, and demand stimulated, by the period's general deconcentration of the population, by the suburbanization of manufacturing as well as private residences. *Midnight Cowboy's* opening shot refers in this way to the dramatic geographic alteration of the U.S. landscape that Fordism produced. The Big Tex Drive-In here becomes a figure for—more specifically, a metonym for—Fordism itself, as is, for that matter, the Fordist Western, as is the commodity in which Joe outfits himself and with which he identifies.

The film's homosexualizing devaluation of Joe's standardized identity in this respect metonymically figures a much larger horizon of devaluation, a devaluation of the regime of accumulation of which this commodity is a part. When Joe travels from suburbanized Texas to New York City, he suddenly finds himself in a place where the automobile is, if anything, a threat: in what has certainly become the film's single most famous sequence, Ratso responds with his fist when a cab nearly runs him down. The urban landscape that Joe encounters, moreover, is palpably contradictory. The film's stylized, critical representation of the metropolis persistently registers similarly extreme degrees of commodification and destitution, the contradictions of capitalism in their most immediately personal, experiential form. Intermittently throughout the film, the motion of wrecking balls and images of condemned or destroyed Manhattan buildings and landscapes, the detritus that capital's perpetual "creative destruction" leaves in its wake, intermingle in a sort of montage with the bright, electric advertisements that hover above Times Square, the billboard advertisements that seem to hover everywhere else, and an endless stream of sales pitches blaring over television and radio frequencies. A destitute Joe and Ratso stumble past a billboard promising "steak for everybody." Advertising slogans and jingles emanate from the radio Joe carries with him ("What do you want more than anything in the world?"), even as he is on the verge of eviction from his hotel room, a turn of events that will soon consign him to Ratso's living quarters in a condemned building. The sorry domestic existence Joe and Ratso then share starkly contrasts with the aural and visual inducements to spend money that bombard them. If the drive-in landscape in the film's opening seconds is a metonym for the Fordist mode of regulation, the contradictory landscape Joe and Ratso negotiate seems itself more abstract and global than the film's literal setting, less "Times Square" or "New York City" than the dazzling, devastating process of capital accumulation as such.

To take a mass commodity on legs like Joe and overwhelm him with a filmic space so immediately indicative of socioeconomic contradiction is to deterritorialize that commodity in a way that makes starkly visible the contradictions successfully managed by Fordism for a generation. In what remains of this section, I want to shift gears a bit, sketching an ultimately global horizon of devaluation, and proposing a way in which the film's devaluation of the standardized cowboy can be understood within it.[39] The slowing of accumulation that began in the mid- to late sixties had its most dramatic results in the seventies, including labor uprisings, that protracted combination of stagnant productivity and inflation called "stagflation," and an accelerated deindustrialization as factory production began to relocate overseas. But by 1969 symptoms of a broad devaluation of Fordism were already evident in the United States, most notably the symptom of rising inflation: a devaluation of the dollar undertaken initially by corporations, and ultimately by the U.S. government through monetary policy, a devaluation that ultimately signified the global devaluation of the Fordist regime of accumulation itself.

Accumulation crisis is typically defined in terms of a situation in which idle capital is accumulated on the one hand and idle labor is accumulated on the other, a situation in which there is no clear outlet for investment, no clear productive way to reunite them. In the late sixties, however, the United States had an extremely low rate of unemployment; so in what sense can this be called an accumulation crisis? This particular period of crisis was characterized by an overaccumulation, in key manufacturing sectors, of capital relative to labor: productive capacity and money capital that could not be invested because of almost full employment, a combination that quickly put the brakes on profitability. Capital's typical first response to falling profits would include innovation in productive technology and labor discipline. But Fordism's general structural inflexibility made such responses difficult if not impossible. U.S. capital had been slow in replacing old equipment with new equipment, and thereby increasing the rate at which relative surplus value is extracted from labor, by the time the profit squeeze set in. Fordism had been a long time producing its own gravediggers: this habituated slow rate of innovation, relative to labor costs especially, made capital unprepared to respond to the increased demand for labor that set in after roughly 1965. U.S. firms had reconciled themselves to the high wages that facilitated mass consumption and consensus, and to investments in the enormous fixed capital mass production required. This complacency was to a great extent a product of the very compact between capital and labor that fueled mass consumption, and by the mid-sixties unions were strong enough to resist any significant increase in labor discipline, at least in the short term. This corporate inflexibility was compounded by the inflexibility of the Keynesian welfare state, by the social entrenchment of a range of entitlement programs, even as declining profits began to limit the possibilities of any additional expansion in the tax base for these programs. The inflexibly thorough social institutionalization of the Fordist regime of accumulation was in these ways the very thing that preempted any short-term response adequate to the crisis that was now clearly under way.

Because this national regime of accumulation could not bend, it broke— or more precisely, it ultimately broke because monetary policy, a manipulation of the dollar's value, was one of the only ways it *could* bend. One of the earliest and most obvious symptoms of this particular crisis was an inflationary erosion of the value of the dollar. The agents of this erosion were initially corporations themselves, who responded to the slowing of profitability by raising prices, by making commodities more expensive. What was initially devalued, in other words, were not the commodities themselves but the dollars with which those commodities were purchased. But the agents of this form of devaluation would soon include not only individual firms but also, through the very monetary policy facilitated by Keynesianism, the U.S. government. And the state's inflationary response was itself further reinforced by international pressure on the United States to devalue the dollar. And in this way, the devaluation of the dollar ultimately signified U.S. Fordism's global devaluation. On the one hand, the United States was the definitive global economic giant during the fifties and early sixties, so much so that it could commit, through the Marshall Plan, to massive state-sponsored investment in securing capital's future by rebuilding the infrastructure of other national economies, primarily in Europe and Japan. The advanced capitalist regions of the globe soon included European and Japanese variations on Fordism itself. This international relationship was enforced by U.S. military power and institutionalized in the 1944 Bretton Woods agreement, which recognized the U.S. financial domination of the globe by turning the dollar into the world's reserve currency and tying global economic development to U.S. monetary policy.[40]

But by the late sixties, given Europe's and Japan's younger, less capital-intensive versions of Fordism, with their lower wages and greater capacity for technological innovation, U.S. capital found itself in competition with the very countries whose forces and relations of production it had played an indispensable role in rebuilding. Internal demand in Europe and Japan reached a saturation point at roughly the same time this happened in the

United States, as, beginning around the mid-sixties, the social demand Fordism had so successfully managed finally began to decline, as markets became increasingly congested with the durables Fordism had so efficiently produced. Underconsumption began in its turn to fuel an unprecedented international import/export competition that wreaked havoc with the national protectionism on which the Fordist boom depended. The U.S. government's devaluation of the dollar vis-à-vis the national currencies of Europe and Japan was in this respect also an attempt to make U.S. goods cheaper for foreign consumers, relative to the goods produced in their own nations, an effort to help U.S. firms make inroads into European and Japanese markets. This strategy also made U.S. imports more expensive, further eroding the capital-labor compact and Fordism's consumption-based mode of regulation: financial life became yet more difficult for U.S. workers, who now faced increasing prices at home as well as relatively little access to goods imported from elsewhere, goods that were now more expensive given the higher value of currency in those other countries vis-à-vis the dollar. In the course of these mutually reinforcing, domestic and global developments, devaluation finally made the Bretton Woods agreement impossible to sustain; it was dissolved in 1973, a development implying a global recognition that the United States no longer had the financial wherewithal to dominate global capitalism. U.S. dependence on imports would double by 1980.[41]

These developments provide another way in which to read Joe's trashing of his costume, a mass commodity that is also a metonym for this faltering regime of accumulation. Though inflation immediately made mass commodities more, not less, expensive, devaluation was a symptom of a crisis of accumulation that was ultimately international in scope. National monetary policy, one of the hallmarks of Fordism as it developed in the United States, in devaluing the dollar relative to other national currencies, ultimately undermined Fordism itself, along with U.S. financial domination of global capital. These are the terms in which what Joe experiences, and what the film figures more broadly, as a general shift in the social valuation of the cowboy, is both a sexual transvaluation and an economic devaluation. The film's narrative of deterritorialization figures these two interpretive horizons together, both of them indicative, as I have tried to suggest, of the crisis of a specific, national aggregation of state and corporate power. As was the case in my discussions, in earlier chapters, of Lukács and Marcuse—at this stage in the book I see no point in not giving away the ending—my final objective in this chapter is to read the reification/totality dialectic against these historically specific developments. Rather than reading this text through the lens provided by Jameson's allegorical hermeneutic, I will read this hermeneutic itself through the lens, as it were, of this text, and in terms of the simultaneously national and global horizons in which I have situated it.

RETHINKING ALLEGORY

Midnight Cowboy's narrative deterritorialization of the cowboy has a figural relation, then, to the contemporaneous historical developments I have highlighted: the gradual congealing and increasing visibility of a national gay male formation, and the uniformity and subsequent crisis of a Fordist regime of accumulation. The most familiar contemporary example of a Marxian, critical interpretive practice that emphasizes the role of figuration is the allegorical practice elaborated by Jameson. For Jameson as for Lukács, "interpretation" refers to a practice that seeks to elucidate conceptually the systemic character of capitalist social relations, a systemic character those social relations themselves actively obscure. The interpretive practice I have enacted in the preceding sections differs from Jameson's in ways that will surely be obvious to readers familiar with his work. This very divergence is intended to raise certain questions about that work. Jameson also shares with Lukács a representation of totality thinking as an "aspiration." In his discussion of conspiracy films in *The Geopolitical Aesthetic,* for instance, films that he characterizes in terms of a totalizing intention, he points out explicitly that it is this intention that is important, "rather than the definitive verisimilitude of this or that conspiratorial hypothesis."[42] In this respect, his work acknowledges that totality thinking posits a certain abstract totality that is abstract precisely in its necessary, historically conditioned exclusion of certain social phenomena. Such an exercise, as Jameson puts it, citing Sartre, is always a "partial summing up":[43] it is nothing more than the necessarily limited attempt to think an objectively, positively totalizing mode of production's complex relations of determination with other levels of the social, an exercise that will inevitably be marked by limitations dictated, at a minimum, by the historical specificity of the exercise. Jameson has emphasized the way in which the necessary abstraction of such an exercise is also a product of the abstraction of the concepts it brings to bear—just as Marx does, this book's introduction argued, in his elaboration of his own method in the *Grundrisse*. In the present context, one example in particular of Jameson's defense of this critical employment of abstraction is worth quoting:

> If historical abstraction . . . is something not given in immediate experience, then it is pertinent to worry about the potential confusion of this concept with the thing itself, and about the possibility of taking its abstract "representation" for reality, of "believing" in the substantive existence of abstract entities such as Society or Class. . . . In the long run there is probably no way of marking a representation so securely *as* representation that such optical illusions are permanently forestalled. . . . Permanent revolution in intellectual life and culture means that impossibility, and the necessity for a constant reinvention of precautions against what my tradition calls conceptual reification. . . . What is needed is . . . the renewal of historical analysis itself, and the tireless reexamination and diagnosis of the political and ideological functionality of the concept, the part it has suddenly come to play in the imaginary resolutions of our real contradictions.[44]

The present study—an effort, again, to grapple with the conceptual reification of reification itself—aspires, as its introduction emphasized, to maintain just this kind of historical critique of abstract categories. To critique Marxian concepts like reification from a queer, historically situated vantage is to critique these concepts from within a history of a certain kind of formation specific to capitalist social relations themselves. Because what follows is a discussion of a certain "conceptual reification" consistently at work in Jameson's allegorical hermeneutic, I want first to underscore not only the necessary openness of any particular hermeneutic of totality to subsequent critical scrutiny, but also that Jameson himself has, as consistently as any practitioner of the form of totality thinking this book considers, emphasized the importance of recognizing the ease with which concepts are hypostatized.

Before addressing the "conceptual reification" of reification itself in Jameson's work, we have to consider the status of another category that plays a central role in his interpretive practice. Especially as Marxist theoreticians go, Jameson, like Marcuse, is by no means inattentive to sexuality.

Throughout his work, sexual desire holds a privileged place precisely in its special capacity to allegorize broader and ultimately global processes of social transformation. This representation of sexuality as a figure is basic to the hermeneutic he develops in relation to literary narrative, for example, where he identifies the political unconscious of immediately private operations at work in the novel.[45] But Jameson has also consistently emphasized the need to articulate the "new social movements" with a broader socialist politics and has devoted more than a little attention to theorizing the relations between these specific movements and this "other" socialist imperative. His reading of *History and Class Consciousness* as an "unfinished project" is only one example. On another occasion, Jameson considers queer political imperatives in particular, localizing them and referring to gay promiscuity as "the badge and sign of microgroup behavior";[46] his point is that this "local" pursuit of tabooed pleasure is a figure for the very objective of Marxist praxis in the broad sense, socialism's critique of the radical unpleasure capital produces. It is not necessary to disagree with this too easily neglected way of characterizing Marxism's best utopian impulses to insist also that, from a queer perspective, this localization of a queer pursuit of pleasure is hard to take seriously, the irreducibly social, public practice of gay promiscuity being also an inherently political practice precisely insofar as there is nothing remotely "local" or "micro" about the normalization of heterosexual desire this practice critiques, arguably by definition. It is precisely the *totality* of heterosexual desire's social normalization that this figural localization of gay sexual/social/political practice abstracts out of the totality it would discern. The part played by sexuality in Jameson's exercises in thinking totality begins here to look a lot like what we found in Marcuse: a representation of sexual desire per se—and, in Jameson's case, also of gay politics—as a figure for something else, something more consequential, more pressing.

This conceptualization of sexuality is a direct product of the way Jameson conceptualizes reification. Jameson situates the sexual on the terrain of immediacy, emphasizing that Lukácsian estrangement of the subjective from the objective, a general "incommensurability" in advanced capitalist regions of the globe, as he puts it in *The Political Unconscious*, "between the private and the public, the psychological and the social, the poetic and the political."[47] This incommensurability, in other words, is ultimately symptomatic of the intensely fragmented totality of capitalist social relations that the concept of reification aspires to grasp, an incommensurability that only becomes more difficult to critique as those relations develop and this differentiation becomes more complex. The critical employment of sexuality as figure is a response within Jameson's work to the difficulty within capital of situating personal experience in relation to the social whole that capital mystifies, a response to capital's cordoning off of what a dialectical perspective would reveal to be in fact continuous. If sexuality is here most saliently a figure for the public, the social, the political, this is a result of Jameson's insistence on the importance of understanding reification's obscuring of the social itself, its privatization of experience in general. This objective impasse within capitalist social relations is exemplified for Jameson by what he has called the persistent epistemological impasse between Freud and Marx.

Sexuality's continuity with the social is undoubtedly obscured by capital. It is also obscured by Jameson's method. Part of the problem here, especially from the perspective of a queer critical practice that still takes seriously Foucault's critique of Freud, is the Freudian vocabulary, however critically appropriated, with which Jameson consistently theorizes sexuality—or, as he is more likely to put it, the "libidinal." While *The Political Unconscious* emphasizes that reification is a condition of possibility for psychoanalysis, Jameson also acknowledges in this same text that a rigorously dialectical development of this insight "would requires us radically to historicize Freudianism itself."[48] And an undeniably radical historicization of Freudianism that, as suggested in chapter 1, a Marxian perspective can further radicalize is the same critique offered by Foucault, where he emphasizes that sexuality has been anything but private, that on the contrary social, institutional, "public" knowledge both produced and mystified the very concept of sexuality, and that in the last century Freudianism has exemplified this production as no other discourse has. But Foucault, for his part, is so concerned to emphasize the objective normalization of bodies *by* knowledge that he obscures the production—by agents, by historically situated laboring subjects—*of* this same knowledge. While Foucault's analysis certainly demystifies the objective operation of these knowledge regimes, it also reinforces the mystification of their status as social labor's highly mediated products. Where Foucault's famous anti-Hegelianism is evident, then, in a certain prioritizing of object over subject, Jameson's famous Hegelianism is evident in his recapitulation of Lukács's methodological prioritizing of subject over object, his tendency to obscure the unpredictable multiplicity of reification's objective results. Though this obscuring is certainly not what it is in Lukács,[49] it is evident in his erasure of the social, entirely "public" institutional normalization of sexuality. Jameson has remarked that "cognitive mapping" was ultimately a "code word for class consciousness":[50] in the context of what I think needs to be characterized as a heroic effort to emphasize the importance of totality thinking in the face of a certain pervasive hypostatization of difference, this indispensable critical emphasis on consciousness's epistemological capacity nonetheless operates at the cost of erasing the complexity of reification's objective social, historical, and epistemological repercussions. In the course of this erasure we lose any sense of the extent to which the social and relatively "total" character of the opposition between heterosexuality and homosexuality gives the lie to this representation of desire's airtight privatization. Even as Jameson acknowledges that reification is a condition of possibility for the Freudian hermeneutic he critically appropriates, his work also participates, with Marcuse, in the historically specific reification of desire Freudianism exemplifies.

To what extent, then, does the irreducibly social character of sexual knowledge require us to rethink also the aspiration to totality Jameson practices, given that his hermeneutic's privileged allegorical vehicle is, repeatedly, an unproblematically privatized sexuality? Jameson's restriction of the sexual to the terrain of immediacy (its own variation, we might say, on Marxian-Freudianism, especially given the hermeneutic centrality in Jameson of the category of the unconscious) methodologically preempts from the beginning any recognition that sexuality is irreducibly social, historical, and political.

Recall that Jameson's ultimate horizon of interpretation, as he unfolds it in *The Political Unconscious*, for example, is an uneven, overlapping sequence of modes of production he identifies with "History" as such, though he certainly specifies a range of phenomena mediating this ultimate interpretive or "semantic" horizon. It is the final horizon of three, the first two noting, respectively, "political history, in the narrow sense of punctual event and a chroniclelike sequence of happenings in time; then of society, in the now already less diachronic and time-bound sense of a constitutive tension and struggle between social classes," shorter-term horizons that intervene between individual, "libidinal" experience and

"History."[51] What this implies in the present context, initially and most obviously, is the need for a substantial multiplication of interpretive or semantic horizons and an accounting for a much broader range of differentiation and mediation. We would have to account for the objective historical impact of reification itself, including that objective sexual normalization of bodies, especially the normalizing production of new kinds of sexual subjectivity. We would have to include, further, social and political practices and formations that presuppose these developments as conditions of possibility, including political practices, like gay liberation or ACT UP, which strive to articulate a subjectivity that is as sexually radical as it is socially radical. While sexuality is never allegorical tenor rather than allegorical vehicle within Jameson's hermeneutic, I have suggested that sexuality operates in *Midnight Cowboy* in precisely this way. At the most obvious, overt level of the film's plot, *Midnight Cowboy* is indeed a story about the private needs and desires of two lonely protagonists. But the film's narrative deterritorialization of the cowboy is also an allegorical vehicle figuring sexuality as an objective, historical interpretive horizon: specifically, a collective working of the homosexual weakness in the norm of masculinity that is inseparable from the coalescence of a national gay male formation, a socialization of sex and a sexualization of the social. If this reading of *Midnight Cowboy* resists the unqualified privatization of sexuality Jameson imputes to the capitalist mode of production, it does so at least in part because of the historically pivotal refusal of gay men to remain isolated, "private," "underground," during the period in question.

I have also suggested that *Midnight Cowboy*'s homosexualization and urbanization of the cowboy have a metonymic relation with this conjuncture, including a devaluation of mass consumption and thus the ultimately global devaluation of Fordism itself; what the film trashes, for example, it also marks as a distinctly Fordist commodity. And the film does not only figure the crisis of a Fordist mode of regulation; it was itself a commodity pitched to a countercultural audience. In response to Jameson's rethinking of allegory, I intend this specifically metonymic figuration to suggest a form allegorical interpretation should take given reification's multiple and unpredictable objective impact, especially given sexuality's broad socialization. Though Jameson does not explicitly frame allegory in relation to the category of metaphor, that figure typically opposed to metonymy, allegory does assume strongly metaphorical implications in his hermeneutic: it serves to make connections, to assert unity and, yes, identity in response to capital's radical differentiation of the social. Though I intend this reading of *Midnight Cowboy* to emphasize the critical power of figuration as a reading strategy, I also intend the operation of metonymy in this reading to suggest the way in which sexuality and capital are more closely, contiguously, and contingently connected by relations of determination than Jameson's situating of sexuality at the greatest possible distance from the horizon of "History" would suggest. These metonymic figurations convey the ways in which sexuality is *not* cordoned off from the social and historical, but is complexly entangled with it at a range of levels.

The interpretive horizon at which we should situate sexuality in this context is itself highly unpredictable: I would identify that interpretive horizon as *national.* The implication of this chapter's argument I want most to emphasize in conclusion is that *Midnight Cowboy's* narrative of deterritorialization serves as an example of what Jameson has called national allegory. His argument about national allegory complicates his model of allegorical interpretive practice by insisting on the relative importance of the national as a mediating category in the literature of the so-called Third World, that this literature tends consciously to allegorize the social and historical in national terms. In contrast, First World texts do this, Jameson argues, only at an "unconscious" level.[52] It would be reasonable enough to respond to Jameson's essay, as many others have, that texts produced in economically and politically dominant nations can also take the form of national allegory: even in these regions of the globe the nation can never simply be taken for granted or consigned to the "unconscious." Here again the problem I would highlight is the tendency to represent the advanced capitalist world in terms of an absolute cordoning off of the "public" and the "private," the "social" and the "libidinal," Jameson's suggestion even that within late capitalism the social as such can only ever be "unconscious." As Michael Moon's reading emphasizes, *Midnight Cowboy* is quite consciously about America, about Vietnam, and about the increasing national visibility of a gay male formation. And as I mentioned previously, the emerging gay male formation the film allegorizes was historically overdetermined by a global wave of decolonization and national liberation struggle, a wave "brought home" most palpably by the Vietnam War. While it would be hard to overstate the importance of Jameson's emphasis on the violent intrusion of the national into the consciousness of nations that have suffered imperial or colonial violence and domination (generalized though it may be) one of the issues this chapter has considered is the perhaps less insistent intrusion of the national into the texts of globally hegemonic nations—especially when those nations find themselves in a contradictory rather than continuous relation with what lies beyond their borders, when they are directly confronted with a national liberation strug- gle elsewhere that makes it harder to mystify their own imperial or colo- nial (or neoimperial or neocolonial) ambitions.

But a national mediation of a gay male politics of liberation as well as a more general emergent gay male formation did not operate only at the level of strong identification with these struggles. To Moon's specification of the ways *Midnight Cowboy* is about America, I have added that it is also about Fordist mass consumption itself. The film's status as a national alle- gory is most importantly the product of the simultaneous legitimation and structural crises of a specific, national regime of accumulation and its attendant mode of regulation. Again, what distinguishes Fordism from the intensive regime of accumulation that emerged in the United States between the wars is precisely the central role assumed by the nation-state in the ultimately global managing of capital. And in the case of the narra- tive of deterritorialization this chapter has considered, it is an historically specific impasse between the national and the global that intervenes most consequentially between the interpretive horizons of sexuality and capital, between the complex historical repercussions of the reification of desire and an unfolding failure in the managing of accumulation. Sexuality, accu- mulation, and the nation-state closely mediate each other here; this late sixties, national-global impasse is the interpretive horizon at which *both* sexuality and capital have to be located in this instance. This is especially the case inasmuch as the emergence into national visibility of a gay male formation is, as I have argued, a dimension of the more general legitima- tion crisis of Fordism's mode of regulation. The cognitive mappings of both sexuality and capital here demand attention to this same "interme- diate" level. This national form of mediation implies another way of figur- ing not just sexuality but capital itself within a hermeneutic of totality; it implies an aspiration to totality emphasizing not only capital's mystifying power but its objectively contradictory, historically embedded develop- ment and the gargantuan amounts of social labor and class struggle that any managing of capital's crisis tendencies will require. Here again, one of the more important lessons of regulation theory is that capital is significantly more volatile than Jameson—or Marcuse, or Lukács, or the discourse of reification generally—tends to suggest.

This chapter has continued a movement from an emphasis on reification to an emphasis on totality begun in the previous chapter, a return to the aspiration to totality that emerges from within the process of reification, by asking what form a critique of mystifying differentiation might take if it tried to account for objective historical effects of the reification of sexual desire. But what about the queer aspiration to totality with which the introduction to this book began? How might we understand the social and practical knowledge queer formations can develop in relation to the social and practical knowledge that reification's subjective moment—which for Lukács is the social vantage of the proletariat—demands? My concluding chapter asks these questions by turning to the subsequent national fallout of Fordism's legitimation and accumulation crises.

chapter 5

NOTES ON A QUEER HORIZON:
DAVID WOJNAROWICZ AND THE
VIOLENCE OF NEOLIBERALISM

The previous chapter tried to suggest some of the ways in which, at a
key moment in the ongoing negotiation of accumulation crisis, capital has
mediated the conditions of possibility for, and the gradual consolidation
of, what we might from a contemporary vantage call a queer social formation. Though just how to characterize the forms of social regulation that
have emerged in the wake of Fordism is a topic of persistent debate, an
increasingly central trend in queer studies over the last decade or so has
been to understand this regulatory conjuncture in terms of the set of state
and corporate policies and normalized social practices called neoliberalism.
Among my objectives here will be to examine neoliberalism from within
a contemporary queer vantage while also emphasizing its status as a product of the crisis of Fordism considered in the previous chapter.

With these objectives in mind, we can make an initial distinction between Fordist and neoliberal forms of social regulation by underscoring
the contradiction between a Fordist regime in which, on the heels of a
depression and a world war, accumulation becomes highly dependent on
the corporate and governmental construction of a certain kind of social
stability, and a neoliberal response to the breakup of Fordism that makes
accumulation increasingly dependent on social *instability.* Fordism prioritized the long-term sustainability of profit making and the containment
of capital's defining tendency toward crisis through a broad and unprecedented state management of accumulation. It presupposed, in other words,
the tendency of unregulated accumulation to falter and emphasized not

short-term profitability but the reproduction of conditions amenable to accumulation over the long term. This meant reproducing the labor force through strategies such as the mass commodification of leisure time and the capital-labor compact that made this commodification possible, as well as a range of entitlement programs including welfare and broad government subsidy of education. Neoliberal state and corporate policy has responded to the crisis of Fordism by prioritizing accumulation over the short term and by making the broad social volatility this crisis reintroduced into a central source of profit. The neoliberal state in the United States and elsewhere is increasingly less able to contain capital's most socially destructive tendencies. This state is the product of the contradiction between the national and the global, highlighted in the previous chapter, that emerged from within Fordism itself.

But far from representing some simple erosion of the nation-state's regulatory power, this relatively new state form remains a powerfully consequential social agent, normalizing social life in terms consistent with the logic of an increasingly global private sector, just as actively as the Fordist-Keynesian state had reined in many of the most brutal tendencies of that sector. Neoliberalism, as Wendy Brown puts it, "involves a normative rather than ontological claim about the pervasiveness of economic rationality and advocates the institution building, policies, and discourse development appropriate to such a claim." Far from referring only to a set of discourses produced by conservative economists like Milton Friedman, for example, discourses that naturalize the market and maintain that government intervention artificially hampers its capacities, neoliberalism is instead "constructed—organized by law and political institutions, and requiring political intervention and orchestration." A neoliberal social logic is one in which "the withdrawal of the state from certain domains and the privatization of certain state functions does not amount to a dismantling of government but, rather, constitutes a technique of governing."[1] Market logic is here a logic the state is compelled to institute and normalize.

Within this new stage in the governmental facilitation of capital accumulation, social volatility—what may indeed look, against a Fordist background, like chronic accumulation crisis—itself becomes increasingly central to profit making, in, for example, the hugely profitable expansion of a social logic of risk that Randy Martin has called the financialization of daily life.[2] The ever wider and deeper expansion of market logic into social regions previously managed in an effort to restrain that logic, an expansion actively facilitated by the state, also expands the horizons of capital's social destructiveness. Actively dismantling what regulation theory sometimes calls the Fordist-Keynesian "institutional fix," the neoliberal state paradoxically imposes a form of social regulation that is also what the regulation theorists Adam Tickell and Jamie A. Peck have called "the *absence* of a new institutional fix."[3] Prioritizing a queer point of view, this chapter will emphasize the way in which Fordism's neoliberal sequel is one in which capital's predations are ever more broadly enlisted in the service of capital's expansion.

A key aspect of the neoliberal state's corrosive power has been the ubiquitous constellation of discourses and practices that goes by the name *privatization,* a broad social renegotiation of the opposition between public and private most widely evident within a U.S. national frame, perhaps, in policy initiatives determined to privatize aspects of the Keynesian welfare state. But privatization, which David Harvey has called U.S. neoliberalism's "cutting edge" both domestically and abroad,[4] also has far wider social implications. A neoliberal form of privatization has been brought to bear, for example, on the same queer social formations that, like that ever more nationally visible gay male formation I discussed in the previous chapter, have gradually emerged in the course of Fordism's rise and fall. Among the effects of capital's profitable forms of destruction in the neoliberal moment is an atomizing dispersal of such formations that has taken a number of different state and corporate forms I will consider here. I have already emphasized the way in which, as I put it in my introduction, queer formations have had among their conditions of possibility the ever more complex internal differentiation of capitalist social relations, in particular a reification of sexual desire that had among its forms a broad social opposition between homosexual and heterosexual subjectivity. In the period under consideration in this final chapter, the very form of queer sociality that Fordism and its crisis facilitated, even as it is enriched by an increasing recognition of its internal racial and ethnic differentiation, now also suffers another, reactionary form of internal differentiation in the interests of capital accumulation. The neoliberal period is one in which, from one perspective, capital has entered a qualitatively new stage without precedent, a stage in which capital is defined as never before by the dizzying, increasingly abstract, ever more global heights of financial speculation.

The same period, from a certain queer vantage, looks instead like one of violent social retrenchment.

The Marxian dialectic of reification and totality, I have contended, has failed to provide a sufficiently historical account of the same horizon of sexuality that it has also, in Marcuse and Jameson, aspired to grasp. This failure, as I proposed in the previous two chapters, is especially a failure to register a history of social formations articulated in opposition to compulsory heterosexuality. But the fundamental framing of so much prominent work in queer studies by the discourse of the public sphere indicates the extent to which queer negotiations of the public, both practical and theoretical, by definition perform a critique of the privatization of sexual intimacy capital has persistently both normalized and disrupted.[5] The privatization of sexuality on which this chapter focuses takes the form of a distinctly punitive reaction against those forms of queer sociality which emerged into broad visibility in the course of Fordism's crisis, a form of reaction that is itself an aspect of a broader neoliberal assault on social collectivity as such.

The queer aspiration to totality to which I referred early in this book's introduction, an aspiration that has characterized queer critical practice since its emergence in the nineties, takes the form of an ever more internally contentious and differentiated critique of sexuality's epistemological particularization in a range of social narratives and knowledges. But this chapter will elaborate a distinct, though not unrelated, aspiration that is also a form of sociality, a praxis disclosing what neoliberal privatization would occlude, and what even the aspirations to totality we have seen in the work of Marcuse and Jameson occlude, notwithstanding their efforts to do the opposite: the inseparability of the sexual from the social.[6] This chapter's primary objective is to suggest the ways in which a distinctly queer vantage on neoliberalism and its repercussions has taken the form of such an aspiration, one that both converges with, and provides a critical perspective on, the aspirations to totality considered in previous chapters. Contemporary queer scholarship sometimes refers to what I am calling queer social formations as instances of queer worldmaking; if the term *formations* emphasizes an objective complex of social practices, the term *worldmaking* emphasizes by contrast the subjective capacities of those practices. Worldmaking refers to the historically embedded production of practical and critical knowledges, the production for example of forms of sexual intimacy irreducible to, and operating in negative relation with, the normalizing privatization of sexual intimacy. I contend that worldmaking, as the term itself already suggests, refers to the production of historically and socially situated, bounded totalities of queer praxis inherently critical of the ultimately global horizon of neoliberalized capital itself. This chapter will consider the various critiques performed by this queer aspiration to totality: critiques of contemporary forms of sexual privatization, of capital in its neoliberal stage, and of the form taken by totality thinking in the Marxian work this book has considered. These three lines of critique converge in the text with which this study concludes: David Wojnarowicz's *Close to the Knives,* that harrowing memoir of the first wholesale crisis of a queer-hating neoliberalism, the murderous government indifference to the AIDS epidemic as it emerged in the eighties.

DISPERSALS

Capital famously begins from the point of view of the most immediate experience of capitalist social relations, relations that appear at first as nothing more than an "immense collection of commodities."[7] Gay politics in the current neoliberal conjuncture—though "politics" is ultimately the wrong word altogether—itself looks at first glance like precisely this kind of chaotic collection of formal equivalents. The difficulty here lies in distinguishing between the relatively immediate horizon of these "politics," resolutely and normatively identitarian as they are, and the horizon of the commodity itself. But of course this is less a difficulty than an impossibility: this is a horizon of interchangeably gay citizen-subjects—"dead" citizen-subjects, as Lauren Berlant puts it[8]—that identifies equality with equivalence. But it is also a historically specific horizon that positions lesbians and gays as what Paul Smith has called subjects of value, subjects whose rights the post-Keynesian state takes care to limit to rights consistent with neoliberalism's intensified normalization of ownership and consumption.[9] Corporate-funded periodicals marketed to lesbian and gay consumers dote on innocuous celebrities and are hailed as the agents of a national and indeed global visibility that itself, we are to understand, represents some kind of political victory. Meanwhile, genuinely radical queer movements like ACT UP, the Lesbian Avengers, or Sex Panic!, movements that in various ways have taken issue with the neoliberal variation on this identitarian logic, have also been largely excluded from the capital-intensive terms of visibility, a visibility that is not historically insignificant so much as "normatively constrained," as Eric Clarke has put it.[10] David Harvey points out that the neoliberal terms of political action, such as they are, tend to be "defined and articulated through non-elected (and in many instances elite-led) advocacy groups for various kinds of rights,"[11] and indeed the most broadly visible lesbian and gay "movements" since the early nineties have been civil rights lobbies like the Human Rights Campaign and the Gay and Lesbian Alliance against Defamation (GLAAD), organizations that prioritize assimilation, privatization, and fund-raising; have more than made their peace with the neoliberal state; and demand the rights to marry and serve in the military, as well as "positive" (i.e., normalized, unthreatening) images of gay life. In the era of what Michael Warner calls "post-liberationist privatization," barely visible sexually radical movements like those just mentioned refuse this privatizing isolation of the sexual from the social, a vision of civil rights that, as Warner puts it, tends to take the sex out of homosexual.[12] The citizens these lobbies propose to speak for are then not merely equivalent citizens but equivalently desexualized citizens, and the agenda they pursue begins to look a lot like the embrace of a closet that pretends not to be. The most prominent national gay spokespeople, a familiar list of names including Larry Kramer, Gabriel Rotello, Andrew Sullivan, Bruce Bauer, and Michelangelo Signorile, define the fight against homophobia as a fight for a sanitized, innocuous right to privacy, a mainstreaming agenda that Lisa Duggan has influentially called "the new homonormativity."[13]

This same desexualizing "collection of commodities" also operates in ways that do not even pretend to be political. Even the overtly sexualized appeal to newly legitimate gay consumers can be strangely asexual. For example, the increasingly unambiguous sexual objectification of the male body in visual advertising since the eighties emerged in part as the result of the decision by a number of corporations and ad agencies to begin targeting the gay market, largely in response to readership surveys done in 1977 and 1980 for the *Advocate* by the marketing firm Walker and Struman Research Inc. The stereotypical image of the privileged white gay male with an excess of disposable income originated as a result of these surveys, surveys that limited the data, obviously, to the *Advocate*'s predominantly privileged, white gay male readership. As Danae Clark pointed out in her important reading of this set of developments, such ads began to reach gay audiences through the mainstream media by way of a marketing strategy called "window advertising": appealing to gay consumers in ways that are sexual but not too sexual, ways intended to avoid alienating straight consumers.[14] Of the kind of ad that has become so routine to U.S. consumers since the eighties—typically black-and-white images featuring models from Olympic pole vaulter Tom Hintinauss to Mark Wahlberg (formerly Marky Mark) to a host of similarly sculpted models whose names may be less familiar—the *Advocate*'s publisher Peter Frisch said as early as 1982 that "you have to be comatose not to realize that it appeals to gay men."[15]

But does some variation on window advertising persist even here? What is the nature of this appeal? Sam Shahid, who was director of Calvin Klein's in-house advertising agency and involved in ad design for the company from 1981 to 1991, including the ad featuring Hintinauss, the first of Klein's underwear ads to receive broad media attention (in part because the campaign was the first to include a five-story version in Times Square), remarked that this photograph was taken "from below, looking up . . . so it made him very majestic, bigger than God."[16] To state the obvious—that the profitably chiseled, airbrushed male body has indeed become a commodity fetish in Marx's sense—is also to say (apparently for Shahid as well as for Marx) that this body is "a very strange thing, abounding in metaphysical subtleties and theological niceties," an object partaking of "the misty realm of religion," "a thing which transcends sensuousness":[17] a value, in other words, a thing that transcends the kind of concrete sensory interaction with other human beings Marx associates with the category of use value. It is important to remember that use value is no narrowly utilitarian category for Marx but a category that refers to the qualitative, concrete, material specificity that is value's opposite, that value "transcends," that contradicts quantitative interchangeability. If this particular commodity, this profitably sculpted male body, could speak—to paraphrase the subjunctively rendered proposition with which Marx concludes his discussion of commodity fetishism—it would say that it has nothing to do with the sensory or sensuous, certainly nothing whatever to do with anything as concrete as physical contact, and everything to do with value, that its meaning lies in its operation within a system of formal exchange.[18] This is another way of saying that this commodity would sound a lot like the typical fantasy man from Andrew Holleran's classic fictional account of

unquenchable desire: "He wanted to keep his life in the realm of the perfect, the ideal. He wanted to be desired, not possessed, for in remaining
desired he remained, like the figure on the Grecian urn, forever pursued. He knew quite well that once possessed he would no longer be en-
chanted—so sex itself became secondary to the spectacle."[19]

The desexualization that constitutes the normalizing terms of this contemporary visibility, and even this abstract, Calvin Klein–wearing body,
becomes more apparent when we move beyond the way in which sexuality seems everywhere framed by contemporary commodity logic, to the
other, less visible side of the commodity's mystification of the social, and
try to locate the forms of sensuous, physical contact this logic elides.
Where is the sex secondary to this spectacle? Where, for that matter, is
the sociality secondary to this spectacle? The contradictory other side of
the formal equivalence of commodity fetishism is found here again in capital's dispersal of the social, though what is most crucial in this case is not
the division of social labor this formal equivalence classically presupposes.
What lies behind this sheen of interchangeable identities and airbrushed
bodies is a horizon of genuinely collective queer movement, as well as the
distinctly neoliberal prospect of its disappearance. During the nineties, for
example, this kind of social contradiction became perhaps easier to see
than usual, at least from a perspective we have to call queer rather than
gay: even as homoerotically titillating, gigantic Calvin Klein underwear ads
hovered in the air nearby, the municipal government of New York City
successfully shut down most sites of public sex in the area around Times
Square.[20] For a number of important interventions in the last decade of
queer studies, this and similar developments are pivotal and have implications far beyond the specific sexual geography of Times Square. Central to
this work has been an emphasis on the importance of sustaining contemporary collective queer formations in the face of a moralizing, normalizing,
and distinctly neoliberal threat to their very existence.

The Disneyfication of Times Square was part of a larger set of developments that included, for example, the zoning ordinance aggressively
pushed by the Giuliani administration and passed by the New York City
Council in 1995, an ordinance that forbade adult businesses from operating within five hundred feet of schools, churches, residential areas, and
other such businesses. As Lauren Berlant and Michael Warner point out
in one of the earlier critical accounts of this development, such ordinances

directly threaten the maintenance of any visible, accessible collective queer world, worlds like the area around Christopher Street; as they put it, "not all of the thousands who migrate or make pilgrimages to Christopher street use the porn shops, but all benefit from the fact that some do. After a certain point, a quantitative change becomes a qualitative change. A critical mass develops. The street becomes queer. It develops a dense, publicly accessible sexual culture." Given the historical embeddedness of gay male formations in the United States, for example, within a history of consumption—always, until recently, local and marginal if not marginally legal circuits of consumption, like those recounted in the previous chapter—the effects of closing and or dispersing these small businesses extend far beyond the businesses themselves. The local commercialization of sex, in spaces like pornographic bookstores, bars, and clubs, has been fundamental to the sustaining of queer formations: this is, for instance, how gay men "have learned to find each other; to map a commonly accessible world; to construct the architecture of queer space in a homophobic environment." What these developments directly threaten are forms of queer social life that have been "accessible, available to memory, and sustained through collective activity."[21] Here again, as in the previous chapter, capital's moment of consumption has been fundamental to, a kind of material substratum for, the development of a range of queer formations. And in both cases the publicizing of pornography, not identity, is a basis for the constitution of queer sociality.

Social policies like this zoning law only reinforce the privatization of sex already inherent in the neoliberal logic of lesbian and gay rights to property and consumption; they threaten not an identity but a world of inherently critical practices and knowledges that directly contradict identity's glossy normalization. The publicly accessible queer worlds that neoliberalism threatens have a negative, determinate relation to these desexualizing articulations of identity. The socially radical character of these worlds abides precisely in the refusal they practice of the very distinction between the sexual and the social, practices critically disclosing this distinction as a mystifying fiction. Duggan usefully glosses the ways in which various movements against compulsory heterosexuality have negotiated the ever shifting divide between private and public since the fifties. Homophile movements expanded the space of personal privacy, insisting on the right not to have one's privacy invaded, the right not to be subject to surveillance, entrapment, or other forms of policing. Gay liberation, refusing to settle for this kind of closeted isolation, then insisted not simply on individual and personal privacy but on the importance of sustaining a collective, accessible, resolutely public gay world, including the public distribution of the kinds of media that could form and inform that world, like those the 1995 zoning ordinance sought to disperse.[22] Gay liberation insisted, indeed, on a radical movement beyond even these limits into a total re-imagining of the social as such, a reimagining ACT UP, in its distinctive way, also insisted on, in its analysis of the murderous indifference of cor-porate and governmental power, for example. It has become precisely a collective, queer social life, a queer public, which the neoliberal wave of privatization has undermined.

And this threat to queer social formations is part of a broader neoliberal attack on those movements that have the legitimation crisis of Fordism—"the sixties"—as one of their most salient, if increasingly distant, contexts. Just as post-Fordist production tends to isolate workers from each other rather than concentrating them on the factory shop floors that character-ized Fordism, this spatial dispersal of a queer population should be under-stood as part of a more general strategy of population dispersal, a strategy that has among its objectives neutralizing the forms of collective praxis of which such populations are capable, privatizing collectivity itself out of existence. This attack has unfolded against a number of neoliberal trends legible in urban geography and familiar to radical scholars and critics of the urban. Following the deindustrialization and deregulatory policies with which U.S. corporations and the U.S. government responded to the crisis of Fordism, those same entities prioritized the accumulation of finance capital, in forms such as debt, rent, insurance, and land and real estate speculation.[23] Urban centers are now increasingly given over to financial services, closely managed spaces of consumption, "public-private partner-ships."[24] Especially in cities like New York, which have become central nodes in global financial networks, real estate has been increasingly dis-invested from small-scale businesses like the ones the zoning ordinance directly attacked, and given over instead to major corporate and consumer developments. If marginal, small-scale capital, like physique pictorials and local porn businesses, had in earlier decades tended to facilitate the emer-gence of queer forms of collectivity, now an ultimately global horizon of speculative capital threatens to eviscerate it.[25]

Critical work on urban space sometimes refers to the contemporary city as a fortress, a space that serves, like rising rates of imprisonment, to isolate and police a "surplus" population that a deindustrializing capitalism, a capitalism that tends to make money from money rather than, say, manufacturing, can increasingly do without. If neoliberalism represents, in contrast with Fordism, a conjuncture in which volatility itself becomes a source of profit, then the governmental policing and dispersal of "redundant" populations in metropolitan centers of accumulation is an effort to ensure that the social costs of this ongoing volatility—including forms of devaluation that are also sources of speculative gain—threaten the prospects of accumulation itself as little as possible. So police and private security forces protect valuable, gentrified urban property while secured skyway systems keep speculators and consumers separated from homeless populations as surely as "gated communities" segregate the affluent from low-income populations.[26] Neil Smith has suggestively referred to this city as a *revanchist* city, a term highlighting a crystallization of economic retrenchment and privatization on the one hand, and discourses of reaction against midcentury developments from the welfare state to the "new social movements" on the other. *Revanchism* underscores not only privatization's social violence but its fundamentally reactionary character, its punitive justification for that violence.[27] Smith uses the term with reference to the neoliberal restructuring of the built environment in particular, focusing, for instance, on the dispersal of New York's homeless population in the eighties and nineties. In contrast to the Keynesian-Fordist emphasis on the social reproduction designed to ensure the long-term prospects of accumulation, revanchism refers to a social reaction indicative of crisis, the "strangling of any radical life" that results from "an environmentalism gone corporate."[28]

The 1995 zoning ordinance has not by any means gone uncontested in the years since, as adult businesses have sought to exploit legal loopholes, for example,[29] but its results have been severe. Martin Manalansan has provided an account of the "spatial politics" of neoliberal New York that can also be read as a highly suggestive, if differently focused, update on Berlant and Warner's account from 1998.[30] Emphasizing the way in which the "free market" logic of contemporary gay rights has remained predicated on the social abjection of large swaths of "others," Manalansan provides an ethnographic study of the impact of this reorganization of the urban space of New York on queers of color especially, an account that considers extensions of this neoliberal logic since 9/11. He recounts, for example, the more recent fate of the area around the Christopher Street piers, a queer space of sex and sociality so powerful in the local and national queer imaginary, and long a gathering site for queer youth of color. This area has become the site of a cluster of condominiums and apartments advertised, among other places, in media pitched to wealthy gay consumers. It has also become an area assiduously protected by police, who congregate in great numbers around the time the bars close to make sure that those who don't live in the area quickly disperse. The area that had long been beyond the means of these groups has now become actively hostile toward them. This rare space that had become queer in a way that was not limited to property owners is now even more intensely privatized, increasingly rid of the "unwanted," a space that, for the queer youth of color whom Manalansan interviews, seems less and less to be theirs.

This analysis deftly juxtaposes policing in the defense of real estate value with the policing of the multiethnic and very queer Jackson Heights area of Queens and emphasizes the increasingly fearful mood that has resulted from governmental monitoring of the area that can be traced back at least as far as the Giuliani administration and is now additionally justified by a post-9/11 logic of national security. Immigration officials are a more noticeable presence; profiling, arrests, and the "rounding up" of Latino, black, South Asian, and Middle Eastern men have intensified; and ever more intimidated residents have as a result become less visible in the streets, driven away from the public areas where they used to congregate. The residents recount stories of the "disappearance" of long-familiar inhabitants of or visitors to this neighborhood; and the disappearance of public queer spaces has been one result of this intensified intimidation. Jackson Heights has in this account become a war zone. Manalansan underscores Jackson Heights' geographic and racial externality to moneyed white gay neighborhoods like Chelsea and notes that during the very period in which the area has been increasingly monitored, it has also been represented as a commodity for tourists from across the river, a place for moneyed urban gays to visit. Manalansan underscores the structural inseparability of the fear produced in areas like Jackson Heights and a practice of "private gay enterprise" taking the form of a kind of neocolonial tourism.[31] Here again normative gay consumption is inseparable from a less visible governmental dispersal of queer formations.

Manalansan's analysis also begins to suggest a possible queer understanding of the way in which the policing of populations in the United States since 9/11 extends a neoliberal social logic.[32] Though this is obviously a contested issue, a number of accounts of the intensely militarized post-9/11 conjuncture emphasize its continuity with a pre-9/11 "free market" neoliberalism.[33] Neoliberalism is sometimes contrasted with the neoconservative war on terror in terms of the divergence between the neoliberal objective of capitalizing on social disorder and the neoconservative objective of imposing social order (of imposing a "new American century," for example). But the new militarism can also be understood in terms of the forcible opening up of new horizons of profitable economic volatility, a violent supplementing of market forces. David Harvey remarks of this simultaneously neoliberal and militarized conjuncture that "the U.S. has given up on hegemony through consent and resorts more and more to domination through coercion," that neoconservatism has transformed "low-intensity warfare" into "dramatic confrontation."[34] Harvey defines this post-9/11 neoliberalism in terms of what he calls "accumulation by dispossession," which extends a history of forcible expropriation and enclosure as old as capital itself. With this term, Harvey emphasizes both what is distinctive about militarized neoliberalism and the way in which it is at the same time only the most recent variation on that form of socioeconomic violence that Marx situates at the birth of capitalism and calls primitive accumulation.[35] Harvey cites Hannah Arendt's contention that "the original sin of simple robbery . . . had eventually to be repeated lest the motor of accumulation suddenly die down": capital must always find new opportunities for investment if it is to negotiate successfully the prospect of accumulation crisis.[36] And it can actively manufacture these opportunities if they are not readily available, as in the familiar contemporary privatization of everything from water to state universities to strands of DNA to formerly nationalized Iraqi industries.

I want to suggest that the contemporary, "homonormative" privatizing of sexuality and the evisceration of queer social formations that accompanies it operate not only within a horizon of neoliberal accumulation, or within a horizon that includes forms of social policing that have become more prevalent in an age of endless war. Might we also understand the contemporary dispersal of queer formations by the neoliberal state, with its effect for instance of making Christopher Street less queer, as itself a form

of accumulation by dispossession, as part of this long history of expropriation definitive of capital itself, a history of violence that has always supplemented "hegemony through consent"? Real estate speculation, through
the buying up of devalued assets like the land that was formerly the site
of the Christopher Street piers, for example—investment that hopes to
generate demand for new condominiums and apartments, provided the
police are out in sufficient force to defend the investment—begins here
to look like a variation on the ongoing speculative raiding of the commons. This at least seems to be the case as far as the young queers of color
Manalansan interviews are concerned, who again feel less and less that the
area belongs to them, notwithstanding their continued efforts to claim it.
If by *queer world* we mean some kind of queer commons, some kind of
public, accessible social formation with some kind of infrastructure, however delicate, in areas like Christopher Street or Jackson Heights, areas
with a queer character both facilitated by local business and irreducible,
as Berlant, Warner, and Manalansan point out, to property ownership as
such—if this is what a term like *queer world* signifies, then the neoliberal
dispersal of that world begins to seem both radically new and just another
chapter in a very old story of dispossession.

TOTALITIES

Queer theory's discourse of worldmaking elaborates a form of collective,
critical labor. Berlant and Warner characterize those queer worldmaking
practices threatened with neoliberal erosion as a form of collective consciousness. These practices manifest "the radical aspirations of queer culture
building: . . . the changed possibilities of identity, intelligibility, culture,
sex, publics, that appear when the heterosexual couple is no longer the ref-
erent or the privileged example of sexual culture." They develop forms of
intimacy which "bear no necessary relation to domestic space, to kinship,
to the couple form, to property, or to the nation,"[37] which are irreducibly
social and experienced as such, which directly contradict the enforced segregation of the sexual from the social. Warner suggestively refers to these
worlds as *counterpublic*;[38] *queer* is here most saliently a negative term, a term
referring less to specific identifiable persons than to socially subordinate,
historically conditioned publics defined by critical practices and knowledges inseparable from the labor of sustaining these publics themselves.

Warner has argued that the practice of worldmaking cannot adequately be understood in the terms of traditional social movements, as the kind of practice that "acquire[s] agency in relation to the state."[39] But this practice does operate in negative relation to the state that grants marriage rights and thereby legitimates some relationships to the exclusion of others, as Warner has himself pointed out,[40] the state that would, through an extension of the logic of marriage, privatize the nonheterosexual practices and knowledges that gay liberation, in the seventies, sought to make so radically public that they might compel a radical rethinking of the very distinction between public and private. These practices counter the state, for example, in their insistence on legitimating the homosexual objectification of the body, in their refusal of representations of promiscuity as inherently dehumanizing or shameful. Queer worldmaking develops "the critical practical knowledge that allows such relations to count as intimate, to be not empty release or transgression but a common language of self cultivation, shared knowledge, and the exchange of inwardness."[41] Douglas Crimp's account of the knowledges of safe sex collectively developed in bathhouses during the AIDS epidemic in the eighties, in those spaces of supposed "empty release" that the neoliberal state has sought to extinguish, remains among the most compelling accounts of a simultaneously sexual and social form of knowledge production that is also inherently critical, critical in this case of the U.S. government's lethal indifference to the dissemination of knowledges that could have mitigated that epidemic.[42]

Berlant and Warner clarify their use of the term "worldmaking": a "project, where 'world,' like 'public,' differs from community or group because it necessarily includes more people than can be identified, more spaces than can be mapped beyond a few reference points, modes of feeling that can be learned rather than experienced as a birthright. The queer world is a space of entrances, exits, unsystematized lines of acquaintance, projected horizons, typifying examples, alternate routes, blockages, incommensurate geographies."[43] Rather than always already minoritized, these worlds are instead improvisational, their frontiers socially and historically dynamic and irreducible to categories of identity. Without in any way denying the obvious divergences between Marxian and queer vantages on the social, it is worth emphasizing that class position operates similarly. If at a certain level of analytic abstraction the systemic distinction between those who own the means of production and those who don't is relatively clear, this distinction is also historically conditioned and dynamic, every bit as characterized by "entrances" and "exits": selling one's labor power or purchasing the labor power of others also has nothing inherently to do with identity or birthright. A proletarian perspective on the social is hardly by definition a communal or identitarian perspective, in spite of Lukács's Hegelian framing of that perspective in terms of a proletarian identical "subject-object of history," and in spite of the fact, for example, that working-class consciousness in the United States has sometimes taken communitarian forms, especially in the nineteenth century and the early twentieth. Like queer formations, proletarian formations have had an improvisational character and have at the same time been defined in relation to certain systemic constraints. For Lukács, the production of a negative, proletarian knowledge of the social emerges from within the activity of that collective, and from within that collective's specific situation within the very totality it aspires to know. Similarly, a certain epistemological critique of the neoliberal conjuncture has become a central aspect of the worlds of queer practice, inasmuch as this critique proceeds from a position conditioned by the privatization of sex within that conjuncture.

This queer critical vantage refers to a structurally subordinated, critical and practical knowledge of the broad heteronormalization of social relations. It has been a product of the reification of sexual desire previous chapters have elaborated, especially as this instance of reification opens up a new horizon of social differentiation, a hierarchical relation between heterosexual and homosexual forms of subjectivity, forms that represent competing, opposed ways of seeing and knowing the social. And the opposed perspectives these two forms of subjectivity name have been conditions of possibility for an ongoing, internally contentious history of collective praxis, for the production and reproduction of knowledges critical of heterosexuality's normalization. If a queer vantage on the social that emerges within a neoliberal conjuncture has, for example, to be contrasted with a contemporaneous gay vantage on the social, this opposition is the product of a neoliberal desexualization of a form of identity that itself carried radically negative implications back when a movement out of the closet was inconceivable except in relation to a movement into the streets, when "coming out" represented a revolutionary publicizing of tabooed sexuality, when the identitarian and the socially radical seemed less persistently at odds.[44] These queer worlds are in this respect historically conditioned *totalities* of social, sexual, epistemological, and critical practice. They are forms of sociality that carry a constitutive capacity for their own, irreducibly distinct variation on the practice Marxism calls totality thinking, an aspiration to comprehend the broader set of social relations within which this specific world of practice and knowledge is situated.

Warner remarks that "little seems to have changed since 1950," that "sex has gone undercover"[45]—suggesting the similarities between neoliberal forms of social regulation like those I have been considering and forms of social regulation characteristic of Fordism that, in enforcing a certain social uniformity, marginalized, kept "undercover," the same gay male social formation that an expanded circuit of consumption also helped consolidate. Two texts by Samuel R. Delany that have been especially important for queer studies, taken together, emphasize both the similarities and the differences between these two periods in which sex appears to go undercover. Each articulates, with reference to a distinct historical moment, a practical, critical aspiration to totality as well as the social forces of dispersal any such aspiration must confront. The first, his memoir *The Motion of Light in Water,* includes a widely discussed passage that registers a dialectic of sexual isolation and collectivity; here I return to this passage because I want to underscore both its similarity to, and its historical distance from, a neoliberal moment. Recounting his first visit to the St. Mark's Baths in the late fifties, Delany writes that he entered a "gym-sized room," where he estimates that there are about 125 people. But "perhaps a dozen of them were standing. The rest were an undulating mass of naked, male bodies, spread wall to wall." This stunning scene, Delany recalls, directly contradicted the way in which he had understood the spatial segmentation of the city's, and indeed the nation's, gay male population, his uncritical absorption of a pervasive representation during that period, in the media and in public opinion, of the city's gay men as a population of "isolated perverts." The dispersal he had taken for granted was now radically challenged by the dizzying scene before his eyes. His first emotional response to this scene, he says, was fear. This moment cognitively negates the isolation he had presupposed; it negates, crucially, a separation of the sexual from the social, denaturalizes that separation, disrupts what he identifies as the pervasive fifties assumption that homosexuality is external to, and in contradiction with, the social as such. This externality is here revealed to be a vigorously enforced fiction.[46]

The only time he had felt this fear before, he tells us, had been during what he experienced as a raid, when he had approached parked trucks at the piers near Christopher Street, where men met other men for sex, and policemen started blowing their whistles. What frightened him was not the raid itself, he points out, but the "sheer number of men" who began running from between the trucks. He had thought that the "abandonment of sex" was the price "that any sense of the social exacted from homosexuals." His experience at the baths, however, is distinctive: "Institutions such as subway johns or the trucks, while they accommodated sex, cut it, visibly, up into tiny portions," making "any apprehension of its totality all but impossible"; the vision he witnesses at the baths, by contrast, provides precisely this otherwise absent sense of a gay male sociality. Delany bears witness here both to a gay male sociality that is irreducibly sexual as well and to its active dispersal by the state. He provocatively and memorably insists that "the first direct sense of political power comes from the apprehension of massed bodies."[47] As Fred Moten puts it, "it's not the fact" of these massed bodies "but the vision" that is important here, the critique of dispersal and isolation this moment makes possible.[48] To aspire to totality is here not merely to wish for social plenitude but to critique social fragmentation.

As José Muñoz's reading of this passage, like Moten's, points out, Delany compares this experienced contradiction between totality and isolation to an experience which might at first appear radically different: that pivotal New York "happening," Allan Kaprow's *Eighteen Happenings in Six Parts*, which Delany witnessed at a location near the St. Mark's Baths, in 1960. Delany experienced at this performance not the "apprehension" of aesthetic totality he had anticipated but its disruption, the performance's refusal to allow any viewers to see the piece as a whole. "The whole was distorted," as Muñoz puts it: "the happening thematized vision to show the ways in which vision is constantly compromised."[49] The encounter in the bathhouse, by contrast, represents in Muñoz's reading a utopian break: this other "happening" made it possible to imagine a queer world. A framing of queer worldmaking practices in terms of Marxian discourses of totality has been increasingly central to Muñoz's work, which articulates a queer aspiration to totality in terms of performative gestures that, as he has more recently put it, represent not a prescribed, preconceived end but "an opening or horizon," "a modality of critique that speaks to quotidian gestures as laden with potentiality."[50] Pursuing continuities between theatrical performance and the practice of worldmaking, Muñoz's analyses turn centrally on the negative potential of "embodied and performed queer politics," on the critical articulation of what he calls, following C. L. R. James, a "future in the present," and following Ernst Bloch, an "anticipatory illumination of a queer world." The term *performance* here designates the labor of constituting queer worlds in the present, labor that anticipates a queer future by performing a break with a sexually normalized and privatized present. Citing Adorno's contention that utopia is "the determined negation of that which merely is," Muñoz suggests both the distinctiveness of queer worldmaking, its qualitative divergence from the broader, heteronormalized totality in which it is situated, and the way in which these divergent worlds are also bound together in a relation of determinate negation.[51]

Muñoz draws on Delany's account of this earlier historical moment in the interests of elaborating the importance of totality thinking in the face of contemporary forms of privatizing violence. State attacks on queer worlds in contemporary New York echo Delany's account of a fragmented queer world; Muñoz underscores the importance of seeing, witnessing, and imagining new queer formations, apprehensions of socially and sexually massed bodies that are increasingly difficult to come by, especially in the context of developments like Giuliani's zoning law. Muñoz also briefly references the second text I want to mention, Delany's more recent argument in *Times Square Red, Times Square Blue,* which elaborates a variation on this same isolation/collectivity dialectic, updated for a neoliberal moment. In the face of the forms of class segregation built into contemporary urban space, *Times Square Red, Times Square Blue* offers a narrative about the overlap of social and sexual "contact" in public spaces like the Times Square that predated the area's so-called redevelopment. Delany advocates both the social and sexual importance of the maintenance of accessible social space. "The class war raging constantly and often silently in the comparatively stabilized societies of the developed world . . . perpetually works for the erosion of the social practices through which interclass communication takes place and of the institutions holding those practices stable." He distinguishes between "interclass contact" and "networking": networking is a class-specific practice largely confined to private spaces, which he contrasts with the more "rewarding" opportunities for interaction between classes available in public spaces. The Times Square Redevelopment Project of the nineties is his key example of the constantly, silently raging class war, while "contact is associated with public space and the architecture and [small-scale] commerce that depend upon and promote it."[52] Recounting the range of public sexual encounters he had in the old Times Square—and echoing Berlant and Warner's point that while not everyone who travels to Christopher Street patronizes the porn shops, all who make this journey benefit from the presence of those businesses— Delany emphasizes that such spaces facilitate all kinds of public, and in many cases noncommercial, encounter. Here again sexual space is indistinguishable from social space; this sexual/social space represents a determinate negation of that form of sexual/social privatization manifest in the "family-oriented" redevelopment of Times Square.

Muñoz points out that while Giuliani has been widely credited with a decrease in crime in New York City, antiqueer violence increased in the years following the implementation of the zoning law. He notes the frequency with which, in the wake of the law, posters pointing out the murder or "disappearance" of queers, more often than not queers of color, began appearing in the city. And in his account of the police suppression of a demonstration after the murder of Matthew Shepard in 1998, Muñoz echoes again the importance of the apprehension of massed bodies, recounting the way in which this massing of enraged bodies in the streets was dispersed by the police. "The state understands the need to keep us from knowing ourselves, knowing our masses."[53] Muñoz insists on the importance of the labor of worldmaking in the face of a dispersal that begins to look a lot like the forms of dispersal recounted in *The Motion of Light in Water*. While these two Delany texts, taken together, convey the enforced isolation basic to the Fordist as well as the neoliberal policing of urban populations, what intervenes historically between these moments is again a coalescence of queer formations and their emergence into national visibility. And what subsequently unfolds is a reaction against these formations, their punitive, revanchist "disappearance." Sex and sociality become secondary to the spectacle of equivalently desexualized identities and five-story airbrushed bodies.

A DIALECTIC OF DIS/INTEGRATION

I want to conclude this chapter and this volume by returning to one more queer instance of the aspiration to totality. David Wojnarowicz's memoir

Close to the Knives remains one of the most compelling accounts of the violence that was the governmental and corporate response, or nonresponse, to the AIDS crisis as it emerged in the United States in the eighties. Wojnarowicz is another crucial figure for queer studies. This frequently homeless artist who died of AIDS-related causes in 1992 was also among the most prominent, acclaimed representatives of the short-lived Lower East Side art scene that flourished in the last decade of his life. *Close to the Knives,* which appeared the year before he died, speaks, as does his work generally, from the vantage of a world of social outcasts, especially the dispossessed and the queer, and articulates an insurgent response. Its subtitle is *A Memoir of Disintegration,* and "disintegration" carries a range of charged implications here. Most explicit is certainly the physical and emotional disintegration Wojnarowicz battles after his diagnosis. But the term refers also to an enforced disintegration of the social itself, an enforcement that in the context of the epidemic begins to look genocidal. While the text is, in formal terms, a radically fragmentary collection of sketches, essays, and polemics of varying styles, most of them composed in the eighties and many of them reproduced in Wojnarowicz's visual art, it is just as fundamentally defined by an impulse of epistemological and indeed visionary integration, an impulse to see beyond the social fragmentation the text both records and formally emulates. *Close to the Knives* registers both enforced social disintegration and a longing for its negation, a longing to see the systemic integration that is disintegration's other, invisible side.

In his introduction to *The Waterfront Journals,* a collection of sketches by Wojnarowicz that appeared after his death, Tony Kushner articulates the central social conflict underpinning Wojnarowicz's work, forestalling any easy middle-class identification with him in the process: "We, the proud citizens of a democracy . . . can only conceive of life lived in the open, in public spaces, as being fugitive-invisible, corrupting, enshrouded in mystery, a danger to us. This is telling, and one thing I think it tells us is that we have been successfully inculcated with a fear of the political potential of public space." If the "proud citizens of a democracy" share anything in common, Kushner suggests, it is a simultaneous access to and mystification of privacy, an understanding of the opposition between public and private as anything but socially and historically determinate, an understanding of this opposition as entirely natural—if not supernatural, as Kushner further suggests when he adds that "only the police can descend into Hell, harrow it, and return," that middle-class civilians "imagine ourselves incapable of this border crossing."[54] The response to this fantasy we encounter in *Close to the Knives* is that of a subject compelled to inhabit public space because he has limited access, at best, to private space. Robert Siegle effectively captures the tone of that response when he remarks that Wojnarowicz's work has an impact "akin to throwing the passengers of suburban sedans through their windshields and out onto the unkind streets."[55] This text articulates, for instance, a fantasy of its own, confrontationally affirming the fears to which Kushner refers:

> In my dreams I crawl across freshly clipped front lawns, past statues and dogs and cars containing your guardians. I enter your houses through the smallest cracks in the bricks that keep you feeling comfortable and safe. I cross your living rooms and go up your staircases and into your bedrooms where you lie sleeping. . . . I will wake you up and welcome you to your bad dream.[56]

My dream, he promises, is your bad dream: if the police descend into hell, here we encounter a fantasy of ascension from hell. In this abolition of social distance Wojnarowicz becomes the middle class's nightmare, intruding on its haven of private intimacy. This passage responds to the contradictory identification of social membership with privacy articulated by Kushner's "proud citizens," responds to the contemporary national fantasy that keeps citizens feeling "comfortable and safe," a personal, intimate identification with the nation even as the Keynesian nation-state withers. *Close to the Knives* refers to this fantasized homogeneity of middle-class, white, private life, a paradoxical identification with a privatized nation, as the fantasy of a "one-tribe nation," a fantasy legitimating and perpetuating what for Wojnarowicz is a national "killing machine" (161). If Wojnarowicz's own fantasy affirms the threatening character of public space from the vantage of public space, he also refuses any mystifying decontextualization of that threat. He answers this normalizing fantasy not only with his own violent equivalent but also by demolishing that fantasy from within, shifting to a vantage internal to privacy itself and raising in the process the question of where hell is, exactly:

> I grew up in a tiny version of hell called the suburbs and experienced the Universe of the Neatly Clipped Lawn. This is a place where anything and

everything can and does take place—and events such as torture, starvation, humiliation, physical and psychic violence can take place uncontested by others, as long as it doesn't stray across the boundaries and borders as formed by the deed-holder inhabiting the house on the neatly clipped lawn. If the violence is contained within the borders of the lawn and does not mess up the real estate in any way that would cause the surrounding [property's] devaluation, anything is possible and everything permissible. (151–52)

This passage answers the fantasized association of proprietary privacy with protection from violence with a personal account of its real violence. These passages together shatter, from opposing directions, a national normalization of privacy, denaturalizing the distinction between public and private and insinuating the broader social enforcement of this opposition. These passages disclose the simultaneous integration and disintegration of a paradoxically privatized, middle-class sociality, suggesting that hell is this simultaneity itself.

This representation of social fragmentation contrasts strikingly with the text's representation of the corporeal contact that Wojnarowicz pursues, a pursuit of pleasure that is also a pursuit of social connection. Wojnarowicz depicts the pursuit of sex as the pursuit of an orgasmic overcoming of the socially engineered privacy that others him, a disintegration of the isolate self that is simultaneous with an integration of bodies. In a ceaseless collective search, discrete bodies give way to physical commingling and "the subtle water movements of shadows," to body parts and motion, alternately vivid and vague, luminous and shadowy images of arms, backs, necks. "I was losing myself in the language of his movements," Wojnarowicz remarks of a tall, anonymous figure he cruises (10). These visceral apprehensions of massed bodies are largely concentrated in a chapter called "Losing the Form in Darkness": images of a fluid corporeal formlessness dominate these passages set along the same Hudson river piers to which this chapter keeps returning, where land meets water: "each desire, each memory so small a thing, becomes a small river tracing the outlines and the drift of your arms and bare legs, dark mouth and the spoken words of strangers." Discrete persons melt into the "discrete pleasures" by which connected bodies are "buoyed" (13, 12).

These passages refuse any isolation of sex from sociality, as do the malevolent fantasies we have also just seen, though in tone and style the former could not diverge more dramatically from the latter. This fragmentary collection of sketches is also characterized by a binarized stylistic tension, a dissonance between highly lyrical and sexual passages on the one hand and passages of enraged social polemic on the other, a dissonance that sits uneasily with the text's simultaneous insistence on the reciprocal constitution of the sexual and the social. In this way *Close to the Knives* begins to assume a formal structure more contradictory, unified, and total than mere fragmentation, a simultaneous identity and nonidentity with itself. If the corporeal, sexual disintegration of the isolated self is on the one hand represented here as an indispensable instance of queer sociality, these spaces of social intimacy are also consistently located in sites like these abandoned piers and warehouses, sites located in capital's wake, capital's destructive motion thereby framing this melting immersion of bodies. These sexual and social practices negate the privatization the neoliberal state enforces even as they are limited and conditioned by it.

No wonder, then, that Wojnarowicz represents his experience of these marginal spaces in such utopian, transcendent terms. He aspires to a place beyond social isolation, these experiences taking the form of a kind of hallucinatory, intoxicating sanctuary. He has said elsewhere that orgasm is "like this loss of time and space and identity and everything,"[57] and here too he represents social/sexual practice as a kind of escape from time, a haven of memory and fantasy that destroys time. Bodily connection becomes, paradoxically, a practice of fantasized interiority that is also a fantasy of exploding the body's material boundaries. These practices take him to a place "that might be described as interior world. The place where movement was comfortable, where boundaries were stretched or obliterated: no walls, borders, language or fear" (108). Cultivated interior homelessness operates here as a defense against the lacerations of literal homelessness: Wojnarowicz's response to social disintegration is an integration of bodies that disintegrates the socially isolated person, and this disintegration produces in turn an integration of an interior world, an imaginary unity attributing an undifferentiated fluidity to that sexual/social totality he finds along the piers, a fantasized assertion of interior mobility in the face of social immobilization, interior freedom in the face of social constraint. Privatization's negation of sexual/social worldmaking is in this respect registered here as concrete and historical, while Wojnarowicz's negation of this negation is abstract and "timeless," taking the form of what we might call, following Jameson, an imaginary reconciliation of real social contradictions.

"Hell is a place on earth," he writes in the book's subsequent sketch, "Heaven is a place in your head" (29). But this internal fantasy of freedom and mobility now takes a literally nomadic form. Here, in a dilapidated car and a series of cheap motel rooms, Wojnarowicz ventures out from the decayed urban interstices to seek this same sexual integration of bodies, this same cultivated interior world, in an infinitely spacious southwestern landscape, a landscape that ostensibly transcends the containment and marginality of the piers. Notwithstanding the arid locale, here too he deploys fluid imagery, a "watery circling of shapes and textures" (25), to depict his search for corporeal contact, the eroticized totality of the desert mirroring, as had the fluid totality within piers and warehouses, his interior totality beyond time. "It was a landscape for drifting," he writes, "where time expands and contracts and vision is replaced by memories" (47); "driving a machine through the days and nights of the empty and pressured landscape eroticizes the whole world" (26).

But how can this landscape be both empty and pressured? "There *is* something in all that emptiness—it's the shape of a particular death that got erected by tiny humans on the spare face of an enormous planet long before I ever arrived, and the continuance of it probably long after I have gone" (42, original italics). He soon recognizes that the desert landscape itself "was slowly being chewed up" and that fantasies "in the form of hermetic exile were quickly becoming less possible" (40). Having gone on the road to escape the city, he now confronts, beyond its boundaries, an extension of the city's landscape of disintegration. He cruises the construction sites he encounters in the desert as relentlessly as he cruises deserted Manhattan buildings: here again the motion of capital conditions and delimits this eroticized landscape. The long-term "death" that is capital is explicitly registered here in terms we have already encountered, in the form of its persistent dynamic of enclosure, of accumulation by dispossession, its ongoing, violent expropriation of the commons[58]—in this case the expropriation of a Native American commons. At a truck stop marked by a "neon-outlined teepee," Wojnarowicz notices an older Native American man sitting in a car, "trapped within the glassed-in diorama of his metallic-and-chrome vehicle, within the museum of his own natural history as viewed through a white boy's eyes" (29–30). Privatization long imposed

on them, they are reduced to selling ersatz local culture: "on the walk-
way by the twin-roofed entrances to the toilets, a Native American family
was seated before two blankets filled with cheap turquoise trinkets and
hunger" (48).

But ultimately concrete history ceases merely to exclude Wojnarowicz
from a paradoxically privatized, middle-class, suburban sociality, ceases
merely to impinge on his abstract, timeless, interior totality. Instead it
violently obliterates that totality: "If there were a disease that appeared to
strike only politicians and religious leaders, would the president hesitate
for more than twenty-four hours to allocate more funds for research and
health care? Would the president hesitate to shift the entire $350 billion
defense budget toward research and health care?" (159). The conditioning
of his pursuit of sexual and social integration by the abstract motion of
capital now becomes, instead, a lethally specific threat to the very possibility of sexual and social integration, a punitive indifference to the spread
of a disease disproportionately affecting the dispossessed and the queer.
Wojnarowicz is brutally thrown from timelessness right back into the Rea-
gan eighties, that revanchist "morning in [neoliberal] America," not by his
contraction of the virus but by the larger social horizon within which that
contraction takes place, by a malign neglect threatening the very existence
of those lacking property or sexual propriety. Close to the Knives directs its
rage at religious leaders, politicians, a government health care bureaucracy
committed to the accumulation of capital—which is to say, at that venge-
ful, punitive state ever more indifferent to ever less profitable investment in
keeping alive those who are, from capital's point of view, ever more super-
fluous. Wojnarowicz watches friends die "slow vicious and unnecessary
deaths because fags and dykes and junkies are expendable in this country"
(161): in this text as in Wojnarowicz's work generally, AIDS signifies nothing more powerfully than the official violence of a queer-hating state and
"civil society" so bent on privatizing sex and property that they appear
ominously on the brink of a return to some premodern regime of sexual
normalization in which homosexuality provokes not "treatment" or even
punishment but extermination. "Some of us are born with the cross hairs
of a rifle scope printed on our backs or skulls" (58).

"Losing the Form in Darkness" concludes with a passage anticipating
this turn, evoking the intrusion of historical violence on a space that refuses
the privatization of sexual intimacy. Initially, the dynamism and fluidity of

desire persist in an abandoned warehouse along the Hudson. "Vagrant frescoes . . . huge murals of nude men . . . coupling several feet above the floorboards" seem suddenly to "come to life" as Wojnarowicz passes them and also glimpses the moving shadows of other men, men of flesh and blood, "in the recesses of a room a series of men in various stages of leaning." The frescoes and the living bodies seem, in Wojnarowicz's vision, to blend into each other—the frescoes themselves are "vagrant"—and these animated images then draw the living bodies toward them, "the intensity of the energy bringing others down the halls where guided by little or no sounds they pass silently over the charred floors" (22). But a tension between motion and stasis, animation and lifelessness again asserts itself as these living bodies "appear out of nowhere and line the walls like figurines before firing squads or figures in a breadline in old times pressed into history" (22–23), and as Wojnarowicz thinks of "the eternal sleep of statues, of marble eyes and lips and the stone wind-blown hair of the rider's horse, of illuminated arms corded with soft unbreathing veins, of the wounding curve of ancient backs stooped for frozen battles" (23). Statues, bread lines, firing squads, ancient battles: the text here evokes not merely the past but a history of covert and overt violence, a nightmare of history that startlingly intrudes on Wojnarowicz's abstract, timeless utopia, solidifying its fluidity, halting its motion even as it introduces into that space a different, less abstract kind of motion, history's own qualitatively different, concrete dynamism.

These words also evoke the specter of sexually objectified men, men with marble eyes and lips and illuminated arms, stooping for battle. After contracting the virus, he writes, "It didn't take me long to realize that I'd contracted a diseased society as well" (114). The wall separating a concrete, dynamic exterior totality, a one-tribe killing machine, from the concrete interior it contains and delimits, those social/sexual practices of queer worldmaking that "Losing the Form in Darkness" depicts, is violently collapsed. And as state violence threatens these practices of sexual/social integration by witnessing passively a lethal invasion of the very bodies that would resist isolation, the text again gives itself over to fantasy, this time in a boldface, frenetic passage from which standard punctuation quickly disappears:

I say there's certain politicians that had better increase their security forces and there's religious leaders and health-care officials that had better get bigger

fucking dogs and higher fucking fences and more complex security alarms
for their homes and queer-bashers better start doing their work from inside
howitzer tanks because the thin line between the inside and the outside
is beginning to erode and at the moment I'm a thirty-seven-foot-tall one
thousand-one-hundred-and-seventy-two-pound man inside this six-foot
body and all I can feel is the pressure all I can feel is the pressure and the
need for release. (162)

Here again the state is inseparable from capital's privatizing segmentation of space, but this time the fantasy is one of reversal, a redirection
of violence outward, a "pressure" rising to confront a "pressurized" landscape of enclosure. The "thin line between the outside and the inside"
becomes a refrain in the longer passage from which this quotation is
taken, a thin line inseparable from the "thin line between thought and
action" (161). The words "close to the knives" begin to signify both a prox-
imity to violent death and the potentially violent self-defense this prox-
imity provokes.

    And just as his body threatens expansion/explosion in the face of the
threat of that body's contraction/implosion, his abstract, interior world disintegrates, and the totalizing impulse that had produced it is itself directed
outward. In this respect, too, the barrier between interior and exterior col-
lapses. As the concrete connections between a totality of queer sexuality/
sociality and a broader totality of sexually normalizing neoliberal violence
become more visible, the text's longing for a totality of free movement
can no longer manifest itself abstractly, can no longer take the form of
an escape from the social and the historical: he begins to "los[e] touch"
with this abstract totality, with "the current of timelessness that drove me
through all my life 'til now" (254). The longing articulated by this text
becomes a longing for a social and sexual integration of bodies with other
bodies—a social and sexual disintegration of the body isolated from other
bodies—which must itself be integrated with its social and historical exterior, an integration that would necessarily entail a concrete negation of that
same exterior. Mapping the external, historical world he inhabits explicitly becomes more crucial: "There is something I want to see clearly, something I want to witness in its raw state. And this need comes from my sense
of mortality" (116). He wants to avoid living the rest of his life in "adapta-
tion" to a mystified and mystifying social world, to what Wojnarowicz refers

to in this text and throughout his work as "the preinvented world." The aspiration to totality we have already seen at work in this text is concretized. The queer perspective on an emergent neoliberal brand of violence instantiated by this text aspires to an integration that is not positive but critical, not abstract but concrete, a response to the total character of social disintegration. The text aspires to unify what is dispersed: "I'm trying to lift off the weight of the preinvented world so I can see what's underneath it all. I'm hungry and the preinvented world won't satisfy my hunger" (117). This insistent tension between a daily negotiation of the segmentation of social life and an aspiration to see beyond this segmentation is also one of the text's basic formal characteristics. This overtly fragmentary, disintegrated collection of sketches at the same time performs an aspiration to integrate the whole, to negate this same dispersal of narrative fragments. I referred earlier to the text's stark stylistic differentiation of polemical from sexual passages. But this opposition also abides, again, within a larger unity, the text's unwavering opposition to a brutal totality of social and sexual isolation.

The autocritique of abstract totality performed by *Close to the Knives* converges in important ways with the critique in previous chapters of the abstract variations on totality thinking in Lukács, Marcuse, and Jameson. These abstract totalities are bound together by their common elision of the concrete history that everywhere conditions them. Marcuse distinguishes between a hopelessly localized and compromised politics of sexuality that constitutes a form of "repressive desublimation" and homosexuality as a figure for revolutionary "derepression." Jameson recapitulates this figural representation of the politics of sexuality, consistently positing a sexuality (in the so-called First World, at any rate) unproblematically privatized by capital. Neither representation is equipped to account for the historically specific and determinate character of antiheteronormative social and political formations. While Jameson's argument that *History and Class Consciousness* is an "unfinished project" productively suggests a different way to think about these formations, it is precisely this historical embeddedness, the historical specificity of the critical perspective on the social these formations sustain, that the figural representation of sexuality and sexual/social movements abstracts out of social totality it aspires to know. To make these movements such a figure is not simply to reduce them to a mere vehicle for something else, a figural means to a qualitatively different end, but actively to cordon them off from that totality, to refuse or fail to learn from their own distinct capacities for critical consciousness. The abstract aspirations served by this figuration of sexuality, like the abstract aspirations both posited and critiqued by *Close to the Knives,* make absolute the wall between queer worldmaking and the rest of the world. These accounts of the location of antiheteronormative formations erase the aspect of Lukács's analysis that Jameson's "unfinished project" essay simultaneously encourages us to discern, the immanent historical development of the practical, critical consciousness that defines them.

To represent entire histories of collective practical opposition to compulsory heterosexuality as mere figures is especially to fail to see the way in which reification is itself a condition of possibility for those histories. The aspirations to totality exemplified by Marcuse and Jameson elide what I have argued is an objective, historically determinate reification of sexual desire, and its subsequent, unpredictable social repercussions. Accounting both for privatizing, mystifying dispersal and for the queer world capital played a role in opening up requires accounting not only for the subjective, critical knowledges to which reification dialectically gives rise but for the historical conditions of these knowledges. It might, for example, be tempting to read these queer worlds in terms of sexual practices that abide in some kind of absolute, dehistoricized opposition to identity or subjectivity, as queer critiques of identity categories sometimes have it, or even in terms of some kind of manifestation of those unmediated "bodies and pleasures" Foucault advocated in his more utopian moments. But these queer worldmaking practices are themselves historical products of the regime of sexual knowledge that Foucault specifies, even as they necessarily struggle both within and against its constraints. A critique of capital that would bring together Marxian and queer vantages on reification has to move historically and immanently through sexuality, through reification's objective unpredictability, to come out, as it were, on the other side. This, at least, is the kind of critique this book has aspired to perform.

Close to the Knives is not a text that presumes to present a bird's-eye view of the whole. It *is* a text that performs an aspiration, a text that articulates both the impossibility of any absolute, timeless social integration, and the absolute historical importance of refusing capital's enforcement of social disintegration. In the postscript to its long concluding essay, Wojnarowicz brings the reader to—of all places—the site we glimpsed in chapter 2's brief consideration of *The Sun Also Rises:* the bullfight arena. But here the spectator identifies with the bull, not the bullfighter. Intercut with passages recounting stories of death—the death of friends ravaged by AIDS, by dispossession, by homelessness—the text recounts Wojnarowicz's experience of a bullfight in Merida, Mexico. "The pain I feel is to see my own death in the bull's death; a projection of my own body's nerve endings and nervous system onto the body of that exhausted and enraged animal" (270): in this case, the bullfight arena metaphorically stages the goading into violence to which our narrator has himself been subject. The bull's "stance and sudden erratic movements are purely motions of survival" (266). As Wojnarowicz leaves, he notices "a line of forty or more people waiting patiently for their turn at a makeshift counter that comprises, along with a metal-poled structure, a spontaneous meat market. Huge dripping sections of dead bulls are impaled on hooks or draped over the table. So little has been quartered that I could almost recognize which animal was which" (275–76). Wojnarowicz empathizes with the bulls especially in death, seeing himself and those this postscript remembers, concrete, irreducibly distinct persons, in hanging carcasses that, as he describes them, seem less interchangeable than the abstract, desexualized citizen-subjects defended by the new homonormativity. The book's final passages develop two insistent, sentence-long refrains, sentences brought together in the text's final words: "We rise to greet the State, to confront the State. Smell the flowers while you can" (276). While the second sentence underscores the sense of impending and accumulating death, the devastation in which the greeting and confrontation of the first sentence is imagined, the "We" of the first sentence, in a text so centrally about isolation, is perhaps surprising. This is not the We that Tony Kushner ventriloquizes but its opposite, that We's *Them,* a We that constitutes the infernalized outside, the negation, of a paradoxically privatized and atomized collective of "proud citizens," a We that unifies Wojnarowicz with the dead. "I felt I stood the chance of going crazy and becoming a windmill of slaughter if I allowed myself the luxury of experiencing each of those deaths with the full weight accorded them." Instead his own isolation, he writes, held these lives and possible deaths in suspension (271). But now this memoir of disintegration refuses the timelessness for which memory had earlier been a vehicle: it brings memory together with history, concretizing memory, negating isolation in death, conjuring a collective out of the dead.

"Only that historian will have the gift of fanning the spark of hope in the past who is firmly convinced that *even the dead* will not be safe from the enemy if he wins":[59] *Close to the Knives* ultimately refuses abstract negation, integrates future with past by historicizing both, aspires to some historical location beyond social disintegration, beyond multiform, privatizing violence.

ACKNOWLEDGMENTS

The work that ultimately resulted in this book began in a very different form, and in what sometimes feels like another life, when I was in graduate school at the University of Iowa. Two educational experiences from those years stand out; both influenced for the better my understanding of what it means to do anything that can be called critical theory in a university setting. One of these experiences was the political education I received after becoming involved with the ultimately successful campaign to unionize the university's graduate employees. The other was my experience with the group of faculty who guided me through the earliest version of this project. Cheryl Herr, Kevin Kopelson, Rob Latham, Tom Lewis, and Dee Morris provided responses to my work that routinely opened up new ways of understanding it, and demonstrated patience with a doctoral candidate whose own patience was sometimes in short supply.

Though the limitations of the arguments in this book are certainly my own, whatever cogency they have is a credit to the quality of engagement provided by these five people and by a number of others as these ideas went through a series of subsequent transformations. Rosemary Hennessy, Fred Moten, and Andrew Parker offered indispensable critique, encouragement, and advocacy on repeated occasions. And over the course of a series of satisfying weekends in which we responded to each other's work, ate well, drank well, and enjoyed the view from the twenty-eighth floor, Kathryne Lindberg, Sheila Lloyd, and Stephen Germic gave trenchant feedback on multiple chapters.

Neil Larsen's detailed response to an early draft of chapter 1 was pivotal, as was my discovery of the venue in which I first met Neil. The Marxist Literary Group Institute on Culture and Society has in the past ten years become a model for me of genuinely collective intellectual and critical work. I have experienced these meetings as a kind of respite from the academic currents of what Marx and Engels called the icy water of egotistical calculation, and I remain immensely grateful for this annual, far too brief opportunity to warm up and dry off.

Two anonymous readers of earlier versions of this manuscript provided tough, incisive comments that pushed me to think through its ideas with greater rigor. At the University of Minnesota Press, Richard Morrison sustained a belief in this project over a longer period of time than I had any right to expect. Duke University Press and Guilford Press kindly provided permission to include revised versions of essays that were previously published in *Social Text* and *Science and Society,* respectively.

For years of unwavering support, I am indebted to several senior colleagues currently or formerly at Kent State University, especially Ron Corthell, Fred Schwarzbach, Mark Bracher, and Ray Craig. I thank the Division of Research and Graduate Studies at Kent State for the research leave that accelerated the completion of the book's first draft.

My gang of friends in and around Kent has sustained me in this work. Magicians all, they somehow managed, twelve months a year, to make northeast Ohio a consistently warm place. For Halloween parties, Thanksgiving dinners, many other dinners, poker, bonfires, antiwar demonstrations, evenings we went to see bands we like and were the oldest people there by far, and the rare instance of pure foolishness people with our educational backgrounds really shouldn't be involved in and which I am certainly not going to divulge here, I thank Tammy Clewell, David Farnan, Patti Dunmire, Joel Woller, Marlia Banning, John Ackerman, Florence Dore, Will Rigby, Donna Lee, Pat Gallagher, Joan Parks, and Tony Alessandrini.

This book is dedicated to my mother, Wanda Hembree, my father, Jerry Floyd, and my brother, Bradley Floyd. What the four of us went through, together and apart, made us stronger, which makes me proud of us.

NOTES

INTRODUCTION

1. Judith Butler, "Merely Cultural," *Social Text* 52–53 (1997): 265–77. This essay was part of a widely noted exchange with Nancy Fraser; see also Fraser, "Heterosexism, Misrecognition, and Capitalism: A Response to Judith Butler," *Social Text* 52–53 (1997): 279–89.

2. Butler's essay reappeared in *New Left Review* 227 (1998): 33–44, and Fraser's response was reprinted in the following issue, *New Left Review* 228 (1998): 140–49.

3. Eve Kosofsky Sedgwick, *Epistemology of the Closet* (Berkeley: University of California Press, 1990); Judith Butler, *Gender Trouble: Feminism and the Subversion of Identity* (New York: Routledge, 1990); Butler, *Bodies That Matter: On the Discursive Limits of "Sex"* (New York: Routledge, 1993); Michael Warner, ed., *Fear of a Queer Planet: Queer Politics and Social Theory* (Minneapolis: University of Minnesota Press, 1993).

4. Relatively recent and variously focused work in queer studies that centrally engages the Marxist tradition includes, for example, José Esteban Muñoz, "The Future in the Present: Sexual Avant-Gardes and the Performance of Utopia," in *The Futures of American Studies,* ed. Donald Pease and Robyn Wiegman (Durham, N.C.: Duke University Press, 2002), 93–110; Miranda Joseph, *Against the Romance of Community* (Minneapolis: University of Minnesota Press, 2002); Eric O. Clarke, *Virtuous Vice: Homoeroticism and the Public Sphere* (Durham, N.C.: Duke University Press, 2000); Rosemary Hennessy, *Profit and Pleasure: Sexual Identities in Late Capitalism* (New York: Routledge, 2000); Matthew Tinkcom, *Working like a Homosexual: Camp, Capital, Cinema* (Durham, N.C.: Duke University Press, 2002); Roderick A. Ferguson, *Aberrations in Black: Toward a Queer of Color Critique* (Minneapolis: University of Minnesota Press, 2004); and Elisa Glick, *Materializing Queer Desire: Oscar Wilde to Andy Warhol* (Albany: SUNY Press, forthcoming).

In addition to Muñoz, Joseph, Hennessy, and Clarke, queer work that takes the contemporary dynamics of capital as a key interpretive horizon figures prominently, for example, in Arnaldo Cruz-Malavé and Martin F. Manalansan IV, eds., *Queer Globalizations: Citizenship and the Afterlife of Colonialism* (New York: New York University Press, 2002); and David L. Eng, Judith Halberstam, and José Esteban Muñoz, eds., "What's Queer about Queer Studies Now?" special issue, *Social Text* 84–85 (2005).

5. A key text here is Lisa Duggan, "The New Homonormativity: The Sexual Politics of Neoliberalism," in *Materializing Democracy*, ed. Russ Castronovo and Dana D. Nelson (Durham, N.C.: Duke University Press, 2002), 175–94.

6. One might object that the Frankfurt school represents an exception to this claim. This is a potential exception I will consider at length in chapter 3, which focuses on the work of Marcuse. There I will contend that the Marxian incorporation of Freud characteristic of Frankfurt school accounts of sexuality has tended to preempt rather than facilitate any genuinely social and historical account of sexuality.

7. Warner, "Introduction," in *Fear of a Queer Planet*, xxi.

8. Sedgwick, *Epistemology of the Closet*, 1.

9. Warner, "Introduction," x, xiii.

10. Steven Best, "Jameson, Totality, and the Poststructuralist Critique," in *Postmodernism/Jameson/Critique*, ed. Douglas Kellner (Washington, D.C.: Maisonneuve Press, 1989), 361.

11. Warner, "Introduction," xxvi.

12. Lee Edelman, *No Future: Queer Theory and the Death Drive* (Durham, N.C.: Duke University Press, 2004).

13. Elizabeth Freeman, ed., "Queer Temporalities," special issue, *GLQ* 13, nos. 2–3 (2007), maps and extends this recent work.

14. See Butler, *Gender Trouble* and *Bodies That Matter;* Leo Bersani, "Is the Rectum a Grave?" in *AIDS: Cultural Analysis/Cultural Activism*, ed. Douglas Crimp (Cambridge, Mass.: MIT Press, 1988), 197–222; and Bersani, *Homos* (Cambridge, Mass.: Harvard University Press, 1995).

15. David L. Eng, Judith Halberstam, and José Esteban Muñoz, "Introduction: What's Queer about Queer Studies Now?" *Social Text* 84–85 (2005): 1; Phillip Brian Harper, Anne McClintock, José Esteban Muñoz, and Trish Rosen, "Queer Transexions of Race, Nation, and Gender: An Introduction," *Social Text* 52–53 (1997): 1. Critiques of the racial, national, ethnic, and colonial blind spots imposed by the term "queer" that have themselves become widely cited within queer thought include Ferguson, *Aberrations in Black;* Cathy J. Cohen, "Punks, Bulldaggers, and Welfare Queens: The Radical Potential of Queer Politics?" in *Black Queer Studies: A Critical Anthology*, ed. E. Patrick Johnson and Mae G. Henderson (Durham, N.C.: Duke University Press, 2005), 21–51; José Esteban Muñoz, *Disidentifications: Queers of Color and the Performance of Politics* (Minneapolis: University of Minnesota Press, 1999); Martin F. Manalansan IV, *Global Divas: Filipino Gay Men in the Diaspora* (Durham, N.C.: Duke University Press, 2003); and Gayatri Gopinath, *Impossible Desires: Queer Desire and South Asian Public Cultures* (Durham, N.C.: Duke University Press, 2005).

16. Georg Lukács, *History and Class Consciousness,* trans. Rodney Livingstone (Cambridge, Mass.: MIT Press, 1994), 198.

17. Fredric Jameson, "History and Class Consciousness as an 'Unfinished Project,'" *Rethinking Marxism* 1 (1988): 64.

18. For an especially cogent defense of feminist standpoint theory, especially in the face of the familiar charges of "essentialism"—a defense that also insists on a distinction I am questioning here, the distinction between "totalizing" and "partial" critical perspectives—see Donna Haraway, "Situated Knowledges: The Science Question in Feminism and the Privilege of Partial Perspective," *Feminist Studies* 14 (1988): 575–99.

19. Jameson, "History and Class Consciousness," 65.

20. Ibid., 70, 67, 66 (original italics).

21. Ibid., 72.

22. Fredric Jameson, *Postmodernism, or, The Cultural Logic of Late Capitalism* (Durham, N.C.: Duke University Press, 1991), 332.

23. Harry Cleaver nicely draws out this implication in *Reading Capital Politically* (Edinburgh, U.K.: AK Press, 2000), 97–105.

24. John D'Emilio, "Capitalism and Gay Identity," in *The Lesbian and Gay Studies Reader,* ed. Henry Abelove, Michèle Aina Barale, and David M. Halperin (New York: Routledge, 1993), 467–76.

25. This range of historically and subculturally specific forms of minority sexual identity is elaborated, for example, in George Chauncey, *Gay New York: Gender, Urban Culture, and the Making of the Gay Male World, 1890–1940* (New York: Basic Books, 1994); and Lillian Faderman, *Odd Girls and Twilight Lovers: A History of Lesbian Life in Twentieth Century America* (New York: Columbia University Press, 1991). On the requirement to identify heterosexually that emerged within the U.S. middle class in the early twentieth century, see Chauncey, *Gay New York,* 111–26.

26. Lauren Berlant and Michael Warner, "Sex in Public," *Critical Inquiry* 24 (1998): 558.

27. Edward Said, "Traveling Theory," in *The World, the Text, and the Critic* (Cambridge, Mass.: Harvard University Press, 1983), 239. For another useful account of the term's tendency toward ever greater degrees of abstraction, see Gillian Rose's discussion of "the lament over reification" in *The Melancholy Science: An Introduction to the Thought of Theodor W. Adorno* (New York: Columbia University Press, 1978), esp. 27–42.

28. Georg Lukács, *The Theory of the Novel,* trans. Anna Bostock (Cambridge, Mass.: MIT Press, 1974).

29. Timothy Bewes, *Reification, or The Anxiety of Late Capitalism* (London: Verso, 2002), 15, 3, 4–5.

30. Ibid., 269, 270, 202 (original italics). For a more recent example of the idealist (though less explicitly religious) capacities of the concept, see Axel Honneth's rethinking of reification in terms of the philosophy of recognition in his *Reification: A New Look at an Old Idea* (New York: Oxford University Press, 2008).

31. Fredric Jameson, *The Political Unconscious: Narrative as a Socially Symbolic Act* (Ithaca, N.Y.: Cornell University Press, 1981), 64, 9.

32. Ibid., 61–68.

33. For treatments of the way in which *History and Class Consciousness* intervened in this specific context, see, for example, Andrew Arato and Paul Breines, *The Young Lukács and the Origins of Western Marxism* (New York: Seabury, 1979), esp. 56, 85–86; and John Rees, "Introduction," in *A Defence of History and Class Consciousness: Tailism and the Dialectic,* by Georg Lukács (New York: Verso, 2000), 1–38.

34. Lukács, *History and Class Consciousness,* 1, 9.

35. Ibid., xxiii–xxiv.

36. Theodor W. Adorno, *Negative Dialectics,* trans. E. B. Ashton (New York: Continuum, 1995).

37. Justin Paulson frames reification as a simultaneously spatial and historical narrative of uneven development in "Uneven Reification," *Minnesota Review* 58–60 (2003): 251–64. Though he recapitulates the representation of reification in terms of a narrative of decline, he also productively distances the concept from the question of consciousness, emphasizing instead the objective determinations to which it refers.

38. Karl Marx, *Grundrisse,* trans. Martin Nicolaus (New York: Penguin, 1993), 100.

39. Ibid., 101.

40. Ibid., 101, 102.

41. Stuart Hall, "Marx's Notes on Method: A 'Reading' of the '1857 Introduction,'" *Cultural Studies* 17 (2003): 128.

42. Karl Marx, *The German Ideology* (New York: International Publishers, 1991), 48.

43. Derek Sayer, *The Violence of Abstraction: The Analytic Foundations of Historical Materialism* (New York: Basil Blackwell, 1987).

44. Foucault represents Marx and Freud as the most significant examples of what he calls "initiators of discursive practices," figures who made possible not only subsequent discourses consistent with their own writings but also discourses that diverge from those writings while also operating within the general discursive field they introduced. See Foucault, "What Is an Author?" in *Language, Counter-memory, Practice: Selected Essays and Interviews,* ed. Donald F. Bouchard, trans. Donald F. Bouchard and Sherry Simon (Ithaca, N.Y.: Cornell University Press, 1977), esp. 131–36.

45. Said, "Traveling Theory," 237, 226–27. Extending and critiquing his earlier argument, Said underscores this point even more emphatically in "Traveling Theory Reconsidered," in *Reflections on Exile and Other Essays* (Cambridge, Mass.: Harvard University Press, 2000), 436–52.

46. The founding text of regulation theory is Michel Aglietta, *A Theory of Capitalist Regulation: The U.S. Experience,* trans. David Fernbach (London: New Left Books, 1979). For useful critical secondary accounts of regulation theory, see Robert Boyer, *The Regulation School: A Critical Introduction* (New York: Columbia University Press, 1990); and Robert Brenner and Mark Glick, "The Regulation Approach: Theory and History," *New Left Review* 188 (1991): 45–119.

47. Brenner and Glick's critique in "The Regulation Approach" is of interest on precisely this point. I read it as emphasizing, ultimately, the way in which the general historical trends this discourse tries to conceptualize were historically much more

uneven than regulation theory tends to acknowledge. Their own explicit position, meanwhile, is that their critique of regulation theory's historical blind spots is significantly more damaging to its most basic conceptual claims.

48. Adam Tickell and Jamie A. Peck, "Social Regulation after Fordism: Regulation Theory, Neo-liberalism, and the Global-Local Nexus," *Economy and Society* 24 (1995): 360.

49. David Harvey, *The Condition of Postmodernity* (Oxford, U.K.: Blackwell, 1990), 127.

50. See especially Antonio Gramsci, "Americanism and Fordism," in *Selections from the Prison Notebooks* (New York: International, 1992), 277–318.

51. But see the way in which Leerom Medovoi brings together the regulationist idea of the mode of regulation with the Foucauldian notion of governmentality in "Global Society Must Be Defended: Biopolitics without Boundaries," *Social Text* 91 (2007): 53–79.

52. Leerom Medovoi, *Rebels: Youth and the Cold War Origins of Identity* (Durham, N.C.: Duke University Press, 2005), 15 (original italics).

1. DISCIPLINED BODIES

1. Georg Lukács, *History and Class Consciousness,* trans. Rodney Livingstone (1923; Cambridge, Mass.: MIT Press, 1994); Michel Foucault, *The History of Sexuality*, vol. 1, *An Introduction,* trans. Robert Hurley (New York: Vintage, 1990).

2. See especially "Nietzsche, Genealogy, History," in *Language, Counter-memory, Practice: Selected Essays and Interviews,* ed. Donald F. Bouchard, trans. Donald F. Bouchard and Sherry Simon (Ithaca, N.Y.: Cornell University Press, 1977), 139–64.

3. Lukács, *History and Class Consciousness,* 88.

4. Ibid., 89.

5. Ibid., 90.

6. Harry Braverman, *Labor and Monopoly Capital: The Degradation of Work in the Twentieth Century* (New York: Monthly Review Press, 1974), 171.

7. Lukács, *History and Class Consciousness,* 88.

8. Ibid., 100.

9. See Foucault, *The Order of Things: An Archaeology of the Human Sciences* (New York: Random House, 1970).

10. On the complex discursive entanglement of sexual "inversion" with biological racism in the nineteenth century, see Siobhan Somerville, *Queering the Color Line: Race and the Invention of Homosexuality in American Culture* (Durham, N.C.: Duke University Press, 2000), 15–38.

11. Foucault, *The History of Sexuality,* 118, 123.

12. Ibid., 119.

13. Sander L. Gilman, *Freud, Race, and Gender* (Princeton, N.J.: Princeton University Press, 1993), 6. See also Gilman's discussion of Freud's epistemological "struggle" with the concept of degeneration in "Sexology, Psychoanalysis, and Degeneration," in *Difference and Pathology* (Ithaca, N.Y.: Cornell University Press, 1985), 191–216.

14. See Karl Marx, *Capital,* vol. 1, trans. Ben Fowkes (New York: Penguin, 1976), 439–639; on the difference between the formal and the real subsumption of labor under capital, see pp. 1019–38.

15. According to Sean Wilentz, for example, the uneven shift from independent artisanship to the earliest stages of industrialization within major urban centers took roughly two decades, from around 1820 to around 1840. See Sean Wilentz, *Chants Democratic: New York City and the Rise of the American Working Class, 1788–1850* (New York: Oxford University Press, 1984).

16. David Montgomery, *Workers' Control in America: Studies in the History of Work, Technology, and Labor Struggles* (New York: Cambridge University Press, 1979), 12–13.

17. Foucault, *Discipline and Punish: The Birth of the Prison,* trans. Alan Sheridan (New York: Vintage, 1979), 145, 143.

18. Michel Aglietta, *A Theory of Capitalist Regulation: The U.S. Experience,* trans. David Fernbach (London: New Left Books, 1979).

19. Braverman, *Labor and Monopoly Capital,* 384.

20. The issues of competition, the relation between the productivity of labor and the demand for labor, and the accumulation of capital on the one hand and a "reserve army" of labor on the other are brought together in a relatively concentrated fashion in *Capital,* vol. 1, 762–802.

21. Braverman, *Labor and Monopoly Capital,* 276.

22. Karl Marx, *Grundrisse,* trans. Martin Nicolaus (Harmondsworth: Penguin, 1973), 408 (original italics).

23. Braverman, *Labor and Monopoly Capital,* 403–4.

24. Lukács, *History and Class Consciousness,* 103. The Frankfurt school's employment of Freudianism in their critique of reification, about which I have more to say in chapter 3, only sometimes registered the status of psychoanalysis as a product of reification. Adorno, for example, did explicitly situate psychoanalysis within what he saw as a mystifying division of epistemological labor, in his critique of Talcott Parsons's efforts to develop a social science that could adequately synthesize the insights of sociology and psychology. Such a synthesis would, for Adorno, be false; it would make less visible, not more visible, the fundamental social divisions that form the basis of the distinction between these intellectual disciplines. If on the one hand, he writes, "the separation of society and psyche is false consciousness," this is because this separation itself has its basis in capital's dispersal of social life; it "cannot be removed by a mere methodological dictum." Theodor Adorno, "Sociology and Psychology," *New Left Review* 46 (1967): 69. See also Adorno, "Sociology and Psychology—II," *New Left Review* 47 (1968): 79–97.

25. Braverman, *Labor and Monopoly Capital,* 281.

26. Eli Zaretsky, "Bisexuality, Capitalism, and the Ambivalent Legacy of Psychoanalysis," *New Left Review* 223 (1997): 84.

27. See Nathan G. Hale, *The Rise and Crisis of Psychoanalysis in America: Freud and the Americans, 1917–1985* (New York: Oxford University Press, 1995).

28. Richard Ohmann, *Selling Culture: Magazines, Markets, and Class at the Turn of*

the Century (New York: Verso, 1996), 231–48. See also T. J. Jackson Lears's considera-
tion of the role of advertising in a more general "therapeutic ethos" during this period,
in "From Salvation to Self-Realization: Advertising and the Therapeutic Roots of the
Consumer Culture, 1880–1930," in *The Culture of Consumption: Critical Essays in
American History, 1880–1980,* ed. Richard Wightman Fox and T. J. Jackson Lears (New
York: Pantheon, 1983), 3–38.

29. Zaretsky, "Bisexuality, Capitalism," 84–85.

30. On Foucault's distinction between science and discursive formation, see *The
Archaeology of Knowledge,* trans. A. M. Sheridan Smith (New York: Pantheon, 1972),
178–95.

31. See, for example, Stuart Ewen, *Captains of Consciousness* (New York: McGraw-
Hill, 1976); William Leach, *Land of Desire: Merchants, Power, and the Rise of a New
American Culture* (New York: Vintage, 1993), 35–38; and Ohmann, *Selling Culture,*
48–61.

32. Aglietta, *Theory of Capitalist Regulation,* 66, 70. Aglietta introduces the distinction between extensive and intensive regimes of accumulation on pp. 65–87.

33. See, for example, Alain Lipietz, *Mirages and Miracles: The Crises of Global
Fordism,* trans. David Macey (London: Verso, 1987), 34–35.

34. Regulation theory often associates what it calls a competitive mode of regulation with the earlier, extensive regime of accumulation, and a monopolistic mode of
regulation with the later, intensive regime of accumulation, emphasizing the way in
which the intensive regime requires a concentration and centralization of capital,
which has the effect of reining in the forces of competition. This account typically
understands the period between the world wars in terms of a continuing dominance
of a competitive mode of regulation, even as an intensive regime of accumulation also
begins to develop. The contradiction between the new regime of accumulation and
the persistence of an older mode of regulation inadequate to it then explains the
depression of the thirties. I am emphasizing, to the contrary, the way in which the new
mode of regulation that will ultimately be adequate to this intensive regime begins
to take shape, however sluggishly and unevenly, at least a quarter century before its
Fordist culmination.

35. Robert S. Lynd and Helen Merrell Lynd, *Middletown: A Study in Modern
American Culture* (Harcourt Brace, 1929), 80–81, 75.

36. Moishe Postone, *Time, Labor, and Social Domination: A Reinterpretation of
Marx's Critical Theory* (New York: Cambridge University Press, 1996), 200–216.

37. The classic account of the development of this experiential disjunction, which
focuses on the case of England, is E. P. Thompson, "Time, Work Discipline, and
Industrial Capitalism," *Past and Present* 38 (1967): 56–97.

38. Lukács, *History and Class Consciousness,* 103.

39. Compare Lukács's account on this point with Walter Benjamin's brief remarks,
for instance, on the way in which psychoanalysis, like the cinema, opens up qualitatively new forms of vision in "The Work of Art in the Age of Mechanical Reproduction," in *Illuminations* (New York: Schocken, 1968), 235.

40. David Harvey considers the way in which the body is deployed as a strategy of capital accumulation within both production and consumption in *Spaces of Hope* (Berkeley: University of California Press, 2000), 97–116.

41. Foucault, *The History of Sexuality,* 109, 106, 110.

42. Ibid., 110, 111.

43. Ibid., 114.

44. Influential accounts of the ideological operation of gender and sexual knowledge in the nineteenth century include Carroll Smith-Rosenberg, *Disorderly Conduct: Visions of Gender in Victorian America* (New York: Oxford University Press, 1985); G. J. Barker-Benfield, *Horrors of the Half-Known Life: Male Attitudes toward Women and Sexuality in Nineteenth-Century America* (New York: Harper and Row, 1976); E. Anthony Rotundo, *American Manhood: Transformations in Masculinity from the Revolution to the Modern Era* (New York: Basic Books, 1993); Michael S. Kimmel, *Manhood in America: A Cultural History* (New York: Free Press, 1996), 13–188; and Dana D. Nelson, *National Manhood: Capitalist Citizenship and the Imagined Fraternity of White Men* (Durham, N.C.: Duke University Press, 1998). Nelson's study remains one of the most detailed available on the role of nineteenth-century sexual and gender science in the ideological naturalization of a range of forms of social hierarchy. A more recent volume that serves as a useful overview of the various forms of exclusion on which this nineteenth-century naturalization of gender difference was based, and continues the ongoing critique of the "separate spheres" metaphor in historical scholarship, is Cathy N. Davidson and Jessamyn Hatcher, eds., *No More Separate Spheres!* (Durham, N.C.: Duke University Press, 2002). And for a fascinating critique of arguments (by Smith-Rosenberg and others) that nineteenth-century intimate and erotic relationships between women were ideologically desexualized as "romantic friendships," see Marylynne Diggs, "Romantic Friends or 'A Different Race of Creatures'? The Representation of Lesbian Pathology in Nineteenth-Century America," *Feminist Studies* 21, no. 2 (1995): 317–40.

45. Foucault, *The History of Sexuality,* 103.

46. Dana D. Nelson, *National Manhood,* 12.

47. Barker-Benfield, *Horrors of the Half-Known Life,* 175–88.

48. In addition to Barker-Benfield, historical treatments of the sexual economy attributed to the nineteenth-century male body include Smith-Rosenberg, "Davy Crockett as Trickster," in *Disorderly Conduct,* 90–108; Nelson, *National Manhood;* and Kevin J. Mumford, "'Lost Manhood' Found: Male Sexual Impotence and Victorian Culture in the United States," in *American Sexual Politics: Sex, Gender, and Race since the Civil War,* ed. John C. Fout and Maura Shaw Tantillo (Chicago: University of Chicago Press, 1993), 75–99.

49. Foucault, *The History of Sexuality,* 113, 108.

50. Eve Kosofsky Sedgwick, *Epistemology of the Closet* (Berkeley: University of California Press, 1990), 82–90.

51. Étienne Balibar provides what is in this respect a useful secondary gloss of this crucial component of Lukács's argument. As Balibar puts it, the modern extension of

NOTES TO CHAPTER I

the commodity form to other social spheres, to scientific discourse, for instance, is for Lukács "based on a separation of the objective and subjective sides of experience (which makes it possible to *subtract* the subjective factor . . . from the world of natural objects and their mathematical laws)." But the subtraction of the subjective from the objective "is merely a prelude to the incorporation of all subjectivity into objectivity (or to its *reduction* to the status of object, as is revealed by the notion of the 'human sciences' or by the techniques of management of the 'human factor' which have progressively been extended to the whole of society)." Balibar, *The Philosophy of Marx,* trans. Chris Turner (London: Verso, 1995), 70 (original italics).

52. Sedgwick, *Epistemology of the Closet,* 85.

53. Ibid., 87.

54. Key texts here include Radicalesbians, "The Woman-Identified Woman," in *Out of the Closets: Voices of Gay Liberation,* ed. Karla Jay and Allen Young (New York: New York University Press, 1992), 172–77; and Adrienne Rich, "Compulsory Heterosexuality and Lesbian Existence," in *The Lesbian and Gay Studies Reader,* ed. Henry Abelove, Michele Aina Barale, and David M. Halperin (New York: Routledge, 1993), 227–54.

55. See Kimmel, *Manhood in America,* 119–20.

56. Esther Newton, "The Mythic Mannish Lesbian: Radclyffe Hall and the New Woman," in *Hidden from History: Reclaiming the Gay and Lesbian Past,* ed. Martin Duberman, Martha Vicinus, and George Chauncey (New York: Meridian, 1989), 286. For a richly detailed historical analysis of the displacement of a nineteenth-century notion of female physiology by the emergent category of female heterosexuality, see Carroll Smith-Rosenberg, "The New Woman as Androgyne," in *Disorderly Conduct,* 245–96.

57. George Chauncey, *Gay New York: Gender, Urban Culture, and the Making of the Gay Male World, 1890–1940* (New York: Basic Books, 1994), 100.

58. Lukács, *History and Class Consciousness,* 92.

59. Ibid., 110–49.

60. See Eric O. Clarke, "The Citizen's Sexual Shadow," in *Virtuous Vice: Homoeroticism and the Public Sphere* (Durham, N.C.: Duke University Press, 2000), 101–25.

61. Ibid., 114.

62. Ibid.

63. Andrew Arato and Paul Breines, *The Young Lukács and the Origins of Western Marxism* (New York: Seabury, 1979), 163–209; John Rees, introduction to *A Defence of "History and Class Consciousness": Tailism and the Dialectic,* by Georg Lukács (New York: Verso, 2000), 1–38. I want to thank Marcia Klotz for a series of exchanges about the *Economic and Philosophical Manuscripts of 1844* (hereafter referred to as the *1844 Manuscripts*) that have made this a stronger analysis than it would otherwise have been. See Klotz's contributions to the forum on Marxism and queer theory in *Rethinking Marxism* (which also included contributions by Rosemary Hennessy and by myself, the latter a different version of the present section of this chapter): Marcia Klotz, "Introduction: Toward a Marxian Sexual Politics," *Rethinking Marxism* 18, no. 3

(2006): 383–86; and "Alienation, Labor, and Sexuality in Marx's 1844 Manuscripts," 405–13.

64. Lukács, *History and Class Consciousness*, xxxvi.

65. Karl Marx, *Economic and Philosophical Manuscripts (1844)*, in *Early Writings*, trans. Rodney Livingstone and Gregor Benton (New York: Penguin, 1975), 387.

66. Lukács, *History and Class Consciousness*, 178 (original italics).

67. Ibid., xviii, xvii. Lukács spoke to this issue in the defense of his book he wrote circa 1925, without claiming that this criticism of the book—a criticism that was indeed made in some of its earliest reviews—was a misreading of it: "Self-evidently society arose *from* nature. Self-evidently nature and its laws existed *before* society (that is to say before humans). Self-evidently the dialectic *could* not possibly be effective as an *objective principle of development* of society, if it were not already effective as a principle of development of nature before society, if it did not already *objectively exist*. From that, however, follows neither that social development could produce no new, equally objective forms of development, dialectical moments, nor that the dialectical moments in the development of nature would be *knowable* without the mediation of these new social dialectical forms." *A Defence of History and Class Consciousness*, 102 (original italics). Lukács responds in a way that seems to move his position from a dismissal of any attribution of a dialectical character to nature to a certain tentative, critical acceptance of this position. But the second sentence of the passage, in the way it juxtaposes the terms "nature," "society," and "humans," still seems to associate "humans" closely, if parenthetically, with "society," simultaneously to distance "humans" from "nature," and thereby to forestall any consideration of the human being as a material, embodied entity.

68. In an analysis of *History and Class Consciousness* that resonates in interesting ways with mine, Guido Starosta suggests that the subjective moment of reification Lukács privileges takes the form of an abstract, formal representation of subjectivity. Arguing that Lukács privileges form over content, Starosta theorizes this privileging in terms of the relation between the formal and real subsumption of labor as Marx elaborates this distinction in *Capital*. See Guido Starosta, "Scientific Knowledge and Political Action: On the Antinomies of Lukács's Thought in *History and Class Consciousness*," *Science and Society* 67, no. 1 (2003): 39–67.

69. Lukács, *History and Class Consciousness*, 145.

70. Andrew Arato, "Lukács' Theory of Reification," *Telos* 11 (1972): 53 (original italics).

71. Lukács, *History and Class Consciousness*, 100.

72. Ibid., 169 (original italics).

73. Marx, *Capital*, vol. 1, 283.

74. Marx, *Economic and Philosophical Manuscripts (1844)*, 390 (original italics).

75. But see also Eric Clarke's critique of what he identifies as a prioritizing of form over content in Foucault's discourse/reverse-discourse formulation—Foucault's positing of these two in a relation of formal equivalence, his erasure of the historically specific and overdetermined character of regulatory norms themselves. Clarke, *Virtuous Vice*, 86–95.

NOTES TO CHAPTER 2

76. Lukács, *History and Class Consciousness,* 185–97.

77. Foucault, *The History of Sexuality,* 131.

78. Judith Butler, *Subjects of Desire: Hegelian Reflections in Twentieth-Century France* (New York: Columbia University Press, 1999), 180.

79. On these friendlier forms of organizing, see Kitty Krupat and Patrick McCreery, eds., *Out at Work: Building a Gay-Labor Alliance* (Minneapolis: University of Minnesota Press, 2001).

80. Lipietz, *Mirages and Miracles,* 15.

81. Timothy Bewes, for example, makes this important point early in *Reification, or The Anxiety of Late Capitalism* (New York: Verso, 2002), 12.

82. Max Horkheimer and Theodor Adorno, *Dialectic of Enlightenment,* trans. John Cumming (New York: Continuum, 1993); Herbert Marcuse, *One-Dimensional Man: Studies in the Ideology of Advanced Industrial Society* (Boston: Beacon Press, 1964); Fredric Jameson, *Postmodernism, or The Cultural Logic of Late Capitalism* (Durham, N.C.: Duke University Press, 1991).

83. Jameson, *Postmodernism,* 47.

2. PERFORMATIVE MASCULINITY

1. The following versions of this critique, for example, are otherwise quite varied in emphasis: Teresa Ebert, *Ludic Feminism and After* (Ann Arbor: University of Michigan Press, 1996), 208–32; Kathi Weeks, "Subject for a Feminist Standpoint," in *Marxism beyond Marxism,* ed. Saree Makdisi, Cesare Casarino, and Rebecca E. Karl (New York: Routledge, 1996), 89–118; Rosemary Hennessy, "Queer Theory, Left Politics," in Makdisi, Casarino, and Karl, *Marxism beyond Marxism,* 214–42; and Paul Smith, "Precarious Politics," in *Primitive America: The Ideology of Capitalist Democracy* (Minneapolis: University of Minnesota Press, 2007), 115–24. See also the exchanges between Butler and Žižek in Butler, Ernesto Laclau, and Slavoj Žižek, *Contingency, Hegemony, Universality* (London: Verso, 2000), esp. 214–23, 263–80, 308–16.

2. Butler, Laclau, and Žižek, *Contingency, Hegemony, Universality,* 277.

3. See, for example, the essays collected in Judith Butler, *Undoing Gender* (New York: Routledge, 2004).

4. Miranda Joseph, "The Performance of Production and Consumption," in *Against the Romance of Community* (Minneapolis: University of Minnesota Press, 2002), 30–68.

5. Butler, Laclau, and Žižek, *Contingency, Hegemony, Universality,* 221.

6. Butler, *Bodies That Matter: On the Discursive Limits of "Sex"* (New York: Routledge, 1993), 232, 225.

7. Ibid., 240 (original italics).

8. George Chauncey, *Gay New York: Gender, Urban Culture, and the Making of the Gay Male World, 1890–1940* (New York: Basic Books, 1994), 80.

9. Edward Said, "Traveling Theory," in *The World, the Text, and the Critic* (Cambridge, Mass.: Harvard University Press, 1983), 226–47.

10. Butler, *Bodies That Matter,* 236.

11. Judith Butler, "Melancholy Gender/Refused Identification," in *The Psychic Life of Power: Theories in Subjection* (Stanford, Calif.: Stanford University Press, 1997), 132.

12. Butler, *Bodies That Matter,* 235–36 (original italics).

13. Judith Butler, "Reply to Adam Phillips's Commentary on 'Melancholy Gender/Refused Identification,'" in *Psychic Life of Power,* 165.

14. Slavoj Žižek, *The Ticklish Subject* (London: Verso, 1999), 271, 269.

15. E. Anthony Rotundo, *American Manhood: Transformations in Masculinity from the Revolution to the Modern Era* (New York: Basic, 1993), 232.

16. On Roosevelt's iconic representation of racialized, manly, imperial progressivism, see Richard Slotkin, *Gunfighter Nation: The Myth of the Frontier in Twentieth-Century America* (New York: Harper Collins, 1992), 29–62; and Gail Bederman, *Manliness and Civilization: A Cultural History of Gender and Race in the United States, 1880–1917* (Chicago: University of Chicago Press, 1995), 170–215.

17. Quoted in Rotundo, *American Manhood,* 235.

18. Slotkin, *Gunfighter Nation,* 37.

19. See Rotundo, *American Manhood,* 239–44.

20. Theodore Roosevelt, *The Strenuous Life: Essays and Addresses* (New York: Century, 1901), 4.

21. Slotkin, *Gunfighter Nation,* 52.

22. Michael Kimmel, *Manhood in America: A Cultural History* (New York: Free Press, 1996), 119.

23. Ibid., 120.

24. On the nineteenth-century emergence of a "biology of sexual incommensurability," see Thomas Laqueur, "Sex Socialized," in *Making Sex* (Cambridge, Mass.: Harvard University Press, 1990), 193–243.

25. Siobhan Somerville, *Queering the Color Line: Race and the Invention of Homosexuality in American Culture* (Durham, N.C.: Duke University Press, 2000), 15–38.

26. Nancy Ordover, *American Eugenics: Race, Queer Anatomy, and the Science of Nationalism* (Minneapolis: University of Minnesota Press, 2003).

27. Chauncey, *Gay New York,* 115–16.

28. Ibid., 100.

29. Ernest Hemingway, *The Sun Also Rises* (1925; New York: Charles Scribner's, 1970), 132.

30. Ibid., 116.

31. Eve Kosofsky Sedgwick, "Privilege of Unknowing: Diderot's *The Nun,*" in *Tendencies* (Durham, N.C.: Duke University Press, 1993), 23–51.

32. Hemingway, *The Sun Also Rises,* 22.

33. Ibid., 163, 177.

34. Ibid., 216.

35. Butler, *Bodies That Matter,* 238.

36. Judith Butler, "'Conscience Doth Make Subjects of Us All': Althusser's Subjection," in *The Psychic Life of Power* (Stanford, Calif.: Stanford University Press, 1997), 117.

37. Ibid., 119 (original italics).
38. Judith Butler, "Beside Oneself: On the Limits of Sexual Autonomy," in *Undoing Gender*, 27. Kathi Weeks considers the question of whether Butler is more appropriately read in ontological or anti-ontological terms in "Subject for a Feminist Standpoint," esp. 96–100.
39. Butler, "'Conscience Doth Make,'" 117.
40. Arnold Gingrich, quoted in Kenon Brezeale, "In Spite of Women: *Esquire* Magazine and the Construction of the Male Consumer," in *The Gender and Consumer Culture Reader*, ed. Jennifer Scanlon (New York: New York University Press, 2000), 227.
41. Ibid., 240.
42. His letters on fishing, for example, were being reproduced in these magazines as early as two years after their original appearance in *Esquire;* see John Raeburn, *Fame Became of Him: Hemingway as a Public Writer* (Bloomington: Indiana University Press, 1984), 51.
43. Brezeale, "In Spite of Women," 227.
44. Erin A. Smith, *Hard-Boiled: Working-Class Readers and Pulp Magazines* (Philadelphia: Temple University Press, 2000), 44.
45. Ibid., 94.
46. Christopher Breu, *Hard-Boiled Masculinities* (Minneapolis: University of Minnesota Press, 2005).
47. Steven M. Gelber, "Do-It-Yourself: Constructing, Repairing, and Maintaining Domestic Masculinity," in Scanlon, *Gender and Consumer Culture Reader*, 75.
48. See T. J. Jackson Lears, *No Place of Grace: Antimodernism and the Transformation of American Culture, 1880–1920* (New York: Pantheon, 1981), 60–96, esp. 91–96.
49. Gelber, "Do-It-Yourself," 74–75 (original italics).
50. Arjun Appadurai, *Modernity at Large: Cultural Dimensions of Globalization* (Minneapolis: University of Minnesota Press, 1996), 67.
51. Joseph, "The Performance of Production and Consumption," 34 (original italics). A concentrated elaboration of the concept of *habitus* can be found in Pierre Bourdieu, *Outline of a Theory of Practice* (Cambridge, U.K.: Cambridge University Press, 1977), 72–95, esp. 78–87.
52. Butler, Laclau, and Žižek, *Contingency, Hegemony, Universality*, 270.
53. Butler, *Psychic Life of Power*, 210.
54. Alain Lipietz, *Mirages and Miracles: The Crises of Global Fordism*, trans. David Macey (London: Verso, 1987), 15.
55. Butler, *Bodies That Matter*, 15.
56. Joseph, "Performance of Production," 34, 40.
57. Butler, *Bodies That Matter*, 227.
58. Dana D. Nelson, *National Manhood: Capitalist Citizenship and the Imagined Fraternity of White Men* (Durham, N.C.: Duke University Press, 1998).
59. See, for example, Nelson, *National Manhood*, 26.
60. Industrialization's challenge to the autonomy claimed by skilled laborers in the nineteenth century—claims that were also consistently claims to manliness—is a

common theme, for example, in these otherwise quite differently focused historical studies: David Montgomery, *Workers' Control in America: Studies in the History of Work, Technology, and Labor Struggles* (New York: Cambridge University Press, 1979); David R. Roediger, *The Wages of Whiteness* (London: Verso, 1991); and Lawrence B. Glickman, *A Living Wage: American Workers and the Making of Consumer Society* (Ithaca, N.Y.: Cornell University Press, 1997).

61. Roediger, *The Wages of Whiteness.*

62. Hemingway, *The Sun Also Rises,* 119–20.

63. Richard Godden, *Fictions of Capital: The American Novel from James to Mailer* (Cambridge, U.K.: Cambridge University Press, 1990), 45.

64. Ibid., 50.

65. I refer here to the passages in the *1844 Manuscripts* in which Marx critiques the alienation of labor in terms of his own identification of unalienated productive activity with "species-being," with human life activity as such. See Karl Marx, *Early Writings,* trans. Rodney Livingstone and Gregor Benton (New York: Penguin, 1992), 326–30.

66. The framing of reification in terms of such a fetishizing of means and suspension of ends is central to the Frankfurt school's rethinking of the concept as instrumental reason. See, for instance, Max Horkheimer, "Means and Ends," in *Eclipse of Reason* (New York: Continuum, 1999), 3–57.

67. Weeks, "Subject for a Feminist Standpoint," 99.

68. Elliott J. Gorn, *The Manly Art: Bare-Knuckle Prize Fighting in America* (Ithaca, N.Y.: Cornell University Press, 1986), 181. During the late nineteenth century, spectator sports were largely the province of the wealthy; but working hours for laborers were sufficiently reduced on a sufficiently general scale by the early twentieth century to provide the majority of the population enough leisure time to participate in what Gorn characterizes as the emerging service economy of spectator sports (181–82). See also John M. Carroll, "The Rise of Organized Sports," in *Sports in Modern America,* ed. William J. Baker and John M. Carroll (St. Louis, Mo.: River City Publishers, 1983), 10. The broad commercialization of sports and their gradual incorporation into an intensive regime of accumulation was certainly uneven in any number of ways: different sports underwent this history at different paces, for instance, baseball being one of the earliest to be commercialized and subject to the dictates of national organizations; the eventual incorporation of prizefighting, meanwhile, legitimated a sport strongly associated throughout the nineteenth century with working-class criminality and immorality (see Gorn, *Manly Art,* esp. 129–47).

69. Carroll, "Rise of Organized Sports," 10.

70. Gorn, *Manly Art,* 205.

71. Allen Gutman, *From Ritual to Record: The Nature of Modern Sports* (New York: Columbia University Press, 1978), 47.

72. For Gorn, the triumph of technical expertise in boxing is epitomized by the heavyweight victory, in the last decade of the nineteenth century, of a young boxer named James J. Corbett, whose "reputation rested totally on glove fights" and "was

based on his abilities as a scientific boxer." Corbett defeated John J. Sullivan, an aging boxer who had made his own reputation, years earlier, on bare-knuckle fights and his overwhelming strength. As a newspaper reporting on the fight put it, "youth, skill, and science" had now triumphed over "brute strength" (Gorn, *Manly Art,* 241, 240, 245).

73. Slotkin, *Gunfighter Nation,* 62. On Buffalo Bill and "the mythic space of American history," see pp. 63–87.

74. See Montgomery, *Workers' Control in America,* 9–31.

75. See Postone, *Time, Labor, and Social Domination: A Reinterpretation of Marx's Critical Theory* (New York: Cambridge University Press, 1996), 200–216.

76. See Marx, *Capital,* vol. 1, trans. Ben Fowkes (New York: Penguin, 1976), 553–64, esp. 553–54.

77. Georg Simmel, quoted in David Harvey, *The Urban Experience* (Baltimore, Md.: Johns Hopkins University Press, 1989), 173.

78. Georg Lukács, *History and Class Consciousness,* trans. Rodney Livingstone (1923; Cambridge, Mass.: MIT Press, 1994), 90.

79. Postone, *Time, Labor, and Social Domination,* 211, 294.

80. Ibid., 214.

81. Butler, *Gender Trouble* (New York: Routledge, 1990), 140–41 (original italics).

82. Fredric Jameson critiques contemporary critical discourses on "the body" along these lines in "The End of Temporality," *Critical Inquiry* 29 (2003): 713.

83. Butler, *Bodies That Matter,* 282 (original italics).

84. Weeks, "Subject for a Feminist Standpoint," 98, 96, 95.

85. Butler, *Bodies That Matter,* 250 (original italics).

86. Ibid., 232, 226, 237 (original italics).

87. Butler, "Gender Regulations," in *Undoing Gender,* 50–52.

88. Andrew Parker, "Praxis and Performativity," *Women and Performance* 8 (1996): 271.

89. Lukács, *History and Class Consciousness,* 88.

90. Fredric Jameson, *The Political Unconscious: Narrative as a Socially Symbolic Act* (Ithaca, N.Y.: Cornell University Press, 1981), 102.

91. Butler, *Bodies That Matter,* 231, 224.

3. REIFICATION AS LIBERATION

1. Herbert Marcuse, "The Affirmative Character of Culture," in *Negations: Essays in Critical Theory* (Boston: Beacon Press, 1968), 116.

2. Herbert Marcuse, *One-Dimensional Man: Studies in the Ideology of Advanced Industrial Society* (Boston: Beacon Press, 1964), 1.

3. This is notwithstanding efforts to question what seems to be a certain tendency to take Marcuse's contemporary irrelevance for granted, efforts to call for some kind of new critical engagement with his work. This call has been made, for example, in Angela Y. Davis, "Marcuse's Legacies," in *The New Left and the 1960s: Collected Papers of Herbert Marcuse,* vol. 3, ed. Douglas Kellner (New York: Routledge, 2005), vii–xiv;

and in Kellner, "Introduction: Radical Politics, Marcuse, and the New Left," also in *The New Left and the 1960s,* esp. 3–4. My impression, at least, is that a "Marcuse Renaissance" has hardly gotten under way in the years since Kellner's publication of an essay by this title (in *Marcuse: From the New Left to the Next Left,* ed. John Bokina and Timothy Lukes [Lawrence: University Press of Kansas, 1994], 245–68). But this doesn't mean there is no potential for one; see, for example, Laura Kipnis's provocative appropriation of the eroticized critical utopianism of *Eros and Civilization:* in the face of a contemporary privatization of political imagination itself, Kipnis brilliantly reads marriage and monogamy as a form of alienated labor in "Adultery," *Critical Inquiry* 24 (1998): 289–327.

4. Marcuse, "Affirmative Character of Culture," 116.

5. Herbert Marcuse, "Existentialism: Remarks on Jean-Paul Sartre's *L'Etre et Le Néant,*" *Philosophy and Phenomenological Research* 8 (1948): 309–36.

6. Ibid., 326.

7. Ibid., 327.

8. Ibid.

9. Ibid., 328.

10. Herbert Marcuse, *Eros and Civilization: A Philosophical Inquiry into Freud* (Boston: Beacon Press, 1966), 212. Hereafter cited in the text.

11. Marcuse, "Existentialism," 329.

12. Ibid. (italics mine).

13. Ibid., 328.

14. For important accounts of the Mattachine Society, see John D'Emilio, *Sexual Politics, Sexual Communities: The Making of a Homosexual Minority in the United States, 1940–1970* (Chicago: University of Chicago Press, 1983); and Dennis Altman, *Homosexual Oppression and Liberation* (New York: Avon, 1971), 70–107. I do not intend to understate the too easily forgotten courage of the homophile movements, who mobilized against police entrapment and other forms of harassment, for example. For a useful critique of the tendency to compare these movements negatively with gay liberation, see Martin Meeker, "Behind the Mask of Respectability: Reconsidering the Mattachine Society and Male Homophile Practice, 1950s and 1960s," *Journal of the History of Sexuality* 10, no. 1 (2001): 78–116.

15. Paul Goodman, *Growing Up Absurd: Problems of Youth in the Organized Society* (New York: Random House, 1960); Marcuse, *One-Dimensional Man.*

16. Paul Robinson, *The Freudian Left* (New York: Harper and Row, 1969), 147–48.

17. For a general overview of this trend, see Kenneth Lewes, *The Psychoanalytic Theory of Male Homosexuality* (New York: Meridian, 1988), 140–72.

18. Quoted in Martin Jay, *The Dialectical Imagination: A History of the Frankfurt School and the Institute of Social Research, 1923–1950* (Berkeley: University of California Press, 1973), 104.

19. Quoted in Robert J. Corber, *In the Name of National Security: Hitchcock, Homophobia, and the Political Construction of Gender in Cold War America* (Durham, N.C.: Duke University Press, 1993), 20.

20. U.S. Senate, "Employment of Homosexuals and Other Sex Perverts in the U.S. Government" (selections), in *We Are Everywhere: A Historical Sourcebook of Gay and Lesbian Politics,* ed. Mark Blasius and Shane Phelan (New York: Routledge, 1997), 242, 244.

21. Ibid., 247, 250.

22. Corber, *In the Name of National Security,* 61 (italics mine).

23. For divergently focused but similarly cogent treatments of this same national, midcentury fear of a spectral, universalized homosexuality, see Lee Edelman, "Tearooms and Sympathy, or The Epistemology of the Water Closet," in *Homographesis* (Durham, N.C.: Duke University Press, 1994), 148–70; and Christopher Nealon's analysis of "the secret public of physique culture" in *Foundlings: Lesbian and Gay Historical Emotion before Stonewall* (Durham, N.C.: Duke University Press, 2001), 99–139. I will have more to say about these readings in chapter 4.

24. U.S. Senate, "Employment of Homosexuals," 243.

25. Martin Jay, *Marxism and Totality: The Adventures of a Concept from Lukács to Habermas* (Berkeley and Los Angeles: University of California Press, 1984), 228.

26. Marcuse, *One-Dimensional Man,* xiii.

27. Fredric Jameson, *Marxism and Form: Twentieth-Century Dialectical Theories of Literature* (Princeton, N.J.: Princeton University Press, 1971), 115.

28. Herbert Marcuse, "Repressive Tolerance," in *A Critique of Pure Tolerance,* ed. Robert Paul Wolff, Barrington Moore Jr., and Herbert Marcuse (Boston: Beacon Press, 1969), 81–123.

29. Paul Breines, "Marcuse and the New Left in America," in *Antworten auf Herbert Marcuse,* ed. Jürgen Habermas (Frankfurt am Main: Suhrkamp, 1968), 133–51. See also Kellner, "Introduction: Radical Politics, Marcuse, and the New Left," in *The New Left and the 1960s,* 1–37.

30. Douglas Kellner, *Herbert Marcuse and the Crisis of Marxism* (Berkeley: University of California Press, 1984), 280. The collected papers of Marcuse, edited and published by Kellner in the last few years, provide additional, fascinating evidence of how quickly and dramatically Marcuse rethought his earlier arguments within a relatively narrow window of time during the mid-sixties. On the one hand, Marcuse develops the argument of *Eros and Civilization* in a more explicitly pessimistic register in a talk at Stanford in 1965, for example; see "The Containment of Social Change in Industrial Society," in *Towards a Critical Theory of Society: Collected Papers of Herbert Marcuse,* vol. 2, ed. Douglas Kellner (London: Routledge, 2001), 83–93. But compare this talk with the very different outlook of "Beyond One-Dimensional Man," in the same volume, 111–20.

31. Breines, "Marcuse and the New Left," 146.

32. Marcuse, *One-Dimensional Man,* 33.

33. Ibid., 256.

34. Herbert Marcuse, *An Essay on Liberation* (Boston: Beacon Press, 1969).

35. Herbert Marcuse, *Counterrevolution and Revolt* (Boston: Beacon Press, 1972).

36. Marcuse, *One-Dimensional Man,* 73 (original italics).

37. Ibid.

38. But see also the way in which, ten years later, Marcuse reclaims the potential of Eros to lead to a new reality principle organized around receptivity and sensuous enjoyment, now framed in terms of what he calls feminist socialism, in "Marxism and Feminism," in Kellner, *The New Left and the 1960s,* 165–72.

39. See, for example, Altman, *Homosexual Oppression and Liberation;* Jeffrey Escoffier, "Sexual Revolution and the Politics of Gay Identity," *Socialist Review* 82–83 (1985): 133–34; Gert Hekma, Harry Oosterhuis, and James Steakley, "Leftist Sexual Politics and Homosexuality: A Historical Overview," *Journal of Homosexuality* 29, nos. 2–3 (1995): 2; and Michael Bronski, *The Pleasure Principle: Sex, Backlash, and the Struggle for Gay Freedom* (New York: St. Martin's, 1998), 3.

40. Hekma, Oosterhuis, and Steakley, "Leftist Sexual Politics and Homosexuality," 2.

41. See, for example, the documents collected in the "Gay People vs. the 'Professionals'" section of Karla Jay and Allen Young, eds., *Out of the Closets: Voices of Gay Liberation* (New York: New York University Press, 1992), 122–69.

42. Martha Shelley, "Gay Is Good," in Jay and Young, *Out of the Closets,* 32, 34, 31.

43. Carl Wittman, "A Gay Manifesto," in Jay and Young, *Out of the Closets,* 330–42.

44. The Red Butterfly, "Comments on Carl Wittman's 'A Gay Manifesto,'" in Blasius and Phelan, *We Are Everywhere,* 389–90.

45. Altman, *Homosexual Oppression and Liberation,* 70, 98, 96.

46. A key statement of this imperative as it applies to nineties movements like Queer Nation, for instance, is Lauren Berlant and Elizabeth Freeman, "Queer Nationality," in *Fear of a Queer Planet: Queer Politics and Social Theory,* ed. Michael Warner (Minneapolis: University of Minnesota Press, 1993), 193–229. See also Cindy Patton's brilliant comparison of a queer politics of space with an analogous spatial imperative on the Christian Right, in "Queer Space/God's Space: Counting Down to the Apocalypse," *Rethinking Marxism* 9, no. 2 (1996–97): 1–23.

47. Matt Bell, "'Your Worst Fears Made Flesh': *The Manchurian Candidate*'s Paranoid Delusion and Gay Liberation," *GLQ* 12, no. 1 (2006): 86.

48. I am grateful to Kathryne Lindberg for first suggesting to me the way in which this effort to refuse resignation can be read as a different kind of resignation.

49. Étienne Balibar, "'Rights of Man' and 'Rights of the Citizen': The Modern Dialectic of Equality and Freedom," in *Masses, Classes, Ideas* (New York: Routledge, 1994), 44, 50. See also Balibar, "Is a Philosophy of Human Civic Rights Possible? New Reflections on Equaliberty," *South Atlantic Quarterly* 103, nos. 2–3 (2004): 311–22.

50. Balibar, "'Rights of Man' and 'Rights of the Citizen,'" 43, 51 (original italics).

51. Ibid., 50.

4. CLOSING A HETEROSEXUAL FRONTIER

1. On transcoding, see Fredric Jameson, *The Political Unconscious: Narrative as a Socially Symbolic Act* (Ithaca, N.Y.: Cornell University Press, 1981), 40. On cognitive mapping, see *Postmodernism, or The Cultural Logic of Late Capitalism* (Durham, N.C.:

Duke University Press, 1992), esp. 391–418, where Jameson represents transcoding as inadequate to a critique of the postmodern. See also Jameson, "Cognitive Mapping," in *Marxism and the Interpretation of Culture,* ed. Cary Nelson and Lawrence Grossberg (Urbana: University of Illinois Press, 1988), 347–60.

2. Michel Aglietta, *A Theory of Capitalist Regulation: The U.S. Experience,* trans. David Fernbach (London: New Left Books, 1979), 161.

3. Allan Bérubé, *Coming Out under Fire: The History of Gay Men and Women in World War Two* (New York: Free Press, 1990).

4. See John D'Emilio, *Sexual Politics, Sexual Communities: The Making of a Homosexual Minority in the United States, 1940–1970* (Chicago: University of Chicago Press, 1983), 40–53.

5. "Growth of Overt Homosexuality Provokes Wide Concern," *New York Times,* December 17, 1963, 1A.

6. Thomas Waugh, *Hard to Imagine: Gay Male Eroticism in Photography and Film from Their Beginnings to Stonewall* (New York: Columbia University Press, 1996), 217, 214.

7. Ibid., 413–14.

8. Ibid., 215, 216, 217.

9. Christopher Nealon, *Foundlings: Lesbian and Gay Historical Emotion before Stonewall* (Durham, N.C.: Duke University Press, 2001), 99–139.

10. Waugh, *Hard to Imagine,* 434n.

11. Ibid., 247–48.

12. Ibid., 228 (original italics).

13. Paul Welch, "Homosexuality in America," *Life,* June 26, 1964, 80.

14. Lee Edelman, "Tearooms and Sympathy, or The Epistemology of the Water Closet," in *Homographesis* (Durham, N.C.: Duke University Press, 1994), 163.

15. Terence Kissack, "Freaking Fag Revolutionaries: New York's Gay Liberation Front, 1969–1971," *Radical History Review* 62 (1995): 111.

16. Huey Newton, "A Letter from Huey to the Revolutionary Brothers and Sisters about the Women's Liberation and Gay Liberation Movements," in *We Are Everywhere: A Historical Sourcebook of Gay and Lesbian Politics,* ed. Mark Blasius and Shane Phelan (New York: Routledge, 1997), 404–6.

17. Kissack, "Freaking Fag Revolutionaries," 110–11.

18. Justin David Suran, "Coming Out against the War: Antimilitarism and the Politicization of Homosexuality in the Era of Vietnam," *American Quarterly* 53 (2001): 466.

19. Ibid., 465.

20. Ibid., 470.

21. Kissack, "Freaking Fag Revolutionaries," 123. See also Steven Dansky, John Knoebel, and Kenneth Pitchford, "The Effeminist Manifesto," in Blasius and Phelan, *We Are Everywhere,* 435–38; and "Rapping with a Street Transvestite Revolutionary: An Interview with Marcia Johnson," in *Out of the Closets: Voices of Gay Liberation,* ed. Karla Jay and Allen Young (New York: New York University Press, 1992), 112–20.

22. Michael Leapman, "Hollywood Diplomacy in Oscar Awards," *Times* (London), April 9, 1970, 12.

23. For a brilliant elaboration of a form of queer labor operating in relation to a circulation of mass commodities, largely during this same period, see Matthew Tinkcom, *Working like a Homosexual: Camp, Capital, Cinema* (Durham, N.C.: Duke University Press, 2002).

24. Andy Warhol and Pat Hackett, *POPism: The Warhol Sixties* (New York: Harcourt Brace, 1980), 280 (original italics).

25. The new MPAA ratings system had replaced decades of institutionalized film censorship only six months before *Midnight Cowboy* opened in New York on May 25, 1969, and anything resembling consensus within the industry on what constituted a G, M, R, or X film was far from settled (M, for "mature audiences," would eventually be replaced by PG). While the widespread identification of the X rating with "adult" films was still a few years away, for many the X rating did signify, at the very least, morally questionable (read: homosexual) material: one review of *Midnight Cowboy* reported that "a number of Texas legislators . . . want to put a 'dirty movie' tax on the film" (H. Elliott Wright, "Cowboys, 1969," *Christian Century*, October 29, 1969, 1401). The X was at least controversial enough to encourage the R-rated rerelease after the film received three Academy Awards in April 1970 (Picture, Director [John Schlesinger], and Adapted Screenplay [Waldo Salt]). Even the story of the rerelease is controversial. Some accounts contend that "shortly after the film went into general release," the rating was changed "because the rating commission tended to interpret the MPAA Code less stringently as time went on." Gene D. Phillips, *John Schlesinger* (Boston: Twayne, 1981), 129. But the film's producer Jerome Hellman has claimed that the MPAA offered to release a slightly revised, R-rated version after the Oscars were handed out, and then released the same film with an R rating after Hellman refused to make even minor changes. "Midnight Cowboy Revisited," directed by Peter Fitzgerald, *Midnight Cowboy*, 25th Anniversary Edition, MGM/UA Home Video, 1994. Hellman's implication, of course, is that the distribution of an X-rated "Best Picture" would, from the Academy's perspective, be oxymoronic or at least embarrassing.

26. See Thomas Frank, *The Conquest of Cool: Business Culture, Counterculture, and the Rise of Hip Consumerism* (Chicago: University of Chicago Press, 1997).

27. Martyn J. Lee, *Consumer Culture Reborn: The Cultural Politics of Consumption* (London: Routledge, 1993), 106. Lee's reference is to Daniel Bell, *The Cultural Contradictions of Capitalism* (London: Heinemann, 1976).

28. Lee, *Consumer Culture Reborn*, 106, 107. For important reconsiderations of this dynamic of youthful rebelliousness in relation to capital's efforts to profit from that rebelliousness—studies that situate youth within Fordist and post-Fordist contexts, respectively—see Leerom Medovoi, *Rebels: Youth and the Cold War Origins of Identity* (Durham, N.C.: Duke University Press, 2005); and Rob Latham, *Consuming Youth: Vampires, Cyborgs, and the Culture of Consumption* (Chicago: University of Chicago Press, 2002).

29. Phillips, *John Schlesinger*, 128.

30. Vito Russo, *The Celluloid Closet: Homosexuality in the Movies* (New York: Harper and Row, 1981), 80–83.

31. Michael Moon, "Outlaw Sex and the 'Search for America': Representing Male Prostitution and Perverse Desire in Sixties Film (*My Hustler* and *Midnight Cowboy*)," in *A Small Boy and Others* (Durham, N.C.: Duke University Press, 1998), 131, 127, 126.

32. Ibid., 132.

33. Richard Slotkin, *Gunfighter Nation: The Myth of the Frontier in Twentieth-Century America* (New York: Harper Collins, 1992), 3, 493, 496.

34. Lee Clark Mitchell's reading of this shift in the Western's tone as the fifties gave way to the sixties—in particular, his suggestion that by this point the cowboy had become not merely a more stoic figure but a kind of *undead* figure—illuminates, I think, the starkly anachronistic character of Joe's comic vitality: "In [the] late phase of the film Western (with the advent of Leone and Peckinpah), masculine restraint has been heightened beyond what [James Fenimore] Cooper had in mind when he invested Natty Bumppo with a self-constraining temperament. Now that temperament occurs as little more than a sign of absence. In a world with no larger vision of progress or of a coherent past, rules no longer apply, and all that distinguishes the hero from anyone else is mere emotional detachment—a style that seems like nothing so much as death itself, with the hero's body become a corpse, as motionless and stark as a desert landscape." Lee Clark Mitchell, *Westerns: Making the Man in Fiction and Film* (Chicago: University of Chicago Press, 1996), 171.

35. See Robert Sklar, *Movie-Made America: A Cultural History of American Movies* (New York: Vintage, 1994), 282–83.

36. Beginning with this film, which he represented as nothing less than an intervention in the struggle against Communism, Wayne's cinematic efforts had taken on an increasingly jingoistic tone. See Slotkin, *Gunfighter Nation,* 512–33. The degree to which Western film references had pervaded the nation's official war vocabulary by the late sixties is additionally suggested by Wayne's incorporation of those references into his second directorial effort, *The Green Berets* (1968), including allusions to characters he had himself previously played, the result a dizzying overlay of counterinsurgency rhetoric with frontier allegory.

37. Moon, "Outlaw Sex and the 'Search for America,'" 126.

38. See Kerry Segrave, *Drive-In Theaters: A History from Their Inception in 1933* (Jefferson, N.C.: McFarland, 1992).

39. What remains of this section draws primarily on the following accounts of the accumulation crisis of the late sixties: Philip Armstrong, Andrew Glyn, and John Harrison, *Capitalism since 1945* (Oxford: Blackwell, 1991), 151–220; Lee, *Consumer Culture Reborn,* 73–85, 101–8; and David Harvey, *The Condition of Postmodernity* (Oxford: Blackwell, 1990), 125–88.

40. U.S. Fordism was a national economy with highly protected markets and minimum import penetration. But corporate interests in the post–World War II United States also wanted to see capital expand globally as quickly as possible—in part because

of the Cold War, because of the potential vulnerability of war-torn economies else-where to revolutionary movements that would, with the support of the Soviet Union, threaten capital's further expansion. This investment in other national infrastructures was also, like suburbanization, a valve for absorbing U.S. capital surpluses.

41. Harvey, *The Condition of Postmodernity,* 165.

42. Fredric Jameson, *The Geopolitical Aesthetic* (London: British Film Institute, 1992), 3.

43. Jameson, *Postmodernism,* 332.

44. Fredric Jameson, "Marxism and Postmodernism," in *The Cultural Turn: Selected Writings on the Postmodern, 1983–1998* (London: Verso, 1998), 36 (original italics).

45. Jameson's reading of Balzac is exemplary here: see *The Political Unconscious,* 151–84.

46. Fredric Jameson, "Pleasure: A Political Issue," in *The Ideologies of Theory: Essays, 1971–1986,* vol. 2 (Minneapolis: University of Minnesota Press, 1988), 62.

47. Jameson, *The Political Unconscious,* 31.

48. Ibid., 62.

49. Jameson also argues, for example, for reification's "Utopian vocation," its autonomization of sensory experience, aesthetic compensations for reification that are themselves a product of reification, compensations he associates with modernism. See the opening chapter of *The Political Unconscious,* 63, as well as the Conrad chapter, 206–80.

50. Jameson, "Marxism and Postmodernism," 49.

51. Jameson, *The Political Unconscious,* 75.

52. Fredric Jameson, "Third World Literature in the Era of Multinational Capital-ism," *Social Text* 15 (1986): 79. This essay is perhaps the most controversial publica-tion of Jameson's long career, practically spawning a minor industry of scholarship in response. The best-known critique of this essay—and it is perhaps more accurate to say that it was this critique that spawned this minor industry—is Aijaz Ahmad, "Jameson's Rhetoric of Otherness and the 'National Allegory,'" in *In Theory: Classes, Nations, Literatures* (London: Verso, 1992), 95–122. More recent interventions in a still-vital discourse on Jameson's notion of "national allegory" include Neil Larsen, *Determinations* (London: Verso, 2001), esp. 18–21; Imre Szeman, "Who's Afraid of National Allegory? Jameson, Literary Criticism, and Globalization," *South Atlantic Quarterly* 100 (2001): 803–27; and Neil Lazarus, "Fredric Jameson on 'Third-World Literature': A Qualified Defence," in *Fredric Jameson: A Critical Reader,* ed. Douglas Kellner and Sean Homer (New York: Palgrave, 2004), 42–61. For a differently focused reading of national allegory in relation to the same mode of regulation I consider here, see the way in which Medovoi contextualizes the canonization of *The Catcher in the Rye* in *Rebels,* 53–89.

5. NOTES ON A QUEER HORIZON

1. Wendy Brown, "Neo-liberalism and the End of Liberal Democracy," *Theory and Event* 7, no. 1 (2003): paragraphs 9, 10, and 17. The first twenty-odd paragraphs

of Brown's essay make a cogent, forceful case for the way in which neoliberalism represents a new logic of governance in which the state is a central player, though by no means the only one. Where the essay becomes less compelling, in my view, is where it becomes primarily a defense of the forms of "liberal democracy" that the neoliberal project is undeniably eroding: "It is liberal democracy," Brown contends, "that is going under in the present moment" (para. 23). This chapter proposes some of the ways in which a great deal more than political liberalism is "going under."

2. Randy Martin, *Financialization of Daily Life* (Philadelphia: Temple University Press), 2002.

3. Adam Tickell and Jamie A. Peck, "Social Regulation after Fordism: Regulation Theory, Neo-liberalism and the Global-Local Nexus," *Economy and Society* 24 (1995): 369 (original italics).

4. David Harvey, *The New Imperialism* (Oxford: Oxford University Press, 2005), 157.

5. See, for example, Lauren Berlant, *The Queen of America Goes to Washington City: Essays on Sex and Citizenship* (Durham, N.C.: Duke University Press, 1997); Eric O. Clarke, *Virtuous Vice: Homoeroticism and the Public Sphere* (Durham, N.C.: Duke University Press, 2000); and Michael Warner, *Publics and Counterpublics* (New York: Zone Books, 2002).

6. But see also Rosemary Hennessy's suggestion, right around the time a distinctly queer perspective on neoliberalism was beginning to emerge, that queer theory as it developed in the nineties operated according to a logic consistent with, rather than critical of, the neoliberal project. Rosemary Hennessy, *Profit and Pleasure: Sexual Identities in Late Capitalism* (New York: Routledge, 2000).

7. Karl Marx, *Capital*, vol. 1, trans. Ben Fowkes (New York: Penguin, 1976), 125.

8. Berlant, *Queen of America*.

9. Smith contends that in the current neoliberal regime of capital accumulation, "capitalist unification in the North can be generalized as one where it has become increasingly necessary, in order to consolidate such a subject as a norm, to *legislate* the subject of value." Paul Smith, *Millennial Dreams: Contemporary Culture and Capitalism in the North* (London: Verso, 1997), 84 (original italics). See also Smith, *Primitive America: The Ideology of Capitalist Democracy* (Minneapolis: University of Minnesota Press, 2007), 27–32.

10. Clarke, *Virtuous Vice*, 49.

11. David Harvey, *A Brief History of Neoliberalism* (Oxford: Oxford University Press, 2005), 78.

12. Michael Warner, *The Trouble with Normal: Sex, Politics, and the Ethics of Queer Life* (New York: Free Press, 1999), 168, 41–80.

13. Lisa Duggan, "The New Homonormativity: The Sexual Politics of Neoliberalism," in *Materializing Democracy: Toward a Revitalized Cultural Politics*, ed. Russ Castronovo and Dana D. Nelson (Durham, N.C.: Duke University Press, 2002), 175–94. See also Lisa Duggan, *The Twilight of Equality? Neoliberalism, Cultural Politics, and the Attack on Democracy* (Boston: Beacon, 2004).

14. Danae Clark, "Commodity Lesbianism," in *The Lesbian and Gay Studies Reader*, ed. Henry Abelove, Michele Aina Barale, and David M. Halperin (New York: Routledge, 1993), 186–201.

15. Quoted in Karen Stabiner, "Tapping the Homosexual Market," *New York Times Magazine*, May 2, 1982, 82.

16. Quoted in Susan Faludi, *Stiffed: The Betrayal of the American Man* (New York: Harper Collins, 1999), 506.

17. Marx, *Capital*, 163, 165, 163.

18. Ibid., 176. But on concrete, material, living commodities who can speak—and resist—see Fred Moten's radically different reading of this same subjunctive moment in Marx in *In the Break: The Aesthetics of the Black Radical Tradition* (Minneapolis: University of Minnesota Press, 2003), esp. 5–18.

19. Andrew Holleran, *Dancer from the Dance* (New York: Bantam, 1979), 35–36.

20. David Serlin notes this contradiction in "The Twilight (Zone) of Commercial Sex," in *Policing Public Sex*, ed. Dangerous Bedfellows (South End, 1996), 45–52.

21. Lauren Berlant and Michael Warner, "Sex in Public," *Critical Inquiry* 24 (1998): 562, 551, 562.

22. Duggan, "The New Homonormativity," 180–81.

23. See Robert Fitch, *The Assassination of New York* (New York: Verso, 1993).

24. Among the vast literature on increasingly privatized U.S. cities, see, for instance, the important early contributions to Michael Sorkin, ed., *Variations on a Theme Park: The New American City and the End of Public Space* (New York: Noonday, 1992); as well as Neil Smith, *The New Urban Frontier: Gentrification and the Revanchist City* (New York: Routledge, 1996); and Susan Christopherson, "The Fortress City: Privatized Spaces, Consumer Citizenship," in *Post-Fordism: A Reader*, ed. Ash Amin (Oxford, U.K.: Blackwell, 1994), 409–27. One of the great case studies in this set of contemporary developments remains Mike Davis, *City of Quartz* (New York: Vintage, 1992).

25. See Samuel R. Delany's eloquent consideration of the impact of the "redevelopment" of Times Square on queer sex publics in *Times Square Red, Times Square Blue* (New York: New York University Press, 1999), of which more hereafter. See also Warner, *The Trouble with Normal*, 149–93.

26. On the contemporary city as a fortress, see Christopherson, "The Fortress City," and Davis, *City of Quartz*, 221–63. For a detailed, cogent account of the violent policing of urban populations in the wake of deindustrialization, an account that situates this policing in relation to the persistence of accumulation crisis since the seventies, see Christian Parenti's indispensable *Lockdown America: Police and Prisons in the Age of Crisis* (New York: Verso, 1999). And see Neil Smith's similarly focused discussion of pre-9/11 Giuliani neoliberalism in New York in "Giuliani Time: The Revanchist 1990s," *Social Text* 57 (1998): 1–20.

27. Smith, *The New Urban Frontier*, 45.

28. Smith, "Giuliani Time," 11.

29. See, for example, Eric Lipton, "Giuliani to Seek Rewritten Law in New Attack on Sex Shops," *New York Times*, March 26, 2001; Richard Pérez-Peña, "Sex-Related

Businesses Lose Two Decisions in Appeals Court," *New York Times,* March 30, 2001; Nicholas Confessore, "Sex-Related Shops Are Making a Comeback in Times Square," *New York Times,* March 15, 2005.

30. Martin F. Manalansan IV, "Race, Violence, and Neoliberal Spatial Politics in the Global City," *Social Text,* nos. 84–85 (2005): 141–55.

31. Ibid., 147–48, 149.

32. On the heteronormativity underpinning the intensified xenophobia in the United States since 9/11, including the intensified heterosexism of immigrants trying to avoid governmental surveillance and brutality by representing themselves as good American patriots, see Jasbir K. Puar and Amit Rai, "Monster, Terrorist, Fag: The War on Terrorism and the Production of Docile Patriots," *Social Text,* no. 72 (2002): 117–48; and Jasbir K. Puar, *Terrorist Assemblages: Homonationalism in Queer Times* (Durham, N.C.: Duke University Press, 2007).

33. The literature on contemporary militarism as an extension of the logic of neoliberalism has been growing rapidly, but for a range of perspectives on this continuity see Harvey, *The New Imperialism;* Retort (Iain Boal, T. J. Clark, Joseph Matthews, Michael Watts), *Afflicted Powers: Capital and Spectacle in a New Age of War* (New York: Verso, 2006); and Randy Martin, *An Empire of Indifference: American War and the Financial Logic of Risk Management* (Durham, N.C.: Duke University Press, 2007).

34. Harvey, *The New Imperialism,* 201.

35. On accumulation by dispossession, see Harvey, *The New Imperialism,* 137–82. On primitive accumulation, see Marx, *Capital,* 873–940. In an argument that in this respect converges with Harvey's, Retort contends that neoliberalism has mutated from "an epoch of 'agreements' and austerity programs to one of outright war" (*Afflicted Powers,* 52), and that war is at the same time constitutive of modernity as such.

36. Harvey, *The New Imperialism,* 142.

37. Berlant and Warner, "Sex in Public," 548, 558.

38. See Warner, *Publics and Counterpublics.*

39. Ibid., 124.

40. See Warner, *The Trouble with Normal.*

41. Berlant and Warner, "Sex in Public," 561.

42. Douglas Crimp, "How to Have Promiscuity in an Epidemic," in *AIDS: Cultural Analysis/Cultural Activism* (Cambridge, Mass.: MIT Press, 1987), 237–71.

43. Berlant and Warner, "Sex in Public," 558.

44. See Simon Watney, *Policing Desire* (Minneapolis: University of Minnesota Press, 1989), 18.

45. Warner, *The Trouble with Normal,* 167, 154.

46. Samuel R. Delany, *The Motion of Light in Water* (Minneapolis: University of Minnesota Press, 2004), 291, 293.

47. Ibid., 292, 293.

48. Moten's is a richly suggestive rethinking of Delany and totality in relation to what Moten calls the sexual cuts and breaks that constitute the improvisational performance of the black radical tradition; the quotation is from Moten, *In the Break,* 157.

49. José Esteban Muñoz, "The Future in the Present: Sexual Avant-Gardes and the Performance of Utopia," in *The Futures of American Studies*, ed. Donald Pease and Robyn Wiegman (Durham, N.C.: Duke University Press, 2002), 96. See also Muñoz, "Ghosts of Public Sex: Utopian Longings, Queer Memories," in Dangerous Bedfellows, *Policing Public Sex*, 355–72. For Delany's account of *Eighteen Happenings in Six Parts*, see *The Motion of Light in Water*, 200–208.

50. José Esteban Muñoz, "Cruising the Toilet: LeRoi Jones/Amiri Baraka, Radical Black Traditions, and Queer Futurity," *GLQ* 13, nos. 2–3 (2007): 360.

51. Muñoz, "Future in the Present," 93, 108.

52. Delany, *Times Square Red, Times Square Blue*, 111, 129. For Muñoz's discussion of this text, see "Future in the Present," 97.

53. Muñoz, "Future in the Present," 107.

54. Tony Kushner, introduction to *The Waterfront Journals*, by David Wojnarowicz, ed. Amy Scholder (New York: Grove Press, 1996), xi–xii.

55. Robert Siegle, *Suburban Ambush: Downtown Writing and the Fiction of Insurgency* (Baltimore, Md.: Johns Hopkins University Press, 1989), 317.

56. David Wojnarowicz, *Close to the Knives: A Memoir of Disintegration* (New York: Vintage, 1991), 81–82. Hereafter cited in the text.

57. Barry Blinderman, "The Compression of Time: An Interview with David Wojnarowicz," in *David Wojnarowicz: Tongues of Flame*, ed. Barry Blinderman (New York: Distributed Art Publishers, 1989), 63.

58. On enclosures in the history of primitive accumulation, see Christopher Hill, *The World Turned Upside Down: Radical Ideas during the English Revolution* (Baltimore, Md.: Penguin, 1975); and Peter Linebaugh and Marcus Rediker, *The Many-Headed Hydra: Sailors, Slaves, Commoners, and the Hidden History of the Revolutionary Atlantic* (Boston: Beacon Press, 2000).

59. Walter Benjamin, "Theses on the Philosophy of History," in *Illuminations* (New York: Schocken, 1968), 255 (original italics).

INDEX

abstraction: action and, 117–18; citizenship and, 148–49; the concrete and, 26–33, 77, 223; Jameson on, 187; of labor, 52, 107; social, 23–25, 29, 80

abstract time, 52–55, 61, 111–12, 116, 151–52, 218–19

accumulation: by dispossession, 207–8, 219; managing, 46–48, 51, 55, 61, 74, 183, 193, 195–97; post–World War II, 155–56; strategies of, 55, 108–9, 111, 113–14. *See also* capital: accumulation of; crisis of accumulation; regimes of accumulation

action, 10, 51, 95, 117–18, 124, 137. *See also* praxis

activism, 173, 177, 179. *See also* civil rights movement; gay liberation movement; homophile movements; praxis; social movements; youth movements

ACT UP, 16, 191, 199, 204

Adorno, Theodor W., 213; on psychoanalysis, 128, 129, 148, 234n24; on reification, 16, 26

Advocate (magazine), 200–201

Aglietta, Michel, 46, 50, 55, 158

agrarian way of life, 51, 52

AIDS epidemic, U.S., 38, 199, 209, 215, 220, 225

alienation, 11, 68–69, 70

allegory: Jameson on, 37, 154, 186–94, 250n52; *Midnight Cowboy* as, 156, 177, 178, 186, 191–94

Althusser, Louis: Butler's analysis of, 94–105

Altman, Dennis, 146

Anger, Kenneth, 171

antiheteronormative perspectives, 2, 3, 37, 68, 153; on Lukács, 25, 67, 71–72, 74, 223–24. *See also* heteronormativity

Appadurai, Arjun, 100–101

Arato, Andrew, 71

Arendt, Hannah, 207

artisanship, 52, 98, 99, 111–12, 234n15

aspiration to totality, 9–12, 17, 193–94, 223; Freudian view, 146; Jameson on, 11–12, 154, 186, 224; Marcuse on, 121, 137, 224; Marxian view, 29, 32; queer, 15, 20, 32, 37, 66, 198–99, 210–11, 212; reification and, 23, 25, 30, 119. *See also* reification-totality dialectic; totality thinking

assimilation, 62, 136, 200

Kevin Floyd is associate professor of English at Kent State University.